GOING LOCAL

Going Local

Experiences and Encounters on the Road

Nick Kontis with John Gottberg Anderson

Published by Trip Rambler Media
Going Local: Experiences and Encounters on the Road

Author: Nicholas C. Kontis
Editor: John Gottberg Anderson
Cover Design: Abdul Mateen
Formatting: Luxe Beat Media
Photo Credits: Miscellaneous photos by Gabriela Ramos, Jane Romanishko, David Noyes, Naw Zin Zin Aye, Michael Stinson, Andrew Zimmern and WOOFF.

ISBN: 978-0-9978947-1-4 (Paperback)
ISBN: 978-0-9978947-2-1 (eBook)
ISBN: 978-0-9978947-3-8 (Hardcover)

The Library of Congress number is available upon request.

For Mom and Dad, who took a chance on
America and thankfully chose San Francisco to raise me.

To my loving wife Gabriela, mother-in-law Maria Teresa, and Viking Dog Odin for
believing in my ability to become an author.

To the great explorers who paved the way for me and other curious modern day wanderers
to get off beaten part and travel the world.

To John Gottberg Anderson for helping to create the best second edition possible of
Going Local.

And to all the fellow pilgrims who enriched and enlightened my continuing life journey.

Praise for Nick

"*Nick Kontis fully showcases a better way to travel by fully immersing into local society*" ~ Richard Bangs – Author, Television Personality, and regarded as the Father of modern Adventure Travel

"*Nick is a great traveler and knows the difference between simply navigating between two points and experiencing the true essence of what's in between. His is a never-ending quest for both understanding different cultures and the search for common ground, and Nick has figured it out and then, thankfully, shares what we all need to know.*" ~Peter Greenberg - Travel Editor - CBS News

"*Nick teaches you why going local when you travel is so rewarding, and he reveals the secrets of doing it.*" ~Francis Tapon – Author, Global Nomad, Public Speaker, Wander Learn.com

"*As full-time world travelers since 2012, we could not agree more with the philosophy of Going Local. For the good of the planet, local communities, and vacationers, it's time to move away from mass tourism. This book surfaces an exciting way forward, toward immersive experiences that change lives and connect us as a people.*" ~Mike & Anne Howard, National Geographic, Author and Founders of HoneyTrek.com

"*Experiential travel is the pulsing heart and soul of Nick's book, of living immersed in the moment with the desperate people and cultures of our world, as Nick and John share in their heartfelt words and images.*" ~Kerrick James, Travel Journalist, Teacher, and Explorer

"*Nick Kontis writes about the way we should be traveling. It's not about package tours and brief stops, but deep immersion into getting to know locals and finding out about why they – and now you – love the places they call home.*" ~Michael Luongo – Award Winning New York based novelist, Freelance Writer and photographer

"*Nick Kontis is committed to the kind of travel that brings peace, communication and joy.*" ~Judith Fein – Award Winning Travel Writer, Speaker and Videographer

"Nick Kontis is championing a travel concept that I have held for decades, "Immersion" in local culture. I believe this is the path to international understanding, and I applaud him for his work." ~James Michael Dorsey – Explorer, Award- Winning Author, Photographer and Lecturer

"Nick doesn't just talk about "eating like a local," but shows how to discover the great finds and how to get advice from the right people who live in a place. He doesn't just discuss the benefits of staying in a real neighborhood and shopping there but provides a long list of services that will get you there." ~Tim Leffel – Travel Journalist, Author

"With more and more people traveling into remote corners of our increasingly accessible and complicated world, it is incredibly valuable to have voices like Nick Kontis to guide us towards a more memorable and enlightening travel experience." ~ David Noyes – Award-winning Travel Writer and Photojournalist

"With more Nick Kontises on the road, we'd have a much more peaceful world. Support his kind of 'going local'." ~John Lamkin – Award-Winning Journalist and Photographer

"The single biggest impact on my children's education is the experiences they share, with locals, around the world. Nick Kontis opens up a world many don't realize is accessible to them." ~Jim Pickell – Ex-President of HomeExchange.com

"If Jules Verne were alive today he would use Nick's Ticket Planet to go "Around the World in 80 days" ~Arthur Frommer – Founder of the Frommer's series of travel guides and *Arthur Frommer's Budget Travel* Magazine

"Many people – Mark Twain included - have noted how travel is a certain cure for bigotry and narrow-mindedness. I hope Nick's book may help persuade people to take the treatment." ~Tony Wheeler – Co-founder of Lonely Planet Guidebooks

"If you've ever considered what it might be like to travel free of resorts and hotels, perhaps for months on end, and experience exotic destinations from the perspective of the citizen of that country, Nicholas Kontis has prepared your road map." ~World Traveler Group

Contents

WHY WE TRAVEL

I travel not to go anywhere but to go. I travel for travel's sake. The great affair is to move. — Robert Louis Stevenson

Travel is fatal to prejudice, bigotry, and narrow-mindedness, and many of our people need it sorely on these accounts. — Mark Twain

The world is a book and those who do not travel read only one page. — St. Augustine

We're Nick and John. And we want to take you traveling.

The quotes above are mantras that have suited us well in our pursuit to see the world. But travel is more than just words. Travel is about finding your personal discomfort zone and diving headfirst into it. Travel asks you to accept a challenge to grow, to acknowledge your fears of the new and unknown, to glimpse or perhaps experience the ways in which other cultures live.

As habitual travelers, we want to tell you a little bit about why we consider ourselves "experts" in travel, and offer some thoughts that may help you.

Here's Nick:

Travel and movement have been instilled in my blood since early childhood. Born on Greece's Santorini Island, I was 3 when my parents moved to San Francisco ... just about the time the "flower power" movement was taking off. Growing up in the Bay Area in the '70s, I was introduced to a far wide range of lifestyles than I might have discovered anywhere else. In the end, impulsiveness, curiosity about people, and spontaneous passions forged my life of travel.

Before I learned my timetables, I learned the capitals of all 50 American states. Maps fascinated me. I would close my eyes and spin the globe, always wondering where my finger would land when I put it down. As I grew older, four years of college didn't teach me as much as a 13-month trip around the world.

If a mere picture is worth 1,000 words, what value can be placed upon an experience? I embrace many travel memories that have lasted a lifetime, and each of them is unique and priceless.

Sounds, smells, sights and tastes evoke those memories. In Cairo, the haunting voice of muezzin calling the faithful to worship from lofty minarets, amid the nonstop honking of cars and people packing the streets. In Paris, the aroma of freshly baked bread wafting from every boulangerie and patisserie on every street. In Bangkok, the scent of orange jasmine and the mouth-watering tang of curries sizzling in chile oil and coconut milk, emanating from the outdoor markets. On east Africa's Serengeti Plain, the colossal sight of 2 million thumping wildebeest, zebras and gazelles racing through the Masai Mara.

Travel opens us to so much of our world, connecting us with people, cultures and nature.

As first-generation Greek immigrants, my parents made sure that my ties to the motherland remained engrained in my heart and soul. "Greece is the birthplace of Western civilization, and you should never forget that," my dear old dad told me on more than one occasion.

Some of my fondest childhood memories were from summer vacations in Greece. In my adolescence and youth, I often stayed in Patras, where my father was born and where most of my relatives lived. I slept in any nook and cranny, on couches in my aunts' and uncles' spare bedrooms, or even in a sleeping bag, sometimes outdoors. I ate home-cooked meals with family, and helped to prepare them. I learned to make new friends of complete strangers. I thumbed rides to the beach, took road trips to Athens with cousins, and sought out new hangouts on my own. I learned that I was meant to tag along where my parents went, discovering something new in every encounter.

I grew up neither wealthy nor poor, but I was rich in experiences. I was taught to cherish the ability to travel. I understood, and respected, that nature and people can thrive together. I traveled experientially before it became in-vogue — in other words, that the experience of travel counts far more than simply checking off a list of sought-after destinations.

John's take:

Like Nick, I grew up in the United States with an immigrant influence, albeit second-generation. Three grandparents came from Sweden, but I was most like my maternal grandpa, who left his Finnish fishing village to become a transatlantic sailor and visited four continents before he was 25.

Except for a couple of vacations in Canada, I made no foreign trips as a youth. But my family took frequent journeys within the U.S., and I did plenty of world travel in books I read and in the stamps I collected. My favorite board game was "Pirate and Traveler." Like Nick, I was fascinated with maps and with spinning the globe. And I did him one better than state capitals: I learned *world* capitals. (How many 8-year-olds in the 1950s knew that Tegucigalpa was the capital of Honduras?)

Two summers of college internships in Hawaii were my introduction to foreign cultures. While the islands are indeed an integral part of the U.S., the blend of Asian and Pacific lifestyles was different than I knew, and something that I embraced. I had been shy and introverted as a young person; now, I was learning something new every day. And when upon graduation I departed for Europe for seven months, and went to work in my mother's cousins' furniture factory in the heart of Sweden, I got a full Scandinavian cultural immersion.

From that point on, I was hooked. After a couple of more years in Hawaii, I bought a round-the-world ticket. I was on the road for nearly three years, picking up odd jobs at bars and restaurants, farms and hotels, teaching skiing and making door-to-door sales calls. This was long before internet and cell phones; I collected letters from home at post offices and scheduled international calls at telephone exchanges. Being truly off the grid can be exhilarating, leaving a traveler no choice but to be self-dependent, to rely upon your own smarts and on the kindness of strangers who often don't speak your language. It's no fun when you're deathly ill, as I was for several weeks in 1976 in Nepal. But just as necessity is the mother of invention, isolation (however self-imposed) taps reserves of strength, courage and creativity that you probably didn't know you had.

I learn more about myself in my travels than I learn about the places I visit. Had I been two generations younger, I would have become a digital nomad. Alas, early in my career as a journalist I still used a manual typewriter. And I've certainly never been rich. But, like Nick, I was blessed with parents who encouraged me to follow my dreams. In the decades that followed, I worked in 11 countries on four continents and traveled in scores more. I studied tango dancing in Buenos Aires and batik art on the Indonesian island of Java. I mushed sled dogs in Alaska and rafted the whitewater of Arizona's Grand Canyon. I worked as a honky-tonk piano player in New Zealand and, with apologies to Nick, as a Greek chef in Vietnam.

The bottom line: SO CAN YOU. In the pages that follow, as we tell our stories, we will encourage you to explore this great wide world on your own terms. You're afraid?

Of course you are. But don't let that stop you. Who was it who said, "Whatever you can dream, you can do."

Adventure awaits.

Modern values

The way we travel has changed. Once upon a time, we relied upon travel advisors to plan our trips. While these expert sellers of travel and guidebooks are still a godsend to many global explorers today, we now also use apps and social media. We search for airfare on metasearch engines like Kayak, Hopper or Momondo to book last-minute flights. Low-cost carriers such as EasyJet, AirAsia, TUI and Norwegian Airlines can offer tremendous savings. So, too, with accommodations: In booking accommodations through Trivago, Agoda, Airbnb and other agencies, travelers save massively. You can even swap homes. And fellow adventurers are always pleased to share guidance in online travel groups, such as on Facebook.

Over the past decade, this shift in travel values is even more pronounced. Travelers find it easier than ever to "live like a local" — to become, however temporarily, part of a family or community. Today it's not as hard to get far off the beaten path as it was a generation (or two) ago. Any more, it seems, no road is "the road less traveled."

Sensory experiences and "Instagram moments" are the ethos for many travelers. But finding hidden locations, and visiting more than just typical tourist sites, should be everyone's goal on any trip. Tourist visits to Ho Chi Minh City (Saigon), Vietnam, for example, too often start and end with "essential" half-day tours to the heavily promoted Cu Chi Tunnels and the nearest edge of the expansive Mekong Delta. Go beyond, to the spiritual center of Tay Ninh, hard by the Cambodian border. Or explore deeper into the Mekong, with its floating markets and inland fishing villages, where you can make friends with families of rice farmers and sample such local delicacies as frogs, eels and fresh (and aromatic) durian fruit.

Like chameleons, we can learn to change our colors to blend into new surroundings. Today's explorers seek exclusive encounters, unique and authentic experiences. "Experiential," "immersion" and "peer-to-peer" travel are no longer cutting-edge buzzwords in the travel industry. But is this style of travel, indeed, unique? No: It's as old as civilization itself.

When Airbnb, the poster child of the "going local" movement, gave travelers the thumbs-up on bunking in private abodes some years ago, a new travel genre burst onto the scene. Today, apps and websites revolve around staying with residents, sharing meals prepared by a home chef, hitching rides, and being guided by the experts who know the lay of the land better than anyone: local residents.

As peer-to-peer (or "P2P") travel continues to make its mark on traditional touring, those who wander are finding far more places to stay than hotels, motels and hostels. In a home or apartment, you might easily score a sofa or a spare room. Universities often have rooms available in residence halls, especially in summer. And don't count out more exotic locales such as lighthouses, wineries, monasteries, boats or treehouses.

Total immersion

Never before has food played such a dominant role in choosing a travel destination. Fifteen years ago, few travelers might have proclaimed themselves "foodies"; now, national cuisine now a fundamental reason for many journeys. Globetrotters seek a greater understanding of their road habitats by means of cooking classes, visits to food markets, and commingling with locals through meal sharing.

Another rewarding way to see the world is by volunteering — traveling the world while helping others. You can work in a village in Africa, teach English in Myanmar, grow organic food in Guatemala, pick tea leaves in Sri Lanka, build houses in a Peruvian village, teach school children in Bangladesh, or take a marine conservation holiday in Thailand. Whether you are helping people, assisting with the environment or protecting animals, there's nothing better than giving back to your community, however great or small, by working side-by-side with the local people.

Wanderers must also be responsible travelers, protecting ecosystems and becoming environmentally and culturally responsible. Tour operators are crafting programs and individual trips to tread lightly, leaving a positive footprint on the places where they guide people. Our mantra: Leave it cleaner or safer than you found it.

In the United States of America, fewer than 50% of citizens own a passport. Our goal is to inspire our countrymen (and women) to you to get out and explore the vast richness of our planet. Please consider "Going Local" as a blueprint to more travel options and ways to enrich your travel experience.

Take off your blinders, travel like a local, and you're sure to return home with a better understanding of yourself and of the world around you.

Travel Better,

Nicholas Kontis

John Gottberg Anderson

Chapter One

PEER-TO-PEER TRAVEL:

A Place to Stay

The real voyage of discovery consists not in seeing new sights, but in looking with new eyes. — Marcel Proust

Proust, a French novelist and essayist, may have been 100 years ahead of his time when he made this observation early in the 20th Century. It certainly resonates well with today's curious, well-informed traveler.

As the number of travelers who immerse themselves in a sharing economy continues to increase, the travel landscape has been transformed. Never before has it been easier to "go local" with new ways to sleep, eat, play, meet, ride and blend into unfamiliar surroundings. Instead of patronizing corporate travel brokers and global hotel chains, travelers are finding they can rely upon the expertise of local residents to get to know a new locale.

While peer-to-peer (P2P) travel platforms lead the traditional tourism industry to reexamine its direction, P2P sites have snowballed. The sharing economy is increasing as users access its various assets. Tens of billions of dollars in venture capital funding have poured into the sector since 2010, disrupting traditional travel bookings as the tourism industry is increasingly driven by technology.

The hotel industry understands that some travelers prefer to stay in a home or apartment, versus a traditional hotel stay. Indeed, non-traditional booking sites pose a real threat to the conventional travel industry, as P2P lodging vanguards Airbnb, Home Away, Home Exchange and CouchSurfing make their mark in the hospitality market in a big way. But peer-to-peer (immersion) travel and hotels can coexist; in fact, many industry analysts believe hotels will make adjustments, remain competitive and grow stronger.

Rachel Botsman refers to this trend as "collaborative consumption." Co-author of *What's Mine Is Yours* (2017), she says: "The story you read in the media — and often echoed by travel industry incumbents — is that (the sharing economy is) a Generation Y thing for price-sensitive travelers. It's a sweeping generalization. If you look at the data, it's simply not true."

She later elaborated in a TED talk: "Something profound is changing our concept of trust. While we used to place our trust in institutions like governments and banks, today we increasingly rely on others, often strangers, on platforms like Airbnb and Uber ... This new era of trust could bring with it a more transparent, inclusive and accountable society — if we get it right. Who do you trust?"

Collaborative consumption. It's not just millennials who choose this style of travel. People of all ages and income levels, in search of experiences ranging from adventurous to indulgent, are engaging in peer-to-peer travel to enhance their journeys. Luxury travelers may seek the same profound encounters as backpackers, embracing surroundings with greater meaning than resort hotel rooms.

Those who enjoy more conventional experiences will stick to major hotel brands. They may prefer to be near the center of a city or close to popular tourist attractions. If you're a traveler in search of a more meaningful visit — one that may include living with friendly residents, eating and perhaps being guided by them while staying in an apartment or home farther from the city center — the peer-to-peer style of travel may be the right one for you.

We are reminded by Skift Global Forums, which tracks worldwide travel trends, that P2P is no longer merely the playground of hitchhikers and backpackers. It has grown into a multibillion-dollar industry thanks to the economic, social and technological changes of the early 21st Century.

Beyond a doubt, modern wanderers search for unique and enriching engagements that reveal a country's diversity. P2P travel amplifies the likelihood of such opportunities. The rise in immersion platforms is here to stay as travelers seek new ways to save money while crafting an authentic holiday.

A family-run homestay occupies an A-frame structure in Kyrgyzstan.

AIRBNB: Airbeds and Breakfast

By now, you've heard the story of how three guys turned renting air mattresses in their apartment into Airbnb, a company worth $83 billion as of July 2023.

In 2007, a large design convention in San Francisco, one of the most expensive cities in the world, had left its hotel rooms nearly sold out. So Brian Chesky and Joe Gebbia, forward thinkers who were barely scraping by after paying their rent each month, asked themselves: "Why not rent out our extra room and advertise it on the conference website?" The struggling flatmates rented out three airbeds on the floor and made a quick and easy buck.

From the simple idea of charging convention attendees for room and board, they would change the world of peer-to-peer travel forever. The whiz kids brought in another friend, computer-tech guru Nathan Blecharczyk, as their third partner, and the empire began. The original name of Airbed & Breakfast was later shortened to Airbnb. Founder Chesky still jokes, "Airbnb is the worst idea that ever worked."

After the first guests, the Airbnb team realized it might have lightning in a bottle. Airbnb rapidly emerged as an early leader in peer-to-peer travel. Along the way, the system model made some revolutionary advances, such as its Instant Book feature that allows people to quickly plan their vacations around P2P experiences. The Airbnb platform will match you up with locals who will rent you their spare room, apartment, or even a whole house. Not only is this a fantastic way to save money on costly hotels; by rooming with a local, you can uncover a whole new world of experiences unrivaled by traditional travel methods.

The Airbnb network offers properties in approximately 100,000 towns and cities in 220 countries. (North Korea, Syria and Iran are among the few not on the list.) Total arrivals have surpassed 1 billion people. Rapidly rebounding from the years of Covid shutdown, the company had more than 6 million active listings and 4 million hosts in 2022.

Today, savvy world travelers, high on creating long-lasting experiences, abandon pricey hotels for cozy, private digs—many of them unique, like houseboats and treehouses. Instead of staying in a hotel in Sydney's Martin Place or New York's Times Square, they choose quieter locations with authentic flavor and ambiance.

They may choose alternative neighborhoods like Psari in Athens, Lapa in Rio de Janeiro or the Mission District of San Francisco for their vibrant nightlife, old-school restaurants or exciting new chefs. Airbnb offers an opportunity to discover an off-the-beaten-path section of a city or to live on the outskirts of town.

Unique encounters happen when cultures blend, as people venture out to explore our amazing world. Travel opens your eyes like nothing else, in no small part due to the long-lasting relationships it creates. P2P sites like Airbnb help to change travelers' and hosts' perceptions of people whose cultures are very different from their own. Indeed, the 2016 launch of Airbnb Experiences has provided visitors with new options for tours (including photo and food tours), cooking classes, outdoor adventures and much more. The proliferation of low-cost airlines, coupled with the growing number of peer-to-peer accommodation options, assures that travel is as easy as ever and does not have to be expensive.

"Professional hobo" Nora Dunn travels the world on the cheap.

Travel stories

There are always exceptions, but it's rare when guests, and rarer when hosts, don't recall a visit with smiles on their faces.

Here are some examples:

- Samantha, an Airbnb host in Toronto, writes: "I have been hosting guests now for a little over two years. Among my early guests were a woman and her teenage son from Singapore. They came to check out Humber College, one of our better universities. Their English was good, but I understood from my travels that getting used to a foreign country is not always easy.

"Being a proud Torontonian, I offered to show them around my lovely city, and soon we became wonderful friends. They had never eaten Greek food, so I took them to my favorite Greek restaurant, Anestis Taverna. They were over the moon trying new cuisine with a local. When they left after a week, they bought me an expensive bottle of wine and some gourmet chocolates. They invited me to visit them in Singapore, and I'm still waiting for the right time to plan my visit."

- Damon and Melissa come from New Zealand, a country well removed from most travel routes. But they have the travel bug, and wanderlust fuels travel, even if it means traveling long and far. They came to rely upon Airbnb in trip planning, and stays in Hawaii, New York, Canada and Central America were all positive experiences. Soon after the birth of their son, Marlo, they adopted a nomadic lifestyle that began with a trip to a friend's wedding in Bali. As they were leaving, their Airbnb host gave Marlo a stuffed animal as a memory. They have been hooked on Airbnb ever since.

As a family, they find that Airbnbs give them a neighborhood familiarity not possible with a hotel room. "We can live in a residential area and have a touch of the experience of a local," Melissa says — "a favorite cafe, learning the supermarket's layout, the familiar characters you meet on the street." And in their apartment, "usually there's a kitchen to have a cozy meal should we feel like a night in."

Often, Airbnb hosts are the first locals you meet. They give you a sense of your new surroundings and the culture, often in immersive ways. When Damon and Melissa, traveling in Canada, booked a room in a house in Québec City, they were surprised to find the host and her daughter spoke only French. It was a "cross-cultural exchange for us all," Damon says. "The usual hand gestures, bad Google translations, and good laughs were enough to get everyone working together, our host included. We were glad to have made the leap."

The Kiwis' top tip: Travel light. "You only need half the stuff you think you do," the pair say. But it goes beyond packing: "Budget tighter to travel longer, step lightly and leave no trace."

- Dave Richards, of Houston, admits that he "was skeptical about the whole idea of staying in someone's home" when he took his maiden excursion into the world of P2P travel. "For my first try, I chose New York City," he recalls. "As anyone who has traveled to New York knows, the city can be costly. But besides saving money, I also wanted to experience a more local lifestyle. I wanted to wake up in a neighborhood as if I were a city resident.

"I opted for a nice apartment in Chelsea. My host, Ken, was a breath of fresh air. Ken even showed me his local coffee shop and some of his favorite restaurants and later took me on a walking tour. The experience was everything I wanted. I woke up in an actual home versus a hotel. I slept in my room with the owner down the hall. It was like living with family.

"Discovering Airbnb has changed my thoughts on travel. I would recommend it to anyone. I truly believe that, more often than not, hosts want to show off their native knowledge of the city, which enhances your experience."

- Meeting locals from other cultures showcases people's kindness and teaches that a better world can be forged through a sharing economy. Dana, whose home is in Cork, Ireland, says travel has opened up her perspective of people and places: "I used Airbnb on four continents on my 14-month trip around the world. I even stayed in a treehouse in Thailand. In almost every case, my hosts have been some of the nicest people I have ever met. They have guided me in directions that I might not have found. That alone is worth using Airbnb. My experiences have only been positive." *Airbnb.com*

HomeAway/VRBO

HomeAway started as a vacation-rental marketplace in 2005. Purchased in 2015 by the Expedia group, it merged in 2020 with VRBO (Vacation Rentals by Owner), and with more than 2 million paid listings in 190-plus countries, it is now the world's largest vacation-rental company connecting hosts and travelers. Like Airbnb, the platform leads guests toward experiences that may otherwise be unavailable to tourists, introducing them to locals and off-the-grid locations.

There is something for every taste and budget. VRBO offers an extensive selection of vacation rental homes, cabins, beach houses and more, providing travelers with memorable experiences and benefits for less cost than traditional accommodations. Indeed, the larger the group, the greater the savings. It's especially geared toward family travel: "The Whole House, The Whole Family," is the Home Away slogan. Kids love sharing their experience of discovery with the entire family.

Lifestyle blogger Heather B. Armstrong used HomeAway to find the perfect place to enjoy spring break in Newport Beach, California, with her two daughters and close friends. She wanted someplace close to the surf, and found a modern home just six houses from the sand. "This house had a balcony, patio and grill, and I loved shopping for food for the five days we were there. On Sunday, we had friends over for a beach date and a sunset barbecue. There were enough boogie boards for all the big kids, and there was a huge umbrella for me where I could watch them play in the sun from afar and be safe in the shade." *Vrbo.com*

HomeExchange

With HomeExchange, you don't just exchange homes; you exchange experiences. Founded in 1992 by Californian Ed Kushins as a printed, mail-order directory, it became a web-based platform four years later. The company was purchased in 2017 for $35 million by French competitor GuestToGuest but still operates under the HomeExchange brand.

"We are convinced the practice of home exchange will become the next big thing in tourism," CEO Emmanuel Arnaud said after the merger. Already, he has seen HomeExchange grow into a social network. As one of the first businesses to adopt the principle of collaborative consumption, it epitomizes the sharing economy.

The concept is very simple: When two homeowners go on vacation, they stay in one another's houses, even if they live a nation or a continent apart. As with other P2P enterprises, this creates meaningful experiences and enriching encounters with local people. Unlike the TV show "Home Swap"; HomeExchange provides an authentic experience on a real, local level. In many cases, home exchangers even meet the neighbors at their new digs.

HomeExchange offers nearly 150,000 home swaps in over 150 countries, including more than 1,000 in Asia; 4,000 in Australia, New Zealand and the Pacific; 1,000 in South America, and almost 500 in Africa. The merging of the two similar brands provides an alternative to Airbnb and HomeAway/VRBO. There are more than 65,000 active users on the site.

Valerie Erde and her family began house swapping over a decade ago. "The lodging is free," she points out. "It's a great way to save money for anyone who wants to travel." But there are numerous other benefits. "When we first started house swapping, our two children were young," she says. "You can exchange with a family who also has kids, and your kids are thrilled because you go to this new place, and they have all these new games and toys! And some people will even swap their cars."

Was Erde nervous about swapping with people she'd never met? Not particularly, she says: "Having a 'stranger' in my home has never bothered me. I wasn't nervous because I'm not that type of person. My husband calls me a 'What, me worry?' We've never had a problem, so we keep swapping." HomeExchange has taken them all over the United States and Canada, as well as England, Ireland and France.

A case study of creating local experiences through exchanging homes.

Travel seems to spawn moments of serendipity far more frequently than everyday life. One day while Nick was sunning by the pool in Puerto Vallarta, Mexico, he met a young couple from the city of Utrecht in The Netherlands. Norbert, a mechanical engineer, and Petra, a child psychologist, were traveling with their two boys, ages 4 and 7. After a bit of small talk, they told Nick they were on their second home exchange.

In August 2015, the Dutch professionals had exchanged homes with a Singapore family to attend the island nation's 50th anniversary festivities. They traded their four-bedroom home, 15 minutes from the center of Utrecht, for a three-bedroom condo near the Botanic Gardens in fashionable Singapore. "We would not have been able to find a hotel five minutes from the Botanic Gardens," Norbert told me. "We had a full home with our own kitchen to cook. We could send the kids to bed and have the evening to ourselves in a large living room. We even had a cleaning lady provided. It just makes more sense than a hotel for us."

"We also had more space in a real neighborhood where there was not a loud disco in a hotel sounding off all night," Petra continued. "We stayed in a real, local area. Our exchange hosts gave us a list of places to see, things to do, and restaurants to eat. We enjoyed the experience better than a hotel. Everybody can find a Starbucks, but not everybody can find an unknown coffee shop on a small street. Our hosts gave us so much information that we would have had difficulty finding otherwise."

As the children continued to splash and play in the condo club pool, I asked Petra how the sharing economy and HomeExchange.com worked out, having two hyperactive young boys. "Our children are becoming world travelers through home exchange," she said. "Our kids now have been on Home Exchange in Asia and Mexico. My oldest is already asking, 'Mom, where are we going next year?' On this trip, he bought a Spanish language book to try to learn some Spanish words. Our 4-year-old was living in Singapore, playing with other young children, and even loving the Asian diet, eating rice three times a day."

Norbert told me the family's three-week stay in Puerto Vallarta included a brand-new pickup truck. "Our new exchange friends have given it to us to use at our leisure," he laughed. "Back home in Holland, if we were to ask to borrow a friend's car for three weeks, they would look at us like we're crazy."

Petra was thrilled with the economy. "For a marginal fee to Home Exchange (now $220 a year with no fee for the exchange), we only need to buy a plane ticket to get somewhere. Our home is watched, and we get to live like a local family lives. HomeExchange has made us discover that people worldwide are very much the same; when you arrive in a new place like here in Mexico, we see that people are people wherever we go."

A lifetime of memories thanks to HomeExchange.com.

William had a dream. It was also his father's dream. "My dad died before he could retire, but he was always a big traveler and dreamed of seeing the world," William said. "So I retired at 59 to see one country for every year of my age. With 83 countries on my list, I've surpassed my goal."

He's done it using HomeExchange.com. Having made over 100 exchanges, William has been able to pursue his wanderlust and explore the world as a traveler, not a tourist. The life-altering first exchange was in San Francisco in the 1990s, before the rise of the internet. Communication was by means of a mail-order catalog of available homes. At that time, William said, even house keys were exchanged by mail.

Travel reveals the kindness of strangers, and William embraces a plethora of memories of positive experiences through the HomeExchange platform. While on an exchange in Hawaii, for instance, his hosts took things up a notch by leaving their car for him at the airport.

One of his most memorable swaps was in Bali: "You couldn't ask for a better setting. The house was fabulous and overlooked rice terraces. They had a staff of five people, including maids, gardeners, a driver and a cook. This was something that I never expected."

He fondly recalls unforgettable exchange in Ethiopia. "It was the only home in Ethiopia on the whole site at the time," William said. "We stayed at a couples casita, and the couple invited us into their home, cooking for us, sharing meals, and taking great pride in showing us around their country."

Without a doubt, the sharing economy and budget-friendly travel contribute to the creation of lifelong friendships. William treasures the friends he has made all over the world. He has even met his exchange families in Romania and Australia. *Homeexchange.com*

Travel encourages new friendships with a wide range of people.

HOTELS IN THE SHARING ECONOMY

Just because you decide to stay in a hotel doesn't mean that you cannot "go local." Hotels have begun to hook their wagons to the collaborative consumption train.

"Experiential travel is what the modern guest is after," acknowledges Sarah Came, marketing manager for GuestRevu, a hotel consulting brand. Hotels, she said, have learned they must "satisfy their clientele's wanderlust and exceed expectations. Hotels need to provide more than just a bed or a room for the night. (They must provide) an experience worth traveling and paying for."

The IceHotel in Jukkasjarvi, Sweden, provides an experience that can only be replicated by staying at other ice hotels, of which there are precious few. Sculpted out of ice from the Torne River, the hotel is a work of art, built only in the winter season with a brand new design each year. Located fewer than 150 miles from the Arctic Circle, this place of solace and silence welcomes guests who want to witness the Northern Lights phenomenon.

The opulent, 800-year-old Ashford Castle in County Mayo, Ireland, is a popular get-away spot for monarchs and movie stars. Guests optimize their historic stay by engaging in archery, falconry, clay-pigeon shooting and horseback riding.

Well aware that modern travelers want more immersion in new environs, hotels are finding ways to provide. Travelers still seek value for price, but they also weigh other factors in choosing their accommodations — not the least of which are the amenities and activities offered by the hotel's food-and-drink establishments. Many hotel restaurants now promote locally sourced products and organize such activities as farm-to-table wine dinners, cooking classes, wine and craft-beer tastings, even market tours with the chef or a local guide. They follow the P2P model by introducing guests to local musicians and artists, coffee producers and distillers.

Concierges and other reception-desk employees are on the front line. They're the ones who will point guests down the road less traveled, further from the city center and its core attractions, as the visitors search for off-the-beaten-path or even trendy neighborhoods away from the financial center — places like Roma, Condesa and Juárez in Mexico City.

Modern boutique hotels may even be located in these gentrified neighborhoods. In Tokyo, travelers may be seen meandering the streets and shops, patronizing hip restaurants and hopping nightclubs, in such neighborhoods as neon-filled Shibuya, energetic Shimokitazawa, or old-fangled Yanaka. Hotel guests increasingly expect a concierge or receptionist to point them toward these sights, sounds and tastes. Hotels are happily rising to the challenge.

Hospitality means making a hotel feel more like home. Just because a hotel is located in an upscale neighborhood does not mean the property cannot take on a home feel. One example of a hotel rising to the challenge is the Athenaeum Hotel & Residences in the swank London borough of Mayfair. Here, guests may borrow on-site bicycles with locks and an interactive map to tour the city. Knowledgeable concierges offer tickets to the newest theater in town, directions to an out-of-the-way pub, or a reminder of a farmer's market or neighborhood flea market.

As hotel executives glance over their shoulders at Airbnb and other P2P sites, they increasingly strive to enhance the guest experience. And it's not just high-end hotels taking notice. Platforms such as Twitter are helping hotels to augment the guest experience. Hotels now monitor most inquiries online. During a recent stay at New York's LUMA Hotel Times Square, guest Darla Rose tweeted that she lost her toothbrush. "I can't begin to tell you the shock on my face when a new toothbrush was brought to my room in a matter of minutes," said Rose.

The Place, Florence, Italy. There may be no finer example of a hotel impersonating a home than The Place (formerly Hotel J.K. Place) in Florence. This precious, hidden gem is located well outside of the city center, the Piazza Santa Maria Novella. A three-year facelift turned this old condominium into exquisite guest quarters — a house that one might expect to find in a posh London neighborhood. Its entrance could be easily mistaken for a Florentine residence.

"We do not want to be considered a hotel," said Claudio Meli, the dapper general manager of The Place. "You ring a bell to get inside: It's like visiting your rich uncle in Florence. Even the chef cooks like my mama cooks. After all, this is your home."

Each of the hotel's 20 rooms is different from the next, Meli said, because the renovating architect had to work with the layout of the original structure. Guests don't check in; they are greeted, seated in the living room, offered a beverage, and directed to the self-serve *cicchetti* (tapas) bar. Meli himself may offer the first welcome. A native Florentine Renaissance man, the manager himself has written a book that showcases hidden corners. In his *Essential Guide To Florence*, you will find all that Meli loves about his city. *Theplacefirenze.com*

Heaven Rwanda Retreat, Kigali, Rwanda. Despite its spectacular national park and famous mountain gorillas, the small central African nation of Rwanda has not been on safari travelers' radar for long. Yet for two decades, an American couple has played a leading role in promoting tourism. This compound of two hotels and a restaurant sits on a quiet road, a short walk from the center of the capital, Kigali.

Josh and Alissa Ruxin first came to Rwanda to work in public health. The tourism industry needed help, especially with regard to hospitality training and gourmet restaurants. So Alissa built Heaven, which quickly became Kigali's top restaurant, from the ground up. As Heaven grew, it spawned a boutique hotel. When luxury operators followed and built incredible resorts close to the gorillas, the Ruxins kept up with the competition: They built The Retreat and its stunning poolside restaurant, Fusion.

When Heaven opened in 2008, it was a pioneer in training young Rwandan adults for careers in the growing tourism sector. Today, Heaven and The Retreat have 120 employees. The mantra is: "Make guests feel welcome and share your culture!" Smiling faces and curiosity now accompany visitors on personalized guided tours of Kigali, native villages, and the breathtaking landscape of Rwanda. *Heavenrwanda.com*

Unexpected visitors drop in on diners at Nairobi's Giraffe Hotel.

COUCH SURFING

Ever since Noah first invited strangers to share his ark, friends and travelers have been crashing on each other's couches or in a spare room. The modern vagabond uses CouchSurfing to save money, meet locals, and perhaps briefly share in their lifestyle. It's overnighting with friends, even when those friends live a world away.

Travel spawns creativity and invention. In this case, 21-year-old Casey Fenton conceived Couchsurfing in 1999. It began with a cheap ticket to Iceland. Taking the travel plunge, he realized that he had no accommodations. Now, Iceland's capital, Reykjavik, is one of the world's most expensive cities: For the young Fenton, pricey hotels were not a viable option. So the tech-savvy traveler hacked into the University of Iceland's list of students and sent emails to over 1,000 students. A lightbulb went on when nearly 100 people responded. Casey returned to San Francisco and co-founded CouchSurfing.

Today, many people consider CouchSurfing as the origin of the P2P economy, even though it wasn't built with a business model in mind. There are now about 12 million couchsurfers in virtually every country and territory in the world. It is one of the most robust P2P social communities today: Exceptionally friendly people, CouchSurfers are changing the way travelers sleep and meet inhabitants. Got a couch or a spare room? Offer it to a new friend who you don't know yet.

Although more popular with younger backpackers, we have both used the site occasionally with relative success. A lovely couple in the old mission town of San Luis Obispo, on the central California coast, hosted Nick for two nights, going above and beyond by taking him on a nearby wine-tasting sojourn. When John offered a sofa to a traveler en route to Seattle from the Amazon jungle, where he had been studying natural botanical medicine, their conversation lasted all night. Nick, on the other hand, barely saw his Russian host during a three-night stay in a spare room at the man's east London apartment.

Travel expert and digital nomad Matthew Kepnes is the author of a popular blog, "Nomadic Matt" *(nomadicmatt.com)*. In his blog entry "How to Crush it on CouchSurfing," Kepnes suggests: "You need a positive attitude and a desire to be part of a community. You can't just want to use people for a free place."

Nomadic Matt offers additional advice on how to approach potential hosts. "Hosts still get inundated with more requests than they can handle, and you have to make yourself stand out," he says. "If you're sending out dozens of requests and no one writes back — even to say no — then something is wrong with your approach. Hosts can usually smell the travelers who want to use them for a free place to stay a mile away (a lesson I learned the hard way early on).

"The people you are reaching out to have real lives and take you into their home for free. The dates might not work and/or they might get so many requests (very true for popular destinations) that they don't have time to respond to them all. So how do you find people who will agree to host you? Show that you want to be involved in the (CouchSurfing) community. That you care."

According to Daniel Hoffer, CouchSurfing's former CEO, couch surfing is remarkably safe. "We have had over 6 million positive experiences, with only a tiny fraction of 1 percent negative," he said.

And anything can happen when you venture out into the sharing-economy world. When 30-year-old Callie hosted Jake, a male CouchSurfer, during a comedy festival, she was surprised when the guy who showed up didn't look or act like his profile information. However, she quickly changed her mind when he gave her tickets to his stand-up routine and she saw how animated he became on stage. Jake stayed a few extra days and came back to see her two weeks later. The couple married the following September, just over a year after their first meeting.

"CouchSurfing was a comfort blanket when I lived in Budapest for a while," said Ben Lee of Edinburgh, Scotland. "Hungarian is one of the hardest languages in

the world to master, so communication was not the best at the start. CouchSurfing meet-ups led me to meet other travelers in the same situation. It's the perfect community without the traditional community caveats of a physical set location."

The movement has grown to epic proportions as a way for cultures to connect. There are members in every country, including North Korea, Pakistan, Vatican City, and even Antarctica. All told, members speak more than 365 languages, including Igbo, Yapese and Khandeshi. Heard of those, have you? *Couchsurfing.com*

OTHER HELPFUL APPS

The sharing economy offers many alternatives to staying in pricy hotels. You can rent an apartment, stay in a hostel, share a room or settle into a couch in a private home, throw down your tent in someone's yard, exchange homes or watch someone's house. The best part is that most options are economical, and some can be free. Whether you're a backpacker, a homeowner, traveling with a family, an LGBTQ traveler, on a short journey or a life-changing trip around the world, the sharing economy makes travel more accessible to all demographics.

In 2006, Nora Dunn sold everything she owned in Canada (including a busy financial planning practice) to embrace her dream of world travel. She has been on the move ever since as a professional traveler through 75 countries (and counting). On her website, The Professional Hobo (*theprofessionalhobo.com*), she helps people travel full-time in creative, rewarding, and (most essentially) financially sustainable ways.

"In my first 12 years of full-time travel, I saved over $100,000 on accommodation expenses and also had some of the most culturally rewarding and immersive experiences in so doing," said Dunn. "I befriended locals and enjoyed opportunities that I would never have found if I were simply staying in hotels.

"Accommodation is the most expensive travel aspect, so when you can get it for free, it's a huge money-saver," she continued. "There are five ways to [stay] for free: volunteering (work exchange), house-sitting, living on boats, hospitality exchanges, and home exchanges. Each is appealing in its way, though I discovered that some are better suited than others to the digital nomad lifestyle."

In her book *How to Get Free Accommodation Around the World*, Dunn shows travelers where to find free lodging gigs and how to sift good opportunities from duds. She offers tips for standing out on applications and provides strategies for staying safe and covering all necessary due diligence. Careful planning pays for itself many times over in your first night of free accommodation, and from that day forward, your travels will never be the same.

No matter your travel style or budget, here are some opportunities beyond Airbnb where you might consider hunkering down on your next adventure.

BeWelcome (hospitality network)

Ever since CouchSurfing came along, like-minded travelers have found ways to connect, share, and save money while exchanging ideas and integrating with generous hosts. BeWelcome is about meeting others. There are over 220,000 members in 221 countries on the platform. BeWelcome believes sharing creates a better world. Hosts and guests may be found everywhere in the world. *Bewelcome.org*

Campspace (camp in someone's yard)

What's better than the great outdoors? If camping is your thing and you're traveling on a budget, Campspace allows you to discover micro-camping as you stay in a local's yard or an open space. Bring your tent or campervan. For the active and adventurous traveler, camping can be a year-round lifestyle. *Campspace.com*

FlipKey (vacation rentals)

A leading site in the vacation rental space is FlipKey from Tripadvisor. Homeowners can list their homes with the world's largest travel community, offering guests a perfect stay for their next vacation. FlipKey is managed by property managers as well as by homeowners. *Flipkey.com*

Hostelworld (hostel stays)

When you stay in a hostel — when you bunk in a dormitory and share your living space — you meet the real world, not the tourist brochure. That's what Hostelworld promotes:

interacting with fellow travelers while seeing the world on a budget. Hostel travelers drive the growth of sustainable travel as "green travelers." This site helps you connect with like-minded global explorers even before you arrive at your destination. *Hostelworld.com*

Hotel Tonight (Last-minute deals)

Even the most meticulous trip planners run into last-minute hotel needs. Acquired by Airbnb, Hotel Tonight is a game-changer in planning your hotel stay or vacation. Most hotels have rooms available on the day of travel or a few days before or after. Hotel Tonight offers stays at some of the world's finest hotels for half the price or more that you might pay on other hotel booking sites. *Hoteltonight.com*

Love Home Swap (home exchange)

One need look no further than the 2017 purchase of this site by Wyndham Worldwide to understand that the hotel industry has embraced alternative travel options—in this case, to the tune of $53 million. The Love Home Swap platform represents a passionate community of traveling homeowners who appreciate saving money by trading homes and creating new travel experiences. They're looking to switch it up, take a local break, or even work from someone else's location. *Lovehomeswap.com*

One Fine Stay (luxury vacation rentals)

If you're seeking extravagance on your next vacation, choose from thousands of luxurious properties in this curated collection of homes, villas, and apartments in the world's most desirable destinations. You may find a beach estate in St. Barts, a townhouse in Manhattan, or a villa in the south of France. Each home is hand-picked for space, character, and comfort. *Onefinestay.com*

Stay in a Pub (Great Britain pub stays)

If you truly want to explore local life in the United Kingdom, you really must head to a pub. It's no accident that many British pubs offer accommodations: The name "pub" is short for "public house," and historically, a pub was designed to offer lodging and simple meals for travelers. The "Stay in a Pub" site lists more than 55,000 pubs, taverns, and inns in the British Isles, and each is fully categorized. *Stayinapub.co.uk*

Third Home (home exchange)

Another home-exchange platform, Third Home rides the sharing economy wave by encouraging travelers to offer weeks in their own homes, in return receiving credits to stay rent-free in other members' homes. As it's a membership organization, families around the world are readily trusted. Third Home presently offers 15,000 homes in more than 100 countries. *Thirdhome.com*

Under Canvas (luxury glamping)

Presently available only in the United States, this is glamping for travelers who enjoy indulgence under the stars. Modeled after opulent African safari camps, Under Canvas couples sumptuous lodging and gourmet dining with unique adventures in or near 11 national parks and monuments across America. These include five parks in Utah's red-rock wilderness, as well as Grand Canyon, Yellowstone, Glacier, Mount Rushmore, Great Smoky Mountains, and Acadia. *Undercanvas.com*

Unique Lodges of the World (sustainable stays)

National Geographic's trusted collection of unique lodging goes far beyond a selection of world-class hotels. Sustainability meets splendor at inspiring properties that create the rarest of travel experiences. Each lodge tells a story deeply rooted in its community and surroundings to protect surrounding habitats and cultures. *Nationalgeographiclodges.com*

Wimdu (vacation rentals)

Another successful vacation rental site that offers worldwide accommodations is Wimdu. Here you'll find a collection of over 350,000 vacation rentals with prices starting at under $15 a night. Whether you're seeking a city apartment in Athens, a spacious loft in Prague, or a beach house in Santa Monica, your next perfect vacation match just might be a rental you discover on Wimdu. *Wimdu.com*

WORKING FARM STAYS

Agricultural tourism, or "agritourism," is one of the fastest-growing sectors of the experiential travel industry. Not everyone is drawn to cities and beaches. Many travelers prefer to stay where the air is fresh and the grass is always green, in the rural countryside. Agritourism welcomes travelers to working farms and ranches that open their doors to guests.

The farm accommodation concept started in Europe — in northern Italy and in the British Isles — in the early 1970s. Today, wherever there are nations with large open expanses and farm fields, the prospect of living (however briefly) in a rural location is a huge draw for travelers young and old. From the United States and Canada to Australia, Brazil, Costa Rica, Taiwan and the Philippines, to name but a few locations, countryside lovers are living out their dreams.

Perhaps best known of several agencies that create these opportunities is WWOOF, "Worldwide Opportunities on Organic Farms." It was launched in 1971 by London secretary Sue Coppard, who was convinced there must be many other people, like herself, who sought the occasion to get out of the city and support the growing organic agriculture movement in the British countryside. An initial trial working weekend on a biodynamic farm in Sussex was the seed that germinated into an international movement. Today hundreds of thousands of WWOOFers trade their labor for food and lodging at farms where sustainable practices are a way of life. *Wwoof.net*

Changing perceptions about sustainable food and dining make this alternative holiday especially attractive for "woke" older wanderers along with naturally aware younger travelers. At an older farm, you might stay in former stables or a separate, detached cottage. Or your accommodation could be in a winery, a large apartment or a bed-and-breakfast room.

The countryside is the perfect destination for a relaxing family holiday. Activities could include working in orchards and fields, harvesting olives or grapes, feeding livestock, curing meats, or picking coffee (in the tropics). And who doesn't enjoy visiting a public market to gather ingredients for the day's meals?

In your free time, you might hike or mountain-bike the nearby hills, ride horses, go birdwatching, or take part in a cooking class. And many properties have now added swimming pools and other luxurious boutique comforts. *Agritourismworld.com*

There are no foreign lands. It is the traveler only who is foreign. – Robert Louis Stevenson

Chapter Two

TESTING THE SHARING ECONOMY

Using Travel Apps

The real voyage of discovery consists not in seeing new sights, but in looking with new eyes. —
Marcel Proust

Early in our lives as world travelers, 40 or 50 years ago, we had to go to post offices, or international telephone exchanges, to stand in line and wait for pay phones. Then we could place collect calls to our parents just to let them know we were alive and well ... or alive and not so well, as the case may have been.

A couple of years back, Nick was parked atop a furry hump in central Australia's spellbinding red-rock desert when his wife called. "Honey, how is your trip going?" she queried. Nick sighed as his gaze settled on the immense monolith of Uluru, once known as Ayers Rock. "Well, it's not the best time to chat," he responded. "Why is that?" "I'm riding on a camel in the Outback." "Wonderful," she said. "Let's Facetime!" And so they did. My, how travel has changed.

The internet has revolutionized the way we plan our travels. Nowadays, apps facilitate every step of the process. A bounty of apps helps us plot everything, from making last-minute flight plans or lodging reservations to determining where to eat, what to see and how to get around.

In our younger years, we traveled with bulky guidebooks (Lonely Planet, as often as not) and unwieldy paper maps — lovely to look at on a dining-room table, but decidedly awkward on a windy street corner. (John still prefers the maps, but he's old school.) Nowadays, travel apps help us to navigate our surroundings after we arrive in a new city or country. Apps can help convert currency, translate or learn a language, make a dinner reservation, book theater or museum tickets, and make new friends.

John has long described himself as a "Third World junkie." His first encounter with the developing world occurred in 1976, when he arrived on the Indonesian isle of Bali after a long hitchhike across Australia and a shorter flight from Darwin. He frankly didn't know what to expect. Guided by Tony Wheeler's original *Southeast Asia on a Shoestring*, which in its first edition was as thin as a shoestring potato, he landed at the Denpasar airport without a hotel reservation and with no greater plan than to find his way to Kuta Beach. Not to worry: As backpackers like himself shuffled through immigration, they were swarmed by dozens of young men whose job was to recruit new guests to their families' *losmen* (guest houses). He succumbed to one youth's charming smile, threw his pack into the back of a motorized *bemo,* and launched a romance with Southeast Asian culture that nearly half a century later still has its shine.

But that was then. This is now. In the 1970s, accommodations and restaurants weren't chosen from cell phones. Indeed, there were no cell phones. We wrapped ourselves in *sarongs* (there's nothing so wrong with a *sarong*) and walked to the beach for mushroom omelets, *bakmi goreng* noodles, and black-rice pudding. Today, the wealth of resources that today's Marco Polo has at his fingertips is mind-boggling. From budget airfares, alternative accommodations, community building, dining, or ... you name it. Wherever you find yourself in the travel-planning process, there's an app for that.

"If you want to know a culture, spend a night in its bars," said Ernest Hemingway.

GETTING OFF THE GROUND

While travel advisors may still play an integral role in trip planning, mobile phones and the internet rule our lives. That's especially true for trip planning.

The deluge of trip planner apps out there not only helps you book a flight, but find a better seat, which credit card to use, how to pack better, organize your documents, find an airport lounge, and join in on travel forums.

AirHelp (flight delays). We've all spent countless hours sitting at airports waiting for our flights to depart. What if your flight is delayed: Are you entitled to compensation? Based in Berlin, Germany, AirHelp is the number one air passenger rights expert. If your flight is delayed more than three hours, contact AirHelp, as you may be entitled to up to $1,000 in reimbursement. *AirHelp.com*

FlightAware (flight tracking). With the FlightAware app, you can check your flights, tracking planes in real-time online for delays and cancellations with a live tracking map. This app allows you to keep up to date on any flight status by airline, flight number, or airport. You can check for gate changes and receive mobile push notifications and flight alerts, even charter and private jets. *Flightaware.com*

Flyer Talk (flyer travel forum). In 1998, Randy Peterson founded the thriving travel community FlyerTalk is, where frequent travelers from around the world exchange knowledge of flights, airlines, and airfare. A forum analysis for investigating frequent flyer programs, hotel loyalty programs, and other related issues mainly delving into the world of flying. *FlyerTalk.com*

Hopper (when to book flights). Many experts agree that booking on Tuesday is the best day of the week to find the least expensive airfares. Hopper, with a 95% accuracy and up to one year in advance, predicts prices, helping you book your flights and even your hotel stays at the right. Hopper has helped over 30 million people secure flights and hotels at the right time, with an average savings of up to 40%. *Hopper.com*

Kayak (flights, hotels, cars). The leader in finding fares on various 3rd party sites is Kayak. Prices come from trusted travel sites. Kayak scans the web for the best deals on flights, hotels, and car rentals. Price alerts allow you to track the lowest prices on flights and hotels with an email or a text message. If you're not where to go, Explore everywhere you can fly and even set your budget. Price Forecast will tell you when to book or wait for a flight. *Kayak.com*

Lounge Buddy (airport lounge access). I've had more extended layovers with uncomfortable or no seating than I can count. American Expres Travel's airport lounge booking platform Lounge Buddy allows you to reserve access to airport lounges. The service will enable you to buy one-time passes entering lounges in 80 airports worldwide. There is no pricey membership fee, meaning you can access Lounge Buddy as you need it. *Loungebuddy.com*

Airside Mobile Passport (global entry). A privacy-first digital identity management tool, Airside enables hassle-free entry for American and Canadian Passport holders to 43 international airports in the U.S., Canada and the Caribbean, as well as four cruise ports. The storage of personal information including passport, driver's license and COVID vaccination information lets travelers avoid long customs lines without screening. Airside is approved by major government agencies, including the Transportation Security Administration (TSA). *Airsidemobile.com*

Momondo (global aggregator). Perhaps especially outside the United States, the free global aggregator Momondo, founded in 2006, based in Copenhagen and managed by Kayak, helps you find the best deals comparing flights, car rentals, hotels and package holidays. With a vision that travel should be affordable to all, Momondo is free with no booking fees and never uses cookies to inflate prices. *Momondo.com*

One Mile at a Time (points and miles). If you're new to miles and points, you'll find a wealth of resources on this flight-centric travel blog. Ben "Lucky" Schlapig was a college student when he launched the site. Since childhood, he has been obsessed with aviation and travel, and he's passionate about airports. Lucky shares his knowledge of how to use airline miles and credit-card points to save money, enhancing the travel experience. Savvy travelers find helpful trip-planning advice on the site. *Onemileatatime.com*

Pack Point (packing for weather). As Mark Twain once wrote, "Everybody talks about the weather, but no one does anything about it." Over 50% of travelers worldwide use weather apps. PackPoint is an intelligent packing list app featured in numerous newspapers and travel publications. The genius app will organize what you should pack based upon how long you will travel — further rationalizing where and when you are traveling, accounting for the weather, and considering the activities you have planned during your trip. *Packpnt.com*

Priority Pass (airport lounge access). I'm thrilled when I find solace with access to a lounge when I'm at an airport. I use Priority Pass to be able to enter nearly 1,400 lounges worldwide. I often get a hot meal, free drinks and free Wi-Fi. Some lounges take it up a notch with offerings like spa treatments, massage rooms, or even sleeping quarters for short-term rest. Priority Pass is free to American Express Platinum members. The great thing is that you're allowed lounge access no matter the class of service you're flying. *Prioritypass.com*

Rome2rio (global trip planning). One of my favorite trip-planning apps is Rome2rio. You can search for any city, town, landmark, attraction, or address across the globe, and it will give you options on how to travel from point A to Point B. Whether you want a flight, train, bus, ferry, rideshare or rental car info, Rio2rio gives estimated prices, journey durations and booking details from over 5,000 companies in more than 160 countries – making it one of the top online travel resources used globally. *Rome2rio.com*

SeatGuru (best flight seating). At one time or another, we've all had horrible seats on airplanes. SeatGuru, a gem in the Tripadvisor family of stellar travel companies, was created to help travelers choose the best seats and in-flight amenities — from extra legroom to the best window views, reclining seats, and comparison of airlines and air-craft. *Seatguru.com*

Going (budget air travel). Established in 2013 as Scott's Cheap Flights, this site promises that you'll never overpay for flights again. Scott Keyes and his team of over 25 airfare experts find deals saving up to 80% off airlines' published fares and provide insider tips on when and where to find them. Over 1 million people subscribe to his daily flight-deal email. Subscribers claim to have paid half the cost of flights. *going.com*

Skyscanner (low-cost air and lodging). Business Insider magazine lauds this travel metasearch engine: "Of all the flight-buying websites, Skyscanner is almost always the cheapest due to its multi-city searches, price trend tracker, and secret 'everywhere' feature." Based in Edinburgh, Scotland, and owned by Trip.com, it is designed to find the lowest cost of airfare and hotels. It is not a virtual travel agent: Provider airlines, hotels or other operators process your payment. Skyscanner's blog offers excellent insights and inspiration. *Skyscanner.com*

Soar (fear of flying). Created by licensed therapist Tom Bunn, a retired airline pilot, the Soar app helps people conquer their fear of flying. The app's simple layout is divided into various relief courses. Classes include all parts of the flying experience including navigating the airport, check-in, boarding, take-off and relaxing in flight. The app is free. *Fearofflying.com*

The Points Guy (points and miles). It's a tricky business keeping up with the constant changes in flying, airlines and saving money on your next journey. Have you ever wondered which is the best plastic to carry? Points and miles expert Brian Kelly researches and analyzes credit cards, airline cards, airlines and more. His blog also evaluates news and deals, road trips, travel tips and gear, and taking off with points and miles. *ThePointsGuy.com*

Time Shifter (minimizing jet lag). As seen in leading travel magazines, any airline can get you from A to B; timeshifter makes sure you arrive refreshed. Even if you flew business class, you lay awake in a bed that's not your own, usually unable to sleep. Timeshifter was developed by world-renowned scientists, taking into account light and time zones, using the latest research on sleep and circadian neuroscience. *Timeshifter.com*

TripCase and Tripit (managing travel bookings). You might book airfare, car rental, theater tickets and a tour on a single holiday. TripCase and Tripit work the same way, managing your trip details into one streamlined itinerary, keeping all of your travel reservations in one place. TripCase can also help with flight delays, booking ground transportation and suggesting nearby activities. Add travel details, forward your confirmations to the app, and let TripCase or Tripit manage your vacation. TripIt stores a detailed, daily itinerary focusing on important dates, times and confirmation numbers, directions, maps, weather and more. *Tripcase.com, Tripit.com*

MANAGING YOUR EXPENSES

Money may not make the world go round, but you'll need to manage your money if your goal is to get around the world. Finding an ATM, knowing the current exchange rate, knowing how much to tip, tracking your expenses, and transferring money is vital to keeping you on the road.

Allpoint (ATM Finder). Somewhere in our travels, most of us have been in need of immediate cash. That means blindly seeking an ATM only to travel around in circles while not finding one. With Allpoint, you find ATMs virtually anywhere in the world. With over 55,000 participating surcharge-free ATMs, you're never too far away from your cash. One of every 12 ATMs in the United States is an Allpoint participant. *Allpointnetwork.com*

Wise (Online Money Transfer Service). The easy-to-use online money transfer service Wise (formerly TransferWise) allows travelers to send and receive money in 77 countries worldwide without the hassle of costly banks and pricey PayPal fees. TravelWise also has a global MasterCard using the exchange rate of the day. The service also is much quicker than a bank, usually sending money within 24 hours. *Wise.com*

XE Currency (Currency App). This all-in-one currency app, part of the Euronet Worldwide group of companies, allows you to track your expenses and foreign-exchange fees when purchasing in different currencies. The XE app provides you with up-to-the-minute exchange rates. You can convert up to 180 currencies on your phone for free. *XE.com*

American idyll - Two young men, a rental trailer, a guitar and a barbecue.

GETTING AROUND (TRANSPORTATION)

Getting around has never been more fun, and nowadays, you can share almost anything. The P2P movement offers an intriguing range of options to rent cars, boats, motorcycles, RVs and trailers. Prices are almost always cheaper than the traditional renting method, with opportunities worldwide. Plus, Uber and its alternatives can provide taxi-style service.

Ridesharing

In Nick's teenage years, he hitchhiked throughout Europe. In his 20s, John thumbed it through New Zealand, Australia, Southeast Asia and northern Europe, as well as the United States. Today, hitchhiking has mostly been replaced by ridesharing, a far safer option.

Sharing expenses with a driver heading the same way as you is a fantastic way to travel long distances. It's especially popular in Europe. Let's say that you want to travel from Madrid to Barcelona. A driver will be heading between two of Spain's most popular cities.

The driver saves on gas while the passenger travels faster than on a bus. Many times, new friendships form on rideshares.

BlaBlaCar (ridesharing). In Europe, the undisputed ridesharing leader is BlaBlaCar. The long-distance car-pooling platform supports a trusted community of 90 million drivers and passengers in 22 countries. (The website is translated in all of their languages). It connects long-haul travelers with drivers headed in the same direction, doubling (or more) the occupancy of the vehicle and creating a carbon-saving network. In addition to Europe, BlaBlaCar operates in Brazil, India, Mexico and Turkey. *Blablacar.com*

Car sharing

GetAround. As an alternative to pricier car rental companies, GetAround is a car-sharing platform powered by GetAround Connect technology. There is no need to meet the owner to exchange keys. Drivers can easily rent and unlock excellent cars, as shared by nearby residents. The site employs key-less technology and instant booking; cars can be opened with your phone. *Getaround.com*

Turo. Formerly CarHopper, Turo is the world's largest car-sharing marketplace, operating in the United States, Canada, England and Australia. An online marketplace, Turo pairs clients with trusted local providers to rent unforgettable luxury and exotic cars. Enhanced cleaning policies require all vehicles to be clean and disinfected. Check-in options are contact-free, and cancellations are flexible. *Turo.com*

Boat sharing

BoatAround, Get My Boat and Nautal. Don't assume a sailing holiday is beyond your budget. Sailing is not solely for the privileged, and many boats sit idle. These three sites, based in the Mediterranean, connect boat owners and vacationers in the same way as other sharing websites.

For glamorous yachting on the cheap, for instance, Get My Boat allows you to search among 130,000 certified boats in 184 countries, without crew-and-skipper options. BoatAround brokers sailing yachts, motorboats and much more in 74 countries from the Baltic to the Caribbean, Tahiti to the Seychelles, for as little as US $28 a day. Nautal works primarily in the Mediterranean and Caribbean. Each of these companies also of-

fers fishing charters, whale watching, dive trips and houseboat rentals. *Boataround.com,*
Getmyboat.com, Nautal.com

Global explorer Patricia Schultz hikes Spain's Camino de Santiago pilgrimage trail.

Regional options

North America

Kangaride. Slightly larger than the United States, with a much smaller population, Canada has a vast amount of open space. Based in Montréal, Kangaride is ideal for long-distance ridesharing through the nation's far-flung provinces. Passengers and drivers post their beginning and end points on the website to make connections. Drivers save on petrol as passengers share the cost of fuel. Cheaper than the bus or train, riders can get insights from a Canadian perspective. *Kangaride.com*

RVShare. Road trips have been around for as long as humans have been mobile. Many people who cherish the open road find self-reflection and inspiration in nature. In the United States and Canada, RVShare has tapped this desire with the world's first and largest peer-to-peer marketplace for rentals of recreational vehicles. Even if you don't own an RV, you can appreciate its advantages by getting off the grid in national parks and forests, mountain and lake regions, and other natural wonderlands. Rather than letting their RV sit idle most of the year, owners are happy to share it with responsible drivers. With key-less entry. *Rvshare.com*

Twisted Road. America's top P2P biking community, Twisted Road links travelers with motorcyclists who are willing to rent out their bikes. Think Turo, but with two wheels instead of four. Who knows: They may even decide to join you on the ultimate road trip. *Twistedroad.com*

Latin America

Cabify. Sometimes a taxi is easier to find than an Uber or Lyft. This mobile app for taxi rides is immensely popular in the Spanish-speaking world. Founded in Madrid in 2011, it now is present in 40 cities in Argentina, Chile, Colombia, Mexico, Peru and Uruguay. While the focus is on automobile taxis, it also provides information on ride shares and scooter travel. *Cabify.com*

Europe

Rail Europe. It's a rite of passage in the world of travel. Remember when you were 18 to 24 years old, making your first overseas journey on a multi-country EuRailPass? It is still the only app available for booking train tickets in the United Kingdom and the rest of Europe. Travelers can get alerts for reduced-cost train tickets and navigate Europe's complicated travel network. The app also reminds you that if you take the train instead of flying, you'll help to cut CO_2 emissions by up to 90 percent. *Raileurope.com*

Trainline. Some of Nick's fondest travel memories as a teenager were hopping on and off European trains. The Trainline app provides information on buses and trains in 36 European countries, so that you can search for trains traversing the continent, book tickets and monitor timetables. You can make seat reservations, compare prices and travel with an e-ticket on your phone. *Thetrainline.com*

Asia

Careem. A ride-sharing and delivery service, Careem is the Uber of the Middle East and the greater Arab world. Established in 2012, acquired by Uber in 2019, Careem operates in more than 70 cities in 10 countries from Pakistan to Morocco. The company also operates Careem Bike, a bike-share service. *Careem.com*

DiDi. Based in Beijing, ride-sharing company DiDi Chuxing is one of the most utilized transportation apps globally. With over 400 cities in China and recent expansions into Australia, Brazil, Mexico, Japan and Taiwan, DiDi claims 550 million users and tens of millions of drivers. Services include social ride sharing, taxi hailing, bike sharing and on-demand delivery. *Didiglobal.com*

Grab. Grab is the Asian answer to Uber. It's little known in the West but is virtually everywhere in Asia. In frenzied urban centers such as Ho Chi Minh City, Vietnam, its taxi services are even eclipsed by motorbike taxis — one-driver, one-rider services that negotiate traffic jams and narrow alleyways far more efficiently than a full-size vehicle. In Cambodia and Thailand, three-wheel tuktuks may be ordered by Grab. The company can also deliver food to your door.

So successful is Grab that many cities have spawned other taxi companies to challenge Grab. (In Vietnam, for instance, these include GoJek and BeBe.) But Grab continues to be the undisputed leader. *Grab.com*

Ola Cabs. In India, whose population is greater even that that of China, Ola controls 80% of the online taxi market. Vehicle types vary from high-end sedans to even tuk-tuks. Ola offers city taxis, inter-city cabs, and local cabs at hourly rates. Headquartered in Bangalore, the company also has captured shares of the taxi market in the United Kingdom, Australia and New Zealand. *Olacabs.com*

Australia-Pacific

DriveMyCar. Australia is a huge nation — a continent, really — with vast open spaces between its (mostly coastal) cities. DriveMyCar is another peer-to-peer service that allows drivers to rent from owners for as little as a day ... or as long as a year. The interchange between owner and renter is vetted for security and safety, creating a pleasant handing-over of keys. *Drivemycar.com.au*

The Kiwi Experience. New Zealand boasts one of the most dramatic landscapes on earth. A hop-on, hop-off, bus service, The Kiwi Experience offers flexible guided bus passes that traverse all of New Zealand. Small group tours cover both the North and South Islands, in all styles of travel, in times ranging from one week to 28 days. Besides transportation, the service includes activities and accommodations. *Kiwiexperience.com*

Maps and Navigation

All Trails. If you're like us and sometimes hike off the beaten path or in an area without signage, All Trails can be a lifesaver. Not only does the app help you find trails; but it also gives you directions, allows you to record your trip, and tells you where you are on or off the path, even without service. Using this app, you can hike obscure trails with confidence. All Trails takes the stress out of adventuring. *Alltrails.com*

Bus Bud. Many travelers find bus travel to be a comfortable budget option. One of the most comprehensive travel transportation apps is Bus Bud, which contains millions of routes for a straightforward search. Whether you're in the Karpathos Mountains of Romania or traveling from Kathmandu to Pokhara in Nepal, there is a bus route. Buses are highly affordable, hassle-free, and a comfortable way to roam the world. (But one negative note: John recently checked Bus Bud for departures from the busy transportation hub of Ho Chi Minh City, and found none listed.) *Busbud.com*

Citymapper. The ultimate transportation app combines various transportation modes such as buses, trains, cars, and bikes. Citymapper covers many of the world's most visited cities, mostly in Europe and North America, from Mexico City to Istanbul, London to New York. The app shows you the quickest routes and most efficient way to reach your destination. *Citymapper.com*

HiiKER. Over 100,000 people have used the HiiKER app, accessing detailed information on many of the world's epic hiking trails. This is an app for backpackers who like to walk long distances, from America's Appalachian Trail to Nepal's Annapurna Circuit, from the GR routes of Europe to the Routeburn Track of New Zealand. Trails are categorized by difficulty (from easy jaunts to strenuous hikes). The app includes the ability to download or print specific maps for better trip planning. You'll also learn how to break walks into various day jaunts. *Hiiker.com*

Maps.me. More than 60 million travelers worldwide use Maps.me for detailed mobile maps that help in planning and navigating. With a variety of helpful features, this app offers the most convenient routes ... in the right direction. It's helpful for driving, walking, biking and touring, as well as locating hard-to-find trails. The site's blog offers travel tips and ideas to guide you all over the world. *Maps.me*

Moovit. Planning to take the train or bus? Then you need Moovit, the world's No. 1 mobility app. Transportation is an integral part of any journey, especially in an urban area. Moovit has guided more than 865 million users in over 3,200 cities worldwide. Train, subway, light rail, metro, bus or ferry—Mooviet is your personal transit assistant. And now it has extended its reach to dockless scooters, bikes and ride-sharing. *Moovit.com*

Roadtrippers. Everyone loves a great road trip. Roadtrippers will help you set up a route to exciting locales and unique stops, from scenic points and historic sites to microbreweries and boutique hotels. The platform allows you to layer and plan your perfect trip, whether a short tour or an extended journey. *Roadtrippers.com*

Sygic Travel. Sygic maps quickly take you a step closer to the best attractions in a destination. Navigate to museums, churches, parks, shops, restaurants, bars and other places of interest in your new surroundings. Created by travel editors and fellow travelers, the app efficiently guides you to hidden treasures. *Travel.sygic.com*

Walk Wellbeyond. When we use Google Maps, half the time we cannot figure out which direction to start walking. Walk Wellbeyond (formerly Mapless) takes us in the right direction every time. The app uses a compass to guide you on the correct path to your destination. Simply input your destination and let WW do the rest. Let's say that you're roaming the streets of New York's Soho and wish to continue to Greenwich Village. Simply input your destination: The app gives you visual cues to get where you're going, how many minutes to arrive, and your estimated time of arrival. It will even count your steps and track your vitals. *Wellbeyond.com/walk*

Global explorers want ambience with luxury, as at Italy's Castel Monastero, a restored medieval hamlet from the 10th century.

Health and Safety

GeoSure. Through risk analysis and safety measurements, GeoSure empowers travelers in over 65,000 locations worldwide to travel safely. Locational awareness and even an individual's fear level are taken into account. Whether you're a solo female traveler in Rome, a businessman in Lagos, or a parent concerned about your child's safety while studying abroad in Barcelona, GeoSure keeps you informed of possible dangerous situations on the road. *GeoSureGlobal.com*

Global Travel Risk Map. The U.S. State Department updates its travel-advisory list daily, letting citizens know where they should *not* be going. (As of September 2023, 16 countries are on the "no go" list for Americans). U.S. travelers can register their trips on the app to receive info on United States embassies and consulates overseas. Should a disaster occur during your travels, the local embassy can contact you with up-to-the-minute information. *Travel.state.gov* OR *Travel-advisory.info*

Mayday Safety. While most trips remain out of harm's way, threatening situations can occur. Mayday is an app for travel safety, helping to empower nearly 25,000 people in over 80 countries. You set up the app before you travel. Let's say someone is following you late at night: Hit the red button on the app three times, and friends and family will be notified of your exact location. *Maydaysafety.com*

Medjet. One in 30 trips ends in a medical emergency or safety concern. Ten million people are hospitalized abroad annually, while 2 million travelers each year require medical transport. Recommended by CBS News travel editor Peter Greenberg for travelers' peace of mind, Medjet puts safety first. It is the premier global air-medical transport and travel-security membership program for travelers. *Medjetassist.com*

CONNECTIONS

Disabled

Access Now: This site aims to make the world's top destinations and sites accessible to people with disabilities, who may otherwise have difficulty finding information. Whether a person's challenges are mobility, visual, auditory or intellectual, travel must find a way to be all-inclusive. This loaded app, with content uploaded by travelers in more than 30 countries, is an important resource to this segment of travelers. *Accessnow.com*

LGBTQ

MisterB&B: An LGBTQ community equivalent of Airbnb, Misterbandb welcomes travelers to more than one million LGBTQ-friendly accommodations in 200 countries. Gay bloggers Nomadic Boys call it their go-to accommodations app — so you know your host is gay or at least gay-friendly. Many times your host can also show around the local gay scene. The website also offers valuable destination gay guides. *Misterbandb.com*

Purple Roofs: The LGBT-centric site was started by husbands Mark and Scott in 1999. The friendly, gay-owned-and-operated lodging site includes LGBT travel agents and tour operators. On Purple Roofs, you'll find thousands of hosted gay-friendly lodging and vacation rental properties around the world. *PurpleRoofs.com*

Pet owners

MindMyHouse:

Need someone to look after your house or pets while you're away? MindMyhouse brings homeowners and house sitters together. Homeowners join for free; housesitters pay only $20 a year, the lowest annual fee on the worldwide web. If you're an animal lover, you can enjoy free holiday accommodation, save on rental payments, and treat yourself. *MindMyHouse.com*

Rover:

It's not too shocking that more than 43 million households in the United States alone own dogs. As most people can't bring their pets on trips, there has been significant growth in demand for house- and pet-sitters. Rover was developed to answer that need. *Rover.com*

Trusted Housesitters: Who keeps an eye on your pup or kitty while you travel? Your house sitter, of course. Pets love their owners, but they also love the stability of a safe home environment, where they will have companionship, food, regular exercise and love. Trusted Housesitters allow people to travel with peace of mind. *Trustedhousesitters.com*

Singles

Backpackr: A community to discover travel buddies, connecting with like-minded backpack travelers across the globe. Backpackr allows you to find others traveling in the same vicinity or country. Browse through the numerous profiles to find the travel companions you want to meet. Ask questions to other explorers in the area at the exact time. *Backpackr.org*

Fairy Trail: Are you looking for a date for your next adventure, or perhaps forever? Fairy Trail matches single travelers for exciting journeys on our beautiful planet. Unlike traditional dating sites, it narrows your search to travel interests. The concept was designed for people opting to live a remote lifestyle. Find a connection and Fairy Trail offers options, perhaps booking a trip of four to 20 people to sail through the Greek Islands or to snorkel off Belize. *Fairytrail.app*

GAFFL: The acronym stands for "Get a Friend for Life." Akib Amin started GAFFL to bring together travelers who were already traveling to the same destination. Registered users in over 150 countries are mostly solo travelers, but anyone can join. Enjoy your life-changing experiences while making long-term friendships, sharing costs during the trip. It's cheaper and safer to travel with someone else or with a group of like-minded individuals. *Gogaffl.com*

Meetup: A meet-up is an informal meeting or gathering. Since 2002, Meetup has been hosting in-person and virtual events throughout the world, in most major cities. With over 50 million members, you're sure to connect with someone of mutual interests. You'll meet locals at a volleyball game on the beach, on a bike ride through the countryside, visiting an art gallery, or at an annual festival. In no time, you'll be immersed in the local landscape. *Meetup.com*

Skout: Most travelers know the power of serendipitous meetings. The fun and engaging Skout community spans over 180 countries and is available in 14 languages. The Skout app allows you to pursue chance encounters and make new friends. You might be enjoying a beer at a neighborhood bar in Amsterdam, stamping your feet at a concert in Sydney, or wandering the discreet back alleys of Athens. Use your mobile device as a guide to meet new people wherever you may roam. *Skout.com*

Wander: Find travel partners wherever you are. Instantly connect in your own city with people planning travel to your chosen destination during the same time frame. You might test the shared-interest waters by meeting to explore local attractions or taking day trips, then create your own faraway journeys and invite others to join. *Get-wanderapp.com*

Women

She's Wanderful: This traveling international sisterhood of women who love to travel has become a trusted global network. With thousands of members in over 50 chapters worldwide, women can get advice on their upcoming trip, find travel buddies, and even have a local community to meet up with wherever they wander. The site's hosting network offers women safe places to stay with other members. Even while not traveling, Wanderful women have an exclusive portal to participate in language circles, travel webinars and more. *Sheswanderful.com*

Tourlina: Another women-for-women site, Tourlina links travelers and locals with a secure network. Solo female travelers enter their destinations and dates of travel to be matched with fellow travelers of similar interests. If you find a match, you swipe right and chat to discuss taking a trip together. *Tourlina.com*

Travel Sisters: Empowering women to travel safely, this app is true to its tagline: "Helping women make the world a better place through travel." Build a profile specifying your interests and style of travel, and meet other women who share your passion for roaming new places. Send meeting requests and, once accepted, mingle with fellow travelers. *Travelsisters.co*

Tours, Guides, Local Advice

Active travelers

Backroads: For many decades, Backroads has hosted thousands of guests on biking, walking and hiking tours. Staying in shape while cycling through fields of blossoming lavender in Provence or the picturesque rice terraces of Bali. Knowledgeable leaders share their passion for discovery as they explore with fellow curious travelers from the Rocky Mountains to the temples of Angkor to the Tuscan countryside. *Backroads.com*

WarmShowers: Life on a bicycle is a straightforward process. Your priorities are peddling, drinking, eating and sleeping. If you travel the world astride a bike, then you know that cyclists are a passionate lot. WarmShowers is a community of eager travelers and a support network. You must be a traveling cyclist to join the community. *Warms howers.org*

Custom guides

Black Tomato: The award-winning creator of one-of-a-kind, personalized travel experiences, Black Tomato is a top-end tour operator that delights in encouraging and indulging its clients' curiosity about the world. Destinations may be places fabled for their human or natural history, such as mysterious cultures like Buddhist Bhutan or remote Madagascar, its jungles home to 5% of the world's wildlife. *Blacktomato.com*

Educational travel

Context Travel: The scholarly experts of Context Travel guide visitors through the architecture, religion, history and cuisine of more than 60 cities and many of the world's cultural capitals across six continents. Storytellers and specialists invite you to skip the lines and experience the world through their eyes. Before the journey, Context offers virtual lectures to satisfy the intellectual curiosity of legions of seekers. *Contexttravel.com*

EF Tours: We learned more during our first lengthy international trips than from four years of university. Indeed, there is no better education than travel. Curated by world travelers, EF Educational Tours' teacher-approved itineraries, most of them eight to 12 days, make learning fun. Students are engaged in responsible and sustainable travel along with lessons in history and culture. *Eftours.com*

Road Scholar: Since 1975, older adults especially have enjoyed the educational travel programs of this nonprofit organization, which changed its name from Elderhostel in 2010. Offering adventures for every age and activity level, Road Scholar's catalog suggests 670 budget-priced trips in 150 countries. *Roadscholar.org*

Tours by locals

Free Tours By Foot: Offering walking tours of American, European and some Asian cities, Free Tours By Foot introduces travelers to local guides — who accept whatever price the traveler wishes to pay. You pay what you can afford or express how much you liked the tour. For nearly 20 years, more than 3 million guests have joined over 200,000 tours around the world. *Freetoursbyfoot.com*

Like a Local Guide: Skip the tourist traps of the world and discover the road less traveled. Like a Local is all about finding the cool, cozy, off-the-beaten path places that only city residents seem to know. Want to know of tasty Chinese restaurant on New York's Lower East Side? Or a clandestine lookout point to photograph the Golden Gate Bridge? There's no better way to "go local" than to get expert tips from the people who sleep, eat, play, ride and dream about your new background. It's also a friendlier way to learn about new places. *Likealocalguide.com*

Showaround: Almost any traveler will tell you: "Locals know best." In Nick's home-town of San Francisco, for instance, he feels he can show off the City by the Bay better than any guidebook. As its name suggests, the Showaround app allows visitors to book a private tour with a local expert, and to choose the guide by personality, hobbies or experience. In

224 countries and almost 14,000 cities, Showaround has over 163,000 local guides who offer their services. *Showaround.com*

Nick dresses to celebrate in Rio de Janeiro's Samba City neighborhood.

Language and Translation

If your goal as a traveler is to mingle extensively with locals, it behooves you to learn a bit of the lingo. Even a minimal effort will be rewarded with respect. The modern Hemingway has access to numerous text, voice and photo-translation apps that cover almost every language on Earth. And a wide range of language-learning apps open the door to unforgettable encounters, memories of which will last a lifetime.

Babbel: More than a million global travelers swear that subscription-based Babbel is the most effective way to learn a foreign language. Babbel contextualizes learning through dialogue and practice, based upon essential vocabulary and grammar for living in a foreign land. Users learn by repeating phrases in lessons of 10 to 20 minutes. Babbel covers 14 languages starting at $6.95 per month. *Babbel.com*

Duolingo: Another favorite language-learning method is Duolingo. The free app builds vocabulary and grammar through daily tutorials, with over 30 language options available. The app uses practical topics such as airports, hotel check-in, family travel needs, and ordering a restaurant meal. The "plus" version allows you to remove ads. *Duolingo.com*

Google Translate: This go-to translation app by Google is probably already on your radar. It allows you to translate more than 100 languages to your own, by typing in a word or phrase. Google Translate works with voice as well as text. In Google's real-time Assistant Interpreter mode, you can carry on conversations with the interpreter when meeting locals on the road in over 40 languages. It's user-friendly, with options to take a photo, draw, type or simply speak. *Translate.google.com*

iTranslate: The highly rated iTranslate Voice app helps navigate new linguistic surroundings with ease. You can translate audio between more than 40 languages. Imagine being lost and needing to ask a local for guidance: Start a conversation by recording in your voice; the app translates back in the local language. Sharpen your skills further with the Pro version: Unlimited translations cost $39.99 per year. *Itranslate.com*

Memrise: This British platform is another useful app. Choose your level of proficiency and learn a language with essential phrases in real-life situations. Courses focus on the repetition of key words and phrases, enhanced by videos. Get acquainted with nearly 25 languages with various subscription options. *Memrise.com*

Waygo: Asian languages are especially difficult for Westerners. The Waygo translator app is language-specific for three countries: China, Korea and Japan. You can easily translate texts from those languages text to English without data connection. This is extremely helpful in daily life, as in discerning restaurant menus, using a coin-operated laundry, or navigating through an airport. *Waygoapp.com*

Travel Photography

Just because we carry multiple cameras, tripods and other equipment around the world doesn't mean you will. Modern iPhones take excellent photos; we can edit images right away and send them off to Facebook or Instagram. Whether you're a professional photographer or a casual social-media user, modern technology has changed how we take pictures. It's never been so easy to take eye-popping photos.

If you're a pro, there are apps for shooting with DSLR cameras as well. There are too many photo-enhancement apps to mention here. There are even sites and apps claiming to show you where to take the best photos in a specific location, and apps that allow you to organize photo shoots in albums along with a travel story.

Lightroom Mobile: Many traveling photographers swear by this free app for smartphones and tablets. Adobe Lightroom Mobile allows easy editing and photo sharing, just like Adobe's PC version. You can also edit RAW images for color correction, or sync photos between Lightroom Mobile and your desktop. The app is preset to allow simple adjustments in exposure and shadows. *Lightroom.adobe.com*

Photo Pills: Packed with photography tools to take the guesswork out of capturing perfect images, Photo Pills will lead you to scores of stunning photos. It plans and prepares your shots, covering everything from depth-of-field to exposure and time-lapse. The app is excellent for night shots: The AR mode used for stargazing intensifies the Milky Way, while a sun tool reminds you of the golden hour's exact time and when the sun will rise. The cost is $12 and it's money well spent. *Photopills.com*

VSCO: Trusted by photographers, bloggers, and anyone serious about their photos, VSCO is one of the best photo editing and sharing apps out there. It's straight-forward and easy to use. Choose between 10 preset adjustment tools (such as clarity, contrast, grain and saturation) or, for more advanced photographers, manual adjustments. Features allow you to add focus and exposure and even choose between three flash modes. *VSCO.com*

Nick bikes the shore of famed Ipanema beach in Rio de Janeiro.

Sustainable Travel

Closca Water: With the worldwide rise in ecotourism, technology plays a massive role in guiding travelers responsibly. Closca Water reminds us how harmful plastic consumption is to the environment. Refilling your water bottle cuts down on plastic waste. Closca takes the guesswork out of finding eco-friendly watering stations. The company claims to have helped to eliminate nearly 400,000 plastic bottles. It also designs foldable helmets for bicyclists. *Closca.com*

Fairtrip: The Fairtrip app highlights lodgings, restaurants, shops and tour businesses that have a favorable social and economic impact on people and the environment. Each business must meet specific guidelines, as rated by its positive contribution. It's a goal of the modern global community to change travelers' behaviors, keeping destinations authentic with a low carbon footprint. *Fairtrip.org*

Native Land: Including a detailed map with links to tribal websites, this app is packed with information about indigenous peoples worldwide, and how to best visit them. For some travelers, these are new worlds. Stories about such peoples as the Inuit of the Canadian Arctic and the Maasai of Kenya's Serengheti Plain will expand your sense of awareness and responsibilit for tribes on all continents. *Native-land.ca*

Servas International: The nonprofit hospitality group Servas International encompasses an international network of hosts and travelers. More than 15,000 households in over 100 countries belong to the platform. The concept of Servas developed in 1949 from a group of Danes who called themselves "Peacebuilders." The network strives to build world peace, goodwill and understanding by linking together people of different cultures. *Servas.org*

Cruises

Since his youth, Nick has been fascinated by voyaging, whether small-boat sailing or traveling by ship. He rhapsodized the age of exploration of the 15th and 16th centuries, and wondered what it must have been like for Columbus to set foot in America, or Vasco de Gama to sail around the Cape of Good Hope to India. As a teenager in Greece, he'd hop aboard vessels of the Blue Star ferry line to explore the Aegean Islands, or depart from his father's hometown of Patras and cross the Adriatic to Ancona, Bari or Brindisi in Italy.

John didn't have the same experience, but it was in his genes: His Finnish grandfather sailed to South Africa in the late 1800s, where he served the British Navy in the Boer War, then settled in New York and competed in the America's Cup race at the start of the 20th Century.

Far from the days of simply relaxing by a pool with a fruity rum drink, modern cruise lovers find time to immerse in local culture. Rather than speed-sailing to multiple countries, today's intensive expeditions focus on slower travel and more all-enveloping experiences.

Cruise Critic: To ensure a fantastic cruise, it helps to get advice from others who previously have been where you're going. Cruise Critic, a Trip Advisor company, is the most trusted name in cruise-line reviews. Whether you're going to Antarctica, the Amazon or the Greek Islands, Cruise Critic can advise which cruise will best suit your needs: stateroom comfort, shipboard meals, kid-friendly excursions, or hidden gems to explore when you disembark in an iconic city or romantic island. *Cruisecritic.com*

Cruise Mapper: Suppose you're seeking information on future cruise itineraries. On Cruise Mapper, you can find schedules for the next year or two, cabins, deck plans, technical specifications, photos and videos. Future cruisers can search a database of more than 20,000 cruises on over 30 cruise lines and 300 ships. *Cruisemapper.com*

CrewSeekers International: What global explorer has not dreamed about channeling their inner Magellan to navigate the world on a maritime adventure? For more than 25 years, CrewSeekers has offered both amateur and professional sailing opportunities on the seven seas. CrewSeekers can lead to everlasting friendships as it pairs skippers looking for crew and crew seeking for sailing experiences. *Crewseekers.net*

Quirky Cruise: If you're seeking to sail on small ships with fewer people, Quirky Cruise will lead you to more than 300 boats, ships and yachts all over the world. Informative reviews include size of rooms, amenities, meals, activities and more to plan your perfect sailing. Reviewers inspect river boats, barges, sailing ships, expedition vessels and private charters. *Quirkycruise.com*

And Also ...

Express VPN: A VPN is a virtual private network that may enable you to access forbidden websites. It provides a direct link between your device and the internet, and should protect you from censors and hackers. You'll need this to use many social media in countries (such as China) where the internet is heavily monitored and censored. With a VPN, you can browse the internet anonymously. You can even watch movies and television on the likes of Netflix. Express VPN is simple to install and has over 160 server locations. *Expressvpn.com*

Get Your Guide: With over 20,000 tours and things to do at your fingertips, this app will help you find, compare and book sightseeing tours — attractions, excursions and fun things to do — in some of the world's most popular locations. From kayaking Amsterdam's iconic canals, taking an airboat tour in Everglades National Park, snaring tickets to the Louvre in Paris, tasting tequila in Mexico, touring Los Angeles by helicopter, or learning to cook Greek food in Athens, the possibilities are almost endless. *Getyourguide.com*

Lonely Planet: Back in the days before smartphones and apps, travelers roamed the planet with sometimes cumbersome travel books. None were more popular than Lonely Planet guides. Now LP has entered the digital age with up-to-the-minute travel information at your fingertips. No matter your travel style: adventure, food-centric, culture-vulture, family, beach vacations, road trip or pure budget, Lonely Planet will assist and inspire you to travel the world. *Lonelyplanet.com*

My Postcard: Have you sent postcards from faraway places only to find out they were never delivered or took weeks or even months to arrive? If you love sending postcards while traveling but don't want to search for postcards, buy stamps, or go to a post office in the digital world, there is a more convenient option. My Postcard guarantees that your postcard will arrive and allows you to send personalized photos off your own phone instead of store-bought images. *Mypostcard.com/en/*

On the Go Tours: With a strong passion for authentic journeys, London-based On the Go Tours has operations in more than 60 destinations worldwide. Besides covering iconic sights like Machu Picchu in Peru and Petra in Jordan, the responsible travel company also guides you into the unknown of lesser-visited hidden gems. You might visit locals at their yurts in Kyrgystan or their riad in Morocco, and immerse in the sights and sounds of a festival such as Holi in India or the world's biggest party, Carnival in Rio. *Onthegotours.com*

TourRadar: The world's largest online marketplace for multi-day tours is Tour-Radar. Compare and book over 40,000 tours. The possibilities are astounding as Tour-Radar works with over 2,500 trusted tour operators in nearly 200 countries. With a strict screening process, you're assured of taking the best quality tours, from river cruising on the Rhine to the best of South African safaris. *Tourradar.com*

WiFiFinder: Possibly your best friend in travel is connectivity. True to its name, WiFiFinder helps you find wireless hotspots and available networks. The app gathers as much information about them as possible and even allows you to download maps for offline use while traveling. All networks are verified, and speed-tested. *Wifimap.io*

No one realizes how beautiful it is to travel until he comes home and rests his head on his old, familiar pillow." – Lin Yutang

Chapter Three

TASTE TEST:

Taking a Bite Out of Society

"An adventurous life does not necessarily mean climbing mountains, swimming with sharks, or jumping off cliffs. It means risking yourself by leaving a little piece of you behind in all those you meet along the way " — Shawna Grapentin

We'll travel just about anywhere for a tasty morsel or fine meal, but the dining experience is much more than an epicurean encounter.

It's also an insight into daily life. As we explore new destinations, food connects us with people and culture. Our one commonality is that no matter where we're from or where we visit, food is at the forefront of all movement. A memorable meal is an everlasting memory.

We like to say that "experiential is the new luxury." Whether we're planning a weekend getaway or a journey through Morocco, we know that food will add depth to our travel experience. Today's traveler is more multi-cultured and food-centric than even 10 years ago.

When Nick wasn't eating Greek food, his youthful dining experience often revolved around burgers and pizza. Even growing up in refined, multi-cultured San Francisco, most people did not venture outside of their comfort zones, perhaps only attempting the typical ethnic cuisines of Italy or China. Japanese sushi, Thai curries, Spanish tapas, even Mexican dishes beyond tacos and burritos, were truly foreign. Myriad other dishes and cuisines that today we can't live without—Turkish kebabs? Vietnamese *pho'*? — were unknown to our taste buds until we were old enough to explore the world. Today, of course, most teenagers have a say in planning family getaways and in choosing destinations like Japan. And they are familiar with the cuisines.

While food travel goes far beyond exclusive restaurants in a new locale, the interest in food often takes center stage in travel planning. Food tourism tells the story of a nation itself; tourist boards and tour operators have noticed. Today they busily create food-centric trips to farms, wineries, fish and farmers' markets, craft breweries or whisky distilleries for a pulse of local society.

Food tourism began to boom in the last decade, beginning around 2010. According to the travel research group Skift, the typical traveler spends about 25 percent of his budget on meals. In a recent Food Travel Monitor report, two-thirds of travelers said their primary motivation for in choosing a specific destination is to taste its flavors.

As travelers pursue their next perfect meal around the globe, destinations are encouraging the merger of palate and planning. Nations, states — indeed, individual cities — are showcasing themselves as places to take gastronomy to another level. Any destination with food and drink to brag about can contribute to the growth of tourism.

Iberia and Aegean. Portugal is a favorite nation for combining a culinary journey with a stunning backdrop. "Portugal's cuisine is as rich and varied as its landscape," said Celina Tavares, Visit Portugal Director for the USA. "The most distinctive feature of Portuguese cuisine comes from the sea. As you enjoy a simple grilled fish, fresh like the seafood that abounds from end to end along the coast, you can be sure that you are in Portugal!

"Cataplanas, bouillabaisses, our salted codfish bacalhau, and other fish or seafood dishes are also excellent choices. For meat dishes, the cozido à Portuguesa, a mix of meats, vegetables and various smoked sausages, is amazing. In the Azores, they even slow-cook it underground, using volcanic heat!"

Greece is Europe's oldest civilization, and the national diet is among the world's most delicious and nutritious. It's no surprise that Greek food tourism is ranked highly among countries offering unique and authentic gastronomic experiences.

"Tourism is one of the main sources of income for Greece. Therefore the development of Greek gastronomy tourism is of great importance for the country," said Maria Athanasopoulou of Respond on Demand, a travel marketing firm, and an ambassador for the World Gourmet Society.

"Oil, wine, honey, Greek pies and many other products are included in Greek cuisine from antiquity to the present day. Greek gastronomy experiences are authentic with their own distinct identity," she continued. "Each region of Greece has special local products and special recipes, so in any destination, the visitor will enjoy a unique combination of experiences.

"In the coming years, we expect the rapid development of gastronomy tourism to continue. Travelers now, for whatever reason they travel, want to live gastronomy experiences, tasting the local recipes and the local drinks."

The increased demand for food-related experiences has already increased the number of companies invested in gastro-tourism. The opportunity to sample new, original, authentic and tasty cuisine is evident throughout modern Greece.

As tourists increasingly choose their destinations with a goal of experiencing new flavors, gastronomy is no longer solely about food. It extends to lifestyle, culture and heritage. One nation that has successfully launched food tourism marketing campaigns is Peru.

I recall visiting Peru in the 1990s. The South American country, gateway to the astonishing Andes mountains, was not vested in its culinary riches and was barely on food trippers' radar. But come the 21st century, Peru put its epicurean campaign on center stage at London's World Travel Market. "When you come to Peru, you will become more enriched by experiences with the nation's gastronomy," said Elizabeth Hakim, Promperu's UK and North American marketing representative.

A chef on Greece's Kimolos island turns down the gas as she banters with a diner.

Food tells tales of a country's history. The popularity of the Bacalhau in Portugal dates back to the 14th century when Portuguese fishermen discovered plentiful cod fish off the coast of Newfoundland, Canada.

It's not porn. It's food porn. Driven by today's intense mealtime social-media activity — "food porn," it's been dubbed by more than one participant — you'd be hard-pressed to find a traveler not photographing their ceviche in Lima, regional barbecue in the United States or sushi nearly everywhere else. Memories of sipping tsampa in Kathmandu, sharing kebabs with new friends in Cairo, or taking photos with a pizza chef in Naples, are everlasting. Food connects us to people and our surroundings.

Nick's native Greece splendidly displays the compatibility of food and travel. Put this in your dream bank: A meal of grilled sea bream accompanied by a Greek salad with a bottle of local wine served at a seaside taverna. To top it off, eye-popping sunsets over the Aegean Sea create a kaleidoscope of colors.

Memories of local cuisine remain in your brain forever: In Paris, a hidden Montmartre bakery that serves standout flaky croissants that you just can't find back home. In Siem Reap, the home-cooked meal prepared by a passionate Cambodian home chef. In Venice, the local fish market that you stumbled upon when you got lost in the maze of streets and canals. Priceless encounters and fond travel memories are created when you immerse in food and drink.

The trend of being led in your travels by tastes and smells is here to stay. Ask any traveler about encounters with locals and food. One may lapse into a reverie of dining on a sweet Keralan curry while meandering the backwaters of Alleppey in an Indian houseboat. Others may be reminded of a dinner in a traditional Masai homestead in Kenya's Masai Mara.

Travelers yearn for a slice of local life, where they can eat what and where local citizens dine. So it's not chef-helmed restaurants leading the way. Street food is the gateway to eating like a local. Heading to the streets and visiting that semi-seedy back alley is an inexpensive way to quench your appetite and experience a region's culture and history.

Anyone who has ventured out of their comfort zone will agree that unforgettable moments happen when societies harmoniously merge over a meal: in some instances, even world peace. In 1979, at the White House, Egypt and Israel signed a historic peace accord — then broke bread and shared a meal.

Many long-lasting friendships begin with a meal. In his 20s, on the Aegean Island of Ios, Nick met a Swedish couple, Sven and Maria from Stockholm, over food and drinks. They became fast friends and later partnered on an introspective journey through India and Nepal.

People rarely forget treasured moments that incorporate food and people. Consider that fleeting moment when you embraced the recommendation of a Thai woman in Bangkok—and wound up at an isolated pagoda with hardly a tourist in sight. Perhaps you met a local at a farmer's market and later ended up at their home, exchanging stories over a beer and a meal.

In the end, the joy of food makes people happy. It brings us closer as a society, as we delve into the history, diverse cultural heritage, similarities and differences that make travel timeless. Travel is therapy. So, too, is eating.

World Food Travel Association. The food tourism industry, formally born in 2003, has seen gastronomy's role in travel planning go from secondary to the spotlight. Food now ranks alongside sightseeing, lodging and weather as the basis for a successful holiday. The World Food Travel Association preserves and promotes culinary cultures through tourism and the hospitality industry.

As a driving force toward conquering uncharted territory, food characterizes the recent experiential movement in travel. People love to travel because they love to learn. World exploration is a crash course in life, as one takes the plunge and dives into unfamiliar worlds.

As culinary travelers take their eating habits on the road, the popularity of food and drink soars to new heights. These passionate consumers add considerable revenue to a destination's economy. Friendly locals want to teach you about their region and culture through their cuisine. From cooking classes to pub crawls, coffee shops to wineries, ventures to local farmer's markets or walking tours, travel and food bring us closer together.

To gain perspective on the importance of food-and-beverage tourism, we spoke to Erik Wolf, founder of the World Food and Travel association. An insider to industry trends, Wolf spoke about the union of spirited foodies and the revenue-hungry destinations that seek to attract them.

Q & A with Erik Wolf

WOLF: Many people think that food tourism is about gourmet restaurants or fancy wineries. Those are just a small subset of the bigger industry. Our vast audience spans over 20 different sectors of the food, drink, travel, and hospitality industries.

GOING LOCAL: What are the current trends driving consumer obsession with food and drink?

WOLF: The media have largely driven that obsession. First, we had cooking magazines and then cooking shows on television. Those morphed into featured chef shows and then chef and cooking reality shows. That, combined with the fact that all travelers eat and drink, has helped expand food tourism interest.

GL: What trade or educational events do you run to educate a destination, tourist board, or other organizations about the importance of food in the travel sector?

WOLF: Few trade events exist to educate our industry. Our own association produces biennial food tourism events to do just this. Occasionally other food or travel industry events will showcase the notion of food tourism, something that we can point to regularly.

GL: Travel has never been easier and cheaper. How are destinations luring tourists to visit through their local cuisine?

Wolf: Some nations are doing a better job than others to captivate holiday makers. Countries like France and Italy are always popular, especially among first-time foodie travelers. As foodies gain more experience, they seek secondary and even tertiary destinations. Video is an essential tool in doing just this — as evidenced by Asheville, North Carolina's video interviews for its Foodtopia campaign, or the Korean National Tourism Office's $10 tour video series.

GL: Who are the current big winners in the race to attract food-forward travelers?

Wolf: The big winners are the usual suspects — the big cities like New York or famous destinations like Italy. Then there is the next tier of popular destinations, such as

Peru, Canada and even Sweden. So much work remains to be done. A list of restaurants available in a destination is usually not the kind of information food travelers are looking for.

GL: Can you name some food nations that are perhaps a bit distant and off the traveler's radar?

Wolf: Up-and-coming foodie destinations include Ecuador with its wonderful fruits and huge variety of soups; Indonesia with its local dishes, wonderful coffee and a chocolate industry ready to explode; and undiscovered foodie destinations such as Armenia, which is home to the oldest winemaking in the world.

GL: Food tours, walks and visits to local markets are a wonderful way to immerse into local society. What are some of your favorite places and experiences?

WOLF: I enjoy roving through local markets like London's Borough Market, or pintxo-bar hopping in the Basque region of Spain, or sampling the wares of various hawker stands in Singapore.

GL: Eric, you're based in the thriving, food-forward city of Portland, Oregon. How has Portland transformed into one of the food capitals of the United States?

WOLF: I moved to Portland in 2001 and was amazed to see the quality of the food and drink. Locals were so unassuming. I knew the city had something extraordinary to offer. I've witnessed Portland go from a completely unknown food destination to one of the top 10 food cities on the planet. The media helped drive consumer opinion. Now Portland's food scene has been at least partly responsible for a mass migration to the city. And what's not to love, with great food and drink available on literally every corner?

GL: One hears a lot about meeting locals over a meal. How is the rise in meal-sharing sites like Eat With changing travelers' perceptions of restaurants and dining out?

WOLF: Like how Airbnb tremendously influenced the lodging industry, meal-sharing sites like Eat With are doing something similar to the dining industry. It's a great way to meet locals, get the inside scoop on a destination, and save the cost of taxes and service charges, which can add 20 to 30 percent to the price of a meal in a restaurant.

To learn more about the food tourism industry and economic development, visit: *Worldfoodtravel.org*

Go where the locals go. In many cultures, life revolves around the pub, a bustling night market, or a taco truck. Locals congregate, and chefs provide an understanding and insight into traditional life.

"The gentle art of gastronomy is a friendly one. It hurdles the language barrier, makes friends among civilized people, and warms the heart." — Samuel Chamberlain

Chapter Four

MEAL SHARING:

A New Generation of Foodies

If more of us valued food and cheer and song above hoarded gold, it would be a merrier world. — J.R.R. Tolkien.

As the P2P movement continues to affect the way we travel, the sharing economy plays a greater and greater role. We are reminded that living like a local is learning from the citizens of the area we're visiting, freely sharing meals or finding local dining companions through meal-sharing apps and agencies.

Anthony Bourdain, the forthright foodie, often reminded his readers and viewers of the power inherent in sharing a meal with a stranger. Enter with a free mind and leave your biases at the door, Bourdain said: "You learn much about someone when you share a meal," said the free-spirited epicurean trailblazer.

Gastronomy has become integral to choosing a travel destination. According to the hotel site Booking.com, nearly 70 percent of globetrotters make food and drink a key factor in choosing their next trip.

From the Food Network to the Travel Channel and beyond, we've seen plenty of star-studded roles taken on by celebrity gourmets and chefs during the last two decades. These food icons promote destinations and influence where travelers go on vacation. By showing us how tourism is enhanced as we experience authentic national and regional cuisines, they also transform the way in which we travel.

Considering the impact these programs have on what and where we eat worldwide, it's worthwhile to pay attention to the trends they set. When a culinary personality travels to a remote destination and learns from locals about their food preparation, eating, drinking and lifestyle habits, it's hard not to want to follow in their footsteps.

If you follow the travels of bombastic chef Gordon Ramsay on his TV show "Uncharted," as he talks about eating the best scallops he's ever had in Norway, or "Top Chef" hostess Padma Lakshmi on her journeys through her native India, featuring everything from markets to bakeries, you may have been inspired to try new foods and travel to the novel destinations to taste foods you had never imagined trying.

What happens when actor Stanley Tucci takes viewers to Rome, Florence and beyond in his Emmy Award-winning "Searching for Italy'? Or when "Iron Chef" Masaharu Morimoto weaves through the animated action of a tuna auction at the famed Toyosu Fish Market in Tokyo, followed by a sake brewery tour and tasting? Discerning chowhounds are lured to follow in their footsteps.

And it's not just happening overseas. When chef Wolfgang Puck calls Chicago the most underrated food city in America, people want to know why. When Guy Fieri traverses America in his classic red 1967 Camaro, we get an intimate glimpse into the lifestyle of "Diners, Drive-ins and Dives." Fieri takes us to hidden gems that we might not find on our own.

Korean-Canadian food hostess Mijune Pak of "Top Chef Canada" has a north-of-the-border contingent hanging on her every word as she describes, in mouth-watering detail, scrumptious Cantonese dim sum on a tour of Chinese restaurants in the immigrant-heavy Vancouver suburb of Richmond, British Columbia.

We might not be nearly as inclined to sample "Bizarre Foods" were it not for TV personality Andrew Zimmern. We might never have imagined a "Naked Chef" were it not for Londoner Jamie Oliver.

Wanderlusting travelers and curious gourmands continue to delve deeper into the local fare, and food is the bridge between cultures. "As interest in food gains traction around the world, it's almost becoming a sport for many people," suggested World Food Travel Association founder Erik Wolf. "People arrive in cities with itineraries of markets to visit, cafes to frequent and, of course, restaurants that have been pre-booked for weeks or months in advance.

"I've long believed that good food, good eating, is all about risk," said Tony Bourdain. To live like a local, he said, you must challenge your senses and eat like one. Every no-name street food stall in Bangkok and swanky Tribeca corner bistro in New York share one commonality: They provide a glimpse into local life.

Sometimes, it's unexpected kindness and generosity that we remember most from our travels. Globetrotting travel writer Penny Frederiksen recalled one such instance from the South Asian island nation of Sri Lanka: "My travel partner and I ... were asked to have lunch with the local Buddhist monks in a very remote village. Little did we know we would be 'served' lunch by the monks! ... Two cracked porcelain teacups, sweet black tea, and a packet of very expensive sweet, store-bought biscuits awaited us in a tiny kitchen." Those memories are indeed precious.

Cuisine allows us a access to a backstage look at a nation's identity, history and culture. Between the two of us, we have been fortunate to spend extended time enraptured by the food in some of the world centers for gastronomy — Athens, London, Paris, Rome, Tokyo, Singapore, Hong Kong, Bangkok, Sydney, Buenos Aires, New York, and of course my cherished San Francisco.

Currently John has a home in Cambodia's tidy Mekong River capital, Phnom Penh, where he delights in the tastes of coconut-creamy fish amok and dishes of marinated beef lok lak, sometimes with an exotic red-ant dressing. Nick keeps his main base 100 miles north of Puerto Vallarta, Mexico, in the sleepy port town of San Blas. His life on the sun-splashed Pacific is a veritable tasting menu of fresh seafood's delectable flavors, especially *mariscos* (shellfish). Hardly a day passes when he's not downing oyster shots or grilling shrimp as he mingles with the locals in the historic town of 12,000.

Amazing things can happen when you take a chance to travel and learn a new culture. Our lives have been meteoric odysseys of one serendipitous moment after another, to the extent that we consider chance encounters a way of life.

"Don't bother with churches, government buildings, or city squares; if you want to know about a culture, spend a night in its bars," said Ernest Hemingway. In our experiences, this is at least partly true.

After a day of surfing on Australia's Bondi Beach, Nick had returned to his simple hotel in The Rocks neighborhood when he happened to visit the Fortune of War, the oldest bar in Sydney. A conversation with a proud Sydneysider named Shane prompted Nick to mention his San Francisco home — and quickly led to an invitation to share a home-cooked meal with Shane at his girlfriend's swank apartment overlooking Darling Harbour.

The friends you make while sharing a meal often rival the collaborative plates themselves. Twenty years ago, perhaps, opening one's home to strangers to share a meal might have seemed strange. No more. In today's peer-to-peer society, commingling over food has never been breezier.

Don't be afraid to venture out of your comfort zone for a home-cooked meal. Indeed, whenever you have an opportunity to do so, accept that offer to a local's home (and kitchen). It's real, unfiltered, everyday life.

And if you're shy about barging into someone's home, there are even meal-sharing apps that can help you connect with home cooks. Voilà:

There's no better place to make new friends than sharing a dinner table.

BonAppetour: From a sushi-rolling session in Osaka to a paella-making workshop in Barcelona, this self-described "community marketplace" is engaged in bringing eager travelers to local chefs' homes. Bon Appetour is out to prove that food brings people closer, as diners share epicurean experiences with home chefs, from appetizers to desserts and including drinks. Guests may choose to participate in meal preparation as culinary students, shopping and haggling at local markets for ingredients fresh daily, or simply select a hosted dining experience. *Bonappetour.com*

Eatwith: This site claims to offer the broadest choice of dining-with-locals opportunities in the world, representing 25,000 host chefs in 130 countries. From dinner parties to food tours, cooking classes to workshops, or even to meet new friends for dining out, Eatwith is the ultimate food-focused app. As a traveler, you will be invited to share home-cooked meals in the home of a passionate chef for far less than what you'd pay in an overpriced restaurant — typically as little as $25. Plan well ahead to find a hosted event that meshes with your intended travel dates, then prepare to be dazzled by inspired home cooking with the freshest ingredients. You might even get a guest list to start mingling with your hosts and other guests before you arrive. *Eatwith.com*

Withlocals: This "experiential travel company" has local representatives in 279 cities and 76 countries. And while food-related experiences constitute a major part of its options — dinner at a citizen's own home in Bangkok, for instance — Withlocals showcases bonding in numerous other shared-life instances, from private tours of local attractions to physically challenging outdoor activities. *Withlocals.com*

Traveling Spoon: "Travel off the eaten path." That's the mantra of this San Francisco-based company, whose co-founders promise "to find you the most meaningful and memorable cultural experiences." They do so in 65 countries on six continents. Travelers are paired with talented home cooks, each one thoroughly vetted, for meals, cooking classes and/or market visits. The cost can be as little as $20 as wandering foodies build international communities and learn to enjoy a simpler, healthier lifestyle.

Chester, a visitor to Indonesia from London, recalled an unforgettable experience with Traveling Spoon in Bali: "Dewa is a gardener at a resort in the village of Ubud. He likes to meet travelers who wish to learn from his wealth of local customs, and also about Balinese cuisine, like where food is sourced in the elegant manicured rice terraces of Keliki.

"He and his wife, Jero, and their extended family, host guests for once-in-a-lifetime encounters. Dewa allows you to help prepare the evening's meal by walking through the garden to pick fresh vegetables and herbs. He is a remarkable host; he even provided round-trip transportation from our hotel in Ubud. It ended up being a 10-course feast. The meal was fantastic. Dewa even gave us a full tour of his village. We learned much about Bali from a real local, not a guide trained only to show a few highlights." *Travelingspoon.com*

"Do we really want to travel in hermetically sealed pope mobiles through the rural provinces of France, Mexico, and the Far East, eating only in Hard Rock Cafes and McDonald's? Or do we want to eat without fear, tearing into the local stew, the humble taqueria's mystery meat, the sincerely offered gift of a lightly grilled fish head?" Anthony Bourdain, *Kitchen Confidential, Adventures in the Culinary*

Chapter Five

DO-IT-YOURSELF

Cooking Classes and Food Tours

Tell me what you eat and I will tell you what you are. — Jean Anthelme Brillat-Savarin, *The Physiology of Taste* (1826)

A man is what he eats. — Ludwig Andreas Feuerbach, *Spiritualism and Materialism* (1863)

You are what you eat! — Victor Lindlahr, *You Are What You Eat* (1942)

If you really want to understand the foreign culture in which you find yourself, indulge in this trick: Eat like the local folk!

If it's your intention to truly understand a culture, don't waste a meal before diving headlong into the local gastronomy. Gone are the days when globetrotters merely traveled to sightsee, then returned to the hotel for a hamburger and French fries. Food is a common bond between those who wander and those who stay. Street food in Saigon, tapas in Madrid, izakaya fare anywhere in Japan: It's these unforgettable moments, when unfamiliar signs and smells are accompanied by a sensory assault on our taste buds, that create a permanent connection to the soul of a destination and to the people who live there.

Nowhere can a civilization's identity be as readily discovered as in its cuisine. Indeed, the celebratory nature of food is universal: Every culture, every religion, uses food as part of their festivals and somber observances.

Throughout the world, interest in food tourism increases year by year, nation by nation — even region by region. Today you can eat your way around the world while exploring Machu Picchu in Peru, Mount Fuji in Japan, the Atlas Mountains in Morocco, or walk right off the Barcelona waterfront into a Catalan kitchen. You can meander the streets of Athens, Rome, Mexico City, Bangkok and Taipei finding tasty street food.

Experiencing unfamiliar cuisine should be an integral part of any journey. It will help you understand the passions and the struggles — often, even, the ethnic histories — of the world's diverse peoples. Never be afraid to try: Embracing unique ingredients and food preparation styles should be essential learning for homes worldwide.

"Good food and good eating are about risk," Anthony Bourdain wrote in his bestseller, *Kitchen Confidential: Adventures in the Culinary Underbelly.*

Consider India, the world's most populous nation. Its cuisine dates back more than 5,000 years. Each region of the sprawling country has its rich and diverse culture and lifestyle, religion and terrain shaping the cuisine. Often spicy, with layers of varying flavors and a burst of fire, the food has given each of those regions an identity of its own. From the subtropics of Tamil Nadu and Kerala in the far south, to the frigid Himalayan climes of Ladakh, Sikkim and Assam in the north, India is a mishmash of a great many customs and traditions.

Thus Indian food is not simply Indian. It is a menu produced by a long and complicated history. The nation has been invaded from border to border, and with each incursion, a little bit of each aggressor was left behind. Still today, the Indian people use spices from all over the world, and many are now grown domestically: cumin, coriander, ginger, clove and pepper, to name a few. In northern India, where winters are cold, meals are robust. Moghul and Afghani invaders introduced such meats as beef and mutton, which remain popular. In the steamy south, menus are often tied to sweet curries and coconut water. Almost a third of Indians are vegetarians.

No country is more multicultural than the United States, beginning with the scores of Native American tribes. Each subsequent wave of immigrants influenced American society in its own way. Every U.S. schoolchild knows the legend of the first Thanksgiving, but in fact almost every nation on the planet has left its mark. Some of the earliest influences were English, French, Spanish, German, Dutch and Swedish. The Irish, Italians, Greeks, Jews and other Europeans played prominent roles in shaping the nation. The African-American and Caribbean communities created a fusion of dishes, from

Southern barbecue to jerk chicken, and extended to Cajun-Creole cuisine, popularized by French-trained chef Paul Prudhomme in New Orleans.

New York was the port of entry to the "promised land" for Europeans. Other cities were gateways in their own right. The oldest Chinatown in America is in San Francisco — where local fishermen, not Italians, created the seafood stew called cioppino. Los Angeles has the largest groups of Mexicans, Koreans, Armenians and Iranians outside those homelands. Texans of Mexican descent (Tejanos) introduced the wildly popular American cuisine now called "Tex-Mex." Chicago is home to thriving Greek and Polish populations, while Scandinavians settled in the upper Great Lakes region. Cubans and Puerto Ricans found a home in Miami.

The cuisine of any destination is an integral part of travel, a bridge to unite people of different cultures and languages. Why do dishes taste even better in the land (and with the ingredients) where they were first born and nurtured? Of course we love them at home, but as travelers we covet the flavors and textures of sushi in Japan, pasta in Italy, lobster in Maine, ceviche in Peru, and dim sum in Hong Kong.

The same is true of drinks — a rioja sangria with tapas in Spain; chalky, licorice-flavored ouzo as a nightcap in Greece; rum caipirinhas with a spear of sugar cane on the beach in Rio; a sweet and creamy mango lassi in India; wine in the Napa Valley or Tuscany, a Guinness in Dublin, sake in Japan or a craft beer anywhere in the world.

The only thing better than discovering impressive local delicacies in an off-the-beaten-track restaurant is finding a local chef who can teach you how to prepare those beloved dishes yourself. When you join a food tour and take cooking classes, you can relive your journey back home — whipping up the meal you learned; tasting, once again, an enchanting memory of your travels.

If you look at National Geographic's Instagram page, you will notice that half the posts are food-related. Many picture a meal or market on a food tour. Indeed, food tours are exquisite ways to take the plunge and capture the flavor of new surroundings. Food tours offer a unique blend of culture and culinary history, often bringing you to ethnic neighborhoods where you otherwise might not venture. Food brings people closer together, and one experiences an authentic taste of local life.

"We are traveling the world one bite at a time," wrote travel icon Rick Steves. "Guided food tours provide thoughtful explanations of the authentic foods we travel so far to taste."

TV food personality Andrew Zimmern inspects a "bizarre" crab claw.

FOOD APPS (General)

Edible Destinations by Epitourean: This search engine for serious foodies offers authentic culinary encounters. Travels are built around edible inspiration. The app will plan your epicurean getaway, from a two- to three-night self-guided tour to a full six-night cooking-tour itinerary. Top chefs in North America and throughout the world share their special tasting menus as they focus on regional cuisines. *Epitourean.com*

Local Eats: A curated dining guide by in-the-know foodies, LocalEats takes you well beyond a Google search. There isn't a single chain or franchise restaurant on the app — only the best locally owned diners, steak houses, pizzerias, barbecue joints, sushi restaurants and more, throughout the United States. Whether you're a traveler or live nearby, LocalEats takes the guesswork out of dining. *Localeats.com*

Open Table: If you've ever arrived at a restaurant only to be turned away without a reservation, you'll be grateful for Open Table. This online reservation service connects diners with more than 60,000 restaurants worldwide. Best of all, it's free! Each month, Open Table users write over one million reviews. *Opentable.com*

Vegan Maps: We all have different tastes and dietary needs. Today, more and more travelers are giving up meat. For them, Vegan Maps is a free one-stop app for finding tasty vegetarian, vegan and raw food on the go. If you're on a plant-based diet, take the hassle out of searching: This app features over 10,000 plant-based restaurants, eateries and cafes in 150 countries. *vegan-map.com*

Withlocals: Satisfying food travelers in their quests for gastronomic experiences is one goal of Holland-based Withlocals. This app offers more than 2,000 unique food- and culture-based experiences in nearly 90 countries. There is something for all types of travelers, not just foodies; for instance, "night owls" tours are based on watering holes and nightlife. There are tours for families, history buffs, personal shopping tours, adventurers, art gallery walks and more. *Withlocals.com*

DRINKING APPS (General)

Untappd: When you're a fan of microbrews, choosing the right beer in a new city or pub can be a daunting process. Nowadays, almost every destination you visit has its local blend of frothy suds — but how do you keep a diary of every beer you've tried? With the Untappd app, lovers of craft beers not only share beers they've discovered; they also share their experiences at breweries and bars with friends old and new. Rate beers from around the world, find new waering holes, and receive recommendations from other beer enthusiasts. *Untappd.com*

Vivino: If you love wine but are unfamiliar with varietals in, say, Slovenia, Armenia or even New Zealand, Vivino does away with the guesswork of finding the right wine. Simply take a photo or scan the label on the bottle, and upload. Ratings up to 5.0 (anything above 4.0 is outstanding) have been registered by scores of other wine enthusiasts who write detailed descriptions. You'll find palate-pleasing wines wherever you travel. *Vivino.com*

A tea expert takes visitors through a curated tasting in San Francisco's Chinatown.

UNITED STATES

Culinary tours

Foods of New York: The Big Apple offers so much in the way of food culture: Its restaurateurs come from just about every country on the planet. Not only are there more than 70 Michelin-starred restaurants; the city that never sleeps is also a leader in the food-truck movement. Whatever your passion — from a thin, cheese-dripping, crunchy-crust slice to craft beer, whiskey distilleries, and every type of cuisine from Greek to Mexican to Japanese — New York knows its food.

For more than 20 years, Foods of New York has chaperoned voracious eaters on walking tours. Guides visit Chelsea and Gansevoort markets; share the gastronomic histories of Greenwich Village, Little Italy and Chinatown; lead half-day tours of the distinctive neighborhoods of Brooklyn. You will walk in the footsteps of musician Bob Dylan, comedian Jerry Seinfeld, writer Allen Ginsburg, and many others who gained their early fame here. *Foodsofny.com*

Taste of the City, San Francisco: "The City by the Bay," which Nick calls home, has always attracted free spirits and creative minds. While the Golden Gate Bridge and cable cars take center stage for tourists, the trend-setting food scene isn't far behind. The Boudin Bakery has been synonymous with San Francisco sourdough since it began feeding gold miners in 1849. Italian fishermen in the North Beach neighborhood invented cioppino, the tomato-based seafood stew, in the late 1800s. Irish Coffee was first concocted at the Buena Vista Café.

Food tours inevitably explore "Little Italy," erstwhile home to the Beat Generation and *The Godfather*. You'll get acquainted with coffee roasteries, bakeries and Ghirardelli chocolate. Learn about the five steps that go into producing quality olive oil as you nosh on cured meats. Visit fish markets and farmers' markets; walk the back alleys of America's oldest Chinatown, see how fortune cookies are made, and enjoy steamed Cantonese dumplings known as dim sum. *Sffoodtour.com*

Savory empanadas are a highlight of culinary tourism in Argentina.

LATIN AMERICA

Cooking Classes

Cooking in Rio: Passionate and witty chef Simone Almeida dances her way through four lively hours in her cozy Copacabana kitchen as she teaches the intricacies of Brazilian cuisine. After being greeted a quintessential sugar-cane Caipirinha cocktail, you'll get to work in small groups, preparing comfort foods like seafood moqueca and pork-and-bean feijoada. It's best to take this class early in your holiday, inspiring you to delve into Carioca culture with a greater understanding of this melting pot of cultures. Simone's passion is a highlight of any trip to Rio. The friendships you make might last for life — and once you're back home, you can prepare a Brazilian feast for your friends. *Cookinginrio.com*

Skykitchen Peruvian Cooking Classes: Peruvian cuisine has skyrocketed to popularity worldwide, and superstar chefs Astrid and Gaston have become ambassadors of the culinary arts in metropolitan Lima. Their throne room for three-hour, hands-on classes in English, Spanish and German is the rooftop Skykitchen, offering sweeping views over Lima's fashionable Miraflores neighborhood. Cook and share a meal with other foodies, then take a market stroll to sample 35 fresh fruits, tart and sweet, many from the Amazon jungle. Classes include an in-depth explanation of the role that various ingredients play in different dishes. *Skykirchen.pe*

Culinary Tours

Pick Up the Fork (Buenos Aires): Allie Lazar came to Argentina in 2006 to study political science in a semester-long exchange program at the Universidad de Buenos Aires. She soon fell in love with the "Paris of South America." The Chicago native's tale of passion resonates with all those who have moved to another country. "Over 10 years later, I'm still here, crazy enough to have fallen in love with this wonderfully chaotic country," she said. "I started writing 'Pick Up the Fork' in 2010 as a hobby to document my love-hate relationship with food in Argentina, attempting to liven up traditional restaurant reviews with a little bit of honesty and a bit of silliness."

The blog sprang from a culinary obsession with the meat-loving nation, which led directly to ultra-customized, private food tours — or anti-food tours. Allie takes her guests to off-the-beaten-path barrios to experience the local food scene through bites of stuffed empanada turnovers, gaucho steaks and cabrito (kid goat) in its simplest form: charcoal-barbecued with tangy chimichurri sauce. *Pickupthefork.com*

Puerto Vallarta Food Tours: Ever since American silver-screen icons Elizabeth Taylor and Richard Burton had a steamy love affair during the 1964 filming of *Night of the Iguana*, the once-sleepy fishing port on Mexico's sun-soaked Pacific coast has become the nation's crown jewel for sea-and-sand lovers. To make it even better, Mexican is one of the world's unique cuisines. Vallarta Food Tours guides ferocious eaters through the flavors of this culinary enclave in a variety of informative tours.

As a part-time resident of this coast, Nick has enjoyed many afternoons and evenings with Vallarta Food Tours — sampling tasty street tacos and fresh seafood, handcrafted cocktails and even cycling tours. His personal favorite is a walk through the clandestine neighborhood of Pitillal. And who knew there are more than 70 types of chilies in Mexico? *Vallartafoodtours.com*

El Carmen Estate Coffee Tour (El Salvador): Many visitors to Central America have their sights set on an eco-tour in Costa Rica, an exploration of the Mayan culture in Guatemala, or a deep dive into the turquoise Caribbean waters of Belize. El Salvador remains off most travelers' radar. That's a shame as the nation shines with excellent beaches for surfing, charming colonial towns, lofty Mayan ruins and plenty of opportunities for adventure.

Globally, coffee is the second most-traded commodity. El Salvador is renowned for its rich and aromatic beans. Taking a coffee tour around a mill provides insight. Outside the brightly colored mural town of Concepción de Ataco, in an idyllic setting facing a verdant mountain backdrop, El Carmen Estate and Coffee Resort showcases the traditional methods of producing gourmet coffee. Learn how coffee cherries are transformed into green beans for exporting; later, taste in-house coffee prepared in a conventional *chorreador* dripper. *Elcarmenestate-hotel.guestcentric.net*

Tastes vary the world over. A culinary melting pot, London challenges the senses.

EUROPE

Cooking Classes

Cooking Ala Turka (Istanbul): Istanbul's first Turkish cooking school, opened in 2002, Cooking Ala Turka is hands-down one of the best culinary experiences you'll find. The school teaches how to prepare a well-balanced, five-course menu, whether you're in a group of two or 10, culminating with a two-hour tasting and wine pairings. Professional chefs unveil a variety of Turkish dishes, including fava, mezze platters, künefe, date pancakes, semolina cakes with hazelnut, and other delicious delights. Cooking Alaturka also provides a wealth of information about Istanbul life and its local restaurant scene. *Cookingalaturka.com*

L'École Ducasse Paris Studio: Not all-superstar chefs share their passion for cooking. But since 1999, the great Alain Ducasse has offered his love of preparing culinary masterpieces, priming the next generation of innovative cooks. Chefs and pastry chefs share their mastery of culinary techniques with amateur food enthusiasts at this Paris institution. Students here should have a basic knowledge of meal preparation; ambitious dishes come straight from Ducasse's cookbooks. They include curried cod and mussels, lobster court bouillon, double-baked cheese soufflé with Parmesan cheese, and roasted langoustines with pepper. *Paris-ecoleducasse-studio.com*

Glorious Greek Cooking School (Ikaria): The people who live on the happy, stress-free island of Ikaria, 150 miles from Athens in the northern Aegean, are known for their longevity: It's not uncommon to meet Greek residents over 100 years old. The islanders' zest for life can also be found in their healthy but tasty diet. Greek-American chef Diane Kochilas makes her home here, offering week-long cooking classes and culinary tours. Her passion for Greek cuisine is evident in such perfect yet innovative dishes as protoyiahni (a tomato chicken-noodle soup), spanokopita mac'n'cheese with olive-oil bechamel, and green-bean salad with chopped onion and diced, smoked pork. *Dianekochilas.com*

Walk About Florence (Italy): Florence was the birthplace of the Renaissance in Italy, the home of Leonardo da Vinci, Michelangelo and the noble Medici family. The Tuscany region is still embraced as home to some of Italy's finest traditional cuisine, with its regional ingredients, family recipes and distinct flavors. Pizza and gelato are two favorites for Italian visitors, and Walk About Florence can teach you how to make both, from scratch, in a three-hour cooking class. Begin with a mound of flour, kneading the dough and adding the proper toppings. While your pizza is bubbling in the oven, you're learn how to make gelato at home. At the finish, you'll be given a recipe booklet to develop your craft once you return home. *Walkaboutflorence.com*

Culinary Tours

Devour Food Tours (Europe): Centuries of invaders — Phoenicians, Romans, Moors and 21st-century tourists — have left a lasting mark on the Iberian Peninsula. While culinary specialist Devour tours in eight European countries, as well as New York and Boston, it is in Spain's four major tourist centers that the company truly shines. The distinctive flavors of Barcelona, Madrid, San Sebastian and Seville yield such opportunities as gourmet tapas and wine-tasting in Madrid, a food-and-market excursion in Barcelona's Gracia neighborhood, an Andalusian taverna tour that gets up-close-and-personal with flamenco dance, and a sampling of small Basque bar snacks, *pintxos*. *Devourtours.com*

Eating Europe: Founded in Rome in 2011, Eating Europe is the most extensive food tour expert on the continent. The company currently offers food immersion in six Italian cities (Florence, Milan, Naples, Palermo and Venice, along with Rome), plus Amsterdam, Athens, Berlin, Lisbon, London, Paris, Porto and Prague. Walk with a local guide beyond the prominent neighborhoods to taste meals in vibrant secluded neighborhoods in many of Europe's most beloved cities. Wander Rome's medieval Trastevere neighborhood, visit the backstreets of Montmartre in Paris, stroll the cobblestone streets of Old Napoli, pair Czech ales with hearty goulash in Prague, or sample rijsttafel on an Amsterdam canal tour. *Eatingeurope.com*

Maison Cailler Chocolate Tour (Switzerland): Many chocolate lovers consider Switzerland home to the world's finest. Maison Cailler, founded in 1819 as the first chocolate factory in the country, is a must-visit for chocoholics. Milk chocolate is said to have originated at its alpine factory at Broc-Gruyère, where fresh cow milk from nearby dairies was blended with fine imported cacao. Now more than 300,000 confections are packaged daily and shipped worldwide. A museum provides greater insight into chocolate's history, from Aztec cacao ceremonies to modern practices. In-depth workshops and classes teach you to make truffles, pralines and chocolate hearts for Valentine's Day. The factory is an easy day trip from Geneva. *Cailler.ch*

Visiting markets like Chichicastenango in Guatemala provides a glimpse into local society.

ASIA

In China, the expression "Open Rice!" symbolizes family and joy. Initially created to link hungry diners with Hong Kong restaurants, the reservation site Open Rice now operates not only in Hong Kong, Macau, Taiwan and the People's Republic of China, but also in Indonesia, Japan, Malaysia, Philippines, Singapore and Thailand. Much like Yelp, the app encourages trusted reviews from passionate eaters. *Openrice.com*

Cooking Classes

Asian Scenic (Thailand): Chiang Mai, Thailand's second-largest city, is near the top of the list of Asian travelers' favorite cities. And Thai cuisine is one of the world's favorite foods. This school is based on an organic, family-run farm outside the city. Students start with a visit to a local market, then harvest healthy ingredients directly from the garden. Such dishes as *som tum* (green papaya salad), *tom sab* (hot-and-sour soup) and *gang keow* (green curry, optionally with chicken) and fried banana meld three to five basic tastes into a single dish: sweet, sour, salty, spicy and/or bitter). Al fresco dining overlooks the farm and the nearby mountains. *Asianscenic.com*

Casa Luna Cooking School, Bali (Indonesia): Many world travelers have a special place in their hearts for Bali. Chef Janet de Neefe is credited with putting island cooking on the map of world-class cuisine. In the busy village of Ubud, she and her Balinese husband run many hospitality hotspots and culinary centers. Casa Luna has been lauded as one of the world's best cooking schools, showcasing authentic insights into Balinese life. Classes begin with local market tours, and at the Second Honeymoon Guesthouse, you'll learn which herbs and spices give each dish its aroma and flavor. You'll learn to prepare *gado gado* (vegetable salad), seafood *nasi goreng* (fried rice), chicken and prawn saté, grilled snapper and minced duck wrapped in a banana leaf. *Casalunabali.com*

Hoi An Eco Cooking Class (Vietnam): Surrounded by lush rice paddies and fertile farmland, the lovely central Vietnamese town of Hoi An welcomes visitors to half-day classes that begin with a market tour. After learning how to navigate in a round bamboo boat, class members paddle through a grove of coconut palms to source water directly from the fruit, then go fishing for purple crabs. Once the cooking class begins, students learn to grind rice to make traditional "paper" for wrapping fresh spring rolls and folding *bánh xèo* (crispy rice pancakes), finishing with banana-flower salad and Vietnam's famous *phở bò* (beef noodle soup). *Hoianecocookingclass.com*

Tokyo Sushi Academy: No matter where you come from, there's a good chance that you've tried sushi. In recent decades, the Japanese diaspora has carried around the world, bringing traditional foods and culinary techniques to new lands, and sushi is a unique element. The Tokyo Sushi Academy, founded in 2002, was the first international sushi school in Japan to teach sushi-making courses in English. Here, you'll learn to kill live fish and prepare them with a Japanese knife, along with other techniques of the noble art of sushi making — thus assuring higher standards abroad, as foreigners learn the traditional ways. To earn a diploma, you must create 12 pieces of sushi in just three minutes. *Sushiacademy.co.jp*

Culinary Tours

Hong Kong Foodie Tours: The culinary repertoire runs deep in food-centric Hong Kong, sometimes called "the world's food fair." On its bustling streets, roadside stalls meet world-class dining, seamlessly merging Cantonese culture with 156 years of British influence. Gourmands learn to eat like locals in working-class enclaves like Sham Shui Po or amid the buzz of the famous night market on Temple Street. Then leave the urban jungle behind, branching out into the New Territories for a Tai Po Market tour. Everywhere you wander, you'll discover small, family-owned restaurants, holes-in-the-walls that only a local would know. *Hongkongfoodietours.com*

Saigon Street Eats (Vietnam): Sometimes obsession is a good thing. Created by dynamic Australian-Vietnamese couple Barbara and Vu, Saigon Street Eats shepherds small groups of curious eaters through Ho Chi Minh City's dizzying back alleys in search of mouthwatering bites. The tours are designed to be as if your local friends are showing you the best grub around, introducing you to vendors who have worked their culinary craft for generations. Get off the beaten path on a morning food walk and discover a *phở* house that has served delicious noodles for over 35 years. In the evening, explore the Seafood Trail, where all you need is a toothpick or sharp stick to sample snails, mussels, scallops and prawns. *Saigonstreeteats.com*

At a cooking class in Rio de Janeiro students bond over aromas and flavors.

AFRICA

Cooking Classes

Café Clock (Morocco): Easily accessible from Spain, Morocco is the gateway to Africa, a land of dizzying souks, Saharan dunes and the high Atlas Mountains. Fabled Tangier, Fez, Casablanca and Marrakesh draw all takers who care to blend into their ancient medinas. London visitor Mike Richardson saw a need for an all-inclusive cultural hangout when he opened Cafe Clock in 2006, naming it after the centuries-old water tower located in the Bou Inania Madrasa in the old city of Fez. Now expanded to Marrakesh and the "blue city" of Chefchaouen, Cafe Clock offers an assortment of bespoke experiences, from cultural lessons to Moroccan cooking classes. Learn to cook a four-course dinner. There is another class on bread baking and a patisserie workshop. *Cafeclock.com*

Cape Town Culinary Tours (South Africa): Small group tours led by passionate Cape Towners encourage visitors to gain a sense of what locals call "the Mother City." Founder Elsje Erasmus, a fellow global explorer, and her talented team of guides will take you on a culinary walk around the city, inspiring you to discover new food options in the historic city center and beyond. There's a reason Cape Town is a favorite city for many travelers; this authentic culinary experience will help you to delve deeper into the Cape City's gastronomic gems. *Capetownculinarytours.com*

AUSTRALIA-PACIFIC

Seit Bush Tucker Tasting Tour (Northern Territory): Of all our world travels, nowhere else have we sat spellbound on a red-rock desert floor, gawking at a rock. Somehow, we are compelled to stare. Uluru is not just any rock; it's Australia's spiritual center, its heart and soul. The Anangu, an Aboriginal tribe, are the traditional and rightful owners of this great monolith and the equally mesmerizing Kata Tjuta National Park.

To Australians transplanted from Europe, "tucker" is food and "bush" is anything outside the cities. In Seit Outback Australia's Bush Tucker Tasting Tour, Anangu guides showcase their traditional food. You'll learn about native seeds, beetles and grubs, and about the local people's struggles to survive in a scalding climate on indigenous plants and animals. The Seit Outback team also crafts other experiences and tours, including painting workshops and primitive rock art in ancient caves. *Seittours.com*

Please be a traveler, not a tourist. Try new things, meet new people, and look beyond what's right in front of you. — Andrew Zimmern, chef and television personality

Chapter Six

RESPONSIBLE TOURISM:

Changing the World

In the end, you won't remember the time you spent working in the office or mowing the lawn. Climb that goddamn mountain. — Jack Kerouac

Just be sure to leave that mountain the same way you found it... or better.

Tourism is the single largest employer on Earth, accounting for nearly 11 percent of global GDP. Our collective response to the COVID pandemic demonstrated the importance of travel to individuals. The wanderlust of traveling the world and discovering new places captivates all of us — or, at least, the "all of us" who are reading these words now.

Hiking in the Alps, wreck diving in the Solomon Islands, learning about medicinal plants in the Amazon jungle or simply exploring the temples of Tokyo, both tourists and tour operators must behave responsibly to alleviate any negative impact on the environment and communities. Responsible and sustainable travel is the present and future of travel. No traveler can immerse in local society, seeking to take home life-changing memories, without learning and respecting the culture of the local community. Leaving people unexploited and lands pristine points to the importance of traveling responsibly.

More than 30 years ago in the safari and wildlife tourism sector, operators and activists wanted to ensure that tourists visiting Kenya, Tanzania, South Africa, Borneo or the Amazon jungle weren't destroying the wildlife and nature that they came to see. Eco-tourism was born with the mantra, "Take only photographs, leave only footprints." But it had a major flaw as it only focused on nature-based tourism, failing to acknowledge its negative effect on local people when travelers and operators failed to act responsibly.

Long before travelers had begun to discuss responsible or sustainable travel, Mexican conservationist and architect Hector Ceballos-Lascurain coined the term "ecotourism." That was in 1983, and he was ahead of his time. In 2000, two other pioneers of sustainable travel, Justin Francis and Dr. Harold Goodwin, created a company called "Responsible," the first to call for protecting people and their lands by reminding both operators and explorers to tread lightly in their world travels. A visit with a tribal elder at Kawaza village in Zambia had inspired Francis and Goodwin to be ethically and socially aware in their wanderings.

Today, responsible travel encompasses all ends of the tourism sector. When local inhabitants prosper, when their lives are enhanced, so too are travelers' experiences. Their encounters in local societies make travelers an integrated part of the equation. A visitor's actions significantly impact the lives of all those with whom they share the moment.

Whether you're on a one-week beach holiday or an extended journey around the world, the same ethics of responsibility apply. Every time you stay in a family-run inn or dine at a locally owned restaurant, whether in the Cotswolds of Wales or a remote village in Cambodia, you are ensuring that your tourism expenditures remain with the residents. We've trekked Nepal's Himalayas and stayed in local communities in Panama, Peru, Sri Lanka and Vanuatu. When we hire a Sherpa or stay at a private guesthouse, we can see how our money works to support a society. We gain a new perspective on life while preserving a culture to be savored by future travelers.

An open mind

The World Tourism Organization guide, "Responsible Tourist and Traveller," cites a global code of tourism ethics that has been compiled from years of expensive research. The report suggests that travel and tourism should be planned and practiced as a means of individual and collective fulfillment. An irreplaceable factor in self-education, mutual tolerance, and learning about the legitimate differences between peoples and diverse cultures, is an open mind. Indeed, respect for cultural traditions and practices, and for human rights, is at the leaving the planet in the best possible shape for future generations.

Chances are, the "travel bug" will follow you forever. As a responsible traveler, you will earn trust and respect and be more readily welcomed by local people and societies.

You never want to exploit people or the environment in any way. Helping to preserve forest and ocean ecosystems keeps the focus on "local." Without your awareness, future generations will never be able to embrace the life-changing experiences that your travels have provided, such as trekking the Inca Trail to Machu Picchu, visiting the penguins of Antarctica, viewing wild orangutans in Borneo, engaging with the Masai tribe in Kenya.

Tread lightly on local society when you travel. Activities such as zip-lining through Monteverde National Park in Costa Rica or climbing Kilimanjaro in Tanzania must be conducted with respect to nature.

Help improve the world by contributing to economic and social development. Purchase local handicrafts and products to support the local economy using fair trade principles (but never buy items made from endangered plants or animals). Practicing these principles keeps the local society more authentic, and bargaining for goods should reflect the understanding of a fair wage.

Study your destination before you go. Learn as much as possible about your new surroundings — the people, customs and history. Be a global citizen by blending in and making friends with locals. Try to "go local" by merging into the society as if it were your home.

Sustainable tourism

No one is better suited to discuss the importance of sustainable tourism than Dr. Goodwin. As managing director of the Responsible Tourism Partnership, Goodwin has worked on four continents with local communities, their governments, and the inbound and outbound tourism industry. An expert on economic development, poverty reduction, conservation and responsible tourism, he has taught everyone from graduate students to conservationists, and consulted with governments, businesses and international organizations. Goodwin founded the International Centre for Responsible Tourism in 2002.

"Responsible and sustainable tourism will be achieved in different ways in different places," Goodwin told us. "Sustainable tourism is the aspiration; the exercise of responsibility is about how the rather vague aspiration of sustainability is achieved. (But) sustainable tourism, like sustainability, defies definition."

Transparency is a key part of a responsible tourism approach, Goodwin said. This starts with analyzing the local situation, identifying the issues and problems that affect communities and their environment, and establishing local priorities where tourism can contribute to improving the situation.

Travel should solicit far greater emotions than those achieved when we stay in an all-inclusive resort or recognized chain hotel. As travelers, it's in our DNA to give back to local societies and to learn as much as possible about people and cultures. Whether we take time to volunteer, move overseas, or simply travel knowing that fragile, diverse ecosystems are not to be tampered with, we must all travel responsibly to preserve unique experiences. A responsible holiday means being aware of our impact on every landscape and seaside that we visit.

An indigenous guide dabs paint on child before a dance performance in Australia's Northern Territory.

ESSENTIAL TERMS AND PRACTICES

Eco-friendly: Products, practices and institutions that aim to reduce harm to the environment. The concept of eco-friendliness encompasses the physical environment, including water and energy conservation, along with the global ecosystem and biodiversity. We fight against resource depletion, toxic and chemical waste, climate change and overpopulation. Being eco-friendly also means that we protect animal rights — not using animal testing for non-medical reasons; not hunting; raising animals in natural conditions with freedom of movement, and not feeding them growth hormones; using all parts of animals killed for meat, including the skin and fur; and, for many people, refraining from using animal products altogether.

Fair trade: Fair-trade products are those whose merchants, artisans and farmers are paid reasonable wages and whose laborers have good working conditions. This is important in responsible tourism, as multinational corporations often force local workers to work extended hours for low wages.

Protecting cultures: The world's myriad cultures and languages add to the rich diversity of human experience. What's more, a vibrant culture gives that people a sense of pride and community. It is crucial to protect and preserve them.

Accessibility: Individuals with disabilities have the same rights to travel as the able-bodied. It's essential that the tourist industry take steps to make any activity available to the disabled. Not only do barriers show disrespect; they also subconsciously encourage the idea that some are less worthy than others.

The spring-fall rule: Travel in shoulder seasons, avoiding high seasons when destinations are overrun by tourists. Although Nick was born on Santorini, arguably the world's most beautiful island, you will not find him in Greece in July or August. Instead, he visits his homeland in September and October. All travelers can combat over-tourism by staying away from cities like Barcelona and Venice during the summer high season.

Go green: Look into flying on such eco-friendly airlines as Alaska Airlines, JetBlue, Delta, Virgin Atlantic, Air France and Lufthansa. When you can, take public transportation to support local economies. You can also depend on trains or private buses. Consider renting a hybrid or electric car if you can't get along without a car.

Educate yourself about your destination and learn a language: You will have more appreciation for the local culture if you pick up a few phrases, and local citizens will be grateful for your linguistic efforts in starting conversations. Choose dozens of tongues and dialects, Swedish to Swahili, from over 30 online language apps.

Research which businesses engage in responsible practices: Hotels, shops, restaurants, tour companies and others should can engage in such practices as recycling, composting, and using environmentally friendly appliances ... just as you would at home.

Buy directly from artisans and farmers: Purchasing from local merchants is good for the economy and helps develop jobs. In addition, it's an eco-friendly option that helps the area's culture flourish and thrive.

Use less energy: Turn off lights when you don't need them. Unplug your mobile phone charger when it's not in use. Surf websites that save energy, like Blackle, which runs the Google search engine on a dark background.

Don't drink from disposable water bottles: Use reusable water bottles or hydration packs.

Conserve water: Take shorter showers and cut back on baths.

Travel leads the way to economic stability. Around the world, tourism is often a destination's single most important employer, one that changes lives for the better. In order to keep exchanges personal and unique, travelers must work together with governments, businesses, tour operators and others to foster mutual respect with local society. Learning from the people should be at the forefront of any journey.

Sunset over the Amazon rainforest sets the skies ablaze.

SUSTAINABLE DESTINATIONS

Responsible tourism should focus on creating improved economic benefits and a better life for a destination and its residents. Here are a handful of places that lead the way in accountability for sustainable development.

NORTH AMERICA

Alaska: In his epic 1903 adventure novel, Jack London wrote of Alaska's lure as "The Call of the Wild." When it comes to untouched nature with wide-open spaces and few people, enormous Alaska is about as far away from mass civilization as one can reach, short of an expedition. More than 100 immaculate national and state parks are sprinkled across the state. So vital is tourism to the economy here that the state's population doubles during the summer travel season. The self-proclaimed "last frontier" has its own sustainable tourism certification program, Adventure Green Alaska, whose standards insist that all tourism businesses use the best sustainable practices while respecting local customs and native cultures.

Canada: Open spaces far outnumber people in the United States' northern neighbor. With nearly 50 national parks, a kaleidoscope of colors in the Northern Lights, whale watching in British Columbia, and a wild kingdom of polar bears on Hudson Bay, the globe's second-biggest country surely does not disappoint adventure travelers. Canada showcases why sustainable travel is vital to tackling climate change and sustainable food sources, protecting oceans and waterways, as it nurtures a better life for locals and visitors alike. The commonwealth strives to preserve animals, environments, forests, communities and local cultures, protecting Canada's natural beauty.

From the Aegean island of Amorgos, the view extends to the edge of the world.

LATIN AMERICA AND CARIBBEAN

Dominica: The Caribbean region is heavily dependent upon inbound travel. In many island nations, in fact, tourism represents 80 percent of the gross domestic product. And green growth has given Dominica, nicknamed "The Nature Island," the fastest-growing economy of any island in the Caribbean. Eco-travelers have taken notice of the nation's progressive social and economic leadership. This unblemished Lesser Antilles gem is glistening with standout biodiversity, from sulfurous Boiling Lake to the world's only resident population of sperm whales in the surrounding waters. Waitukubuli National Trail extends 115 miles (185 km) through rainforest-shrouded Morne Trois Pitons National Park. What's more, the population includes the most significant community of native people in the Caribbean region.

    Guyana: South America's best-kept ecotourism secret may be culturally diverse Guyana. Few places offer unspoiled adventures and a Caribbean vibe that extends to the dense forest Amazon jungle. Of its nearly 800,000 inhabitants, nearly 90 percent live along the coast, leaving its towering waterfalls and lush jungle ripe for exploration. Guyanese communities work hard to conserve their wildlife and forests to ensure an authentic travel experience. The nation was recently named "Best in Sustainable Tourism" by the Latin American Travel Association at the world's largest travel trade fair, ITB Berlin.

As winter arrives, California Gray Whales migrate away from the frigid waters of Alaska to the warmer waters of Mexico.

EUROPE

Azores (Portugal): Like a collection of unblemished diamonds rising from the sea, the Azores archipelago is sprinkled in the mid-Atlantic, 900 miles from mainland Portugal. Still considered a part of Europe, the nine volcanic islands are rugged and remote, with lofty peaks and stunning coastlines. The plan is for them to remain so, as the Azores are the first archipelago to achieve international certification from the Global Council for Sustainable Tourism. The verdant islands of the Azores continue to maintain an environmentally friendly lifestyle. Sustainable fishing is a way of life, and almost any meal on the islands comes from locally sourced products.

Iceland: Over the past decade, the popularity of Iceland as a tourism magnet has skyrocketed. The underpopulated volcanic island in the North Atlantic is supercharged with gushing geysers, plunging waterfalls, never-ending volcanic movement, soothing geothermal pools and the rainbow of colors in the Northern Lights, or *aurora borealis.* With popularity come pressures and challenges. Environmentally conscious Icelanders are coping with success, managing over-tourism by promoting new areas to draw travelers to the island nation.

Scandinavia: Many travelers know that the Nordic countries of Denmark, Norway, Sweden and Finland are global leaders in sustainability. It all begins with its environmentally conscious citizens, who continue to use renewable energy. All four nations are progressing rapidly toward carbon neutrality. Norway, in fact, is on track to achieve that lofty goal by 2030. Denmark is on course to eliminate one-third of fossil-fuel emissions from cars and buses. Finland aims to reduce greenhouse gases by half in the next decade, creating a low-carbon societies. The region's successes will encourage other countries to investigate ambitious climate actions and realize opportunities to achieve green, climate-resilient growth.

ASIA

Bhutan: The tiny landlocked Himalayan kingdom has been declared the world's most eco-friendly nation. The only carbon-negative country in the world, nestled between superpowers China and India, prides itself on its sustainable approach to tourism. (It helps that tourists were not permitted to enter before 1974.) About 70 percent forested, powered by hydroelectricity from mountain streams, Bhutan promises low-volume but high-value tourism priced at about $250 per day per person. A progressive king devised a

Gross National Happiness index to guide the country's economy, based up on a philosophy of sustainable development.

Raja Ampat, Indonesia: Scuba divers know something of the 1,500 sparsely populated islands of Raja Ampat, off the northwest tip of West Papua (Irian Jaya). The waters are renowned for healthy and diverse coral reefs that nurture an abundance of marine life so rich, it is considered to have the greatest biodiversity on the planet. Protecting this underwater paradise, said to contain 75 percent of the world's coral species, is essential. Part of the forward-thinking conservation approach extends to banning the sale and use of plastic bottles and requiring permits to enter the island region and its forests. Patrol boats monitor fishing restrictions. As a result of marine protections, Raja Ampat attracts more responsible divers and eco-adventurers.

Singapore: Asia's leading sustainable city-state, a mere 17 miles long and 31 miles wide, is densely populated Singapore. A city with a growing population creates new demands for waste management, but Singapore remains Asia's greenest city due to exceptional urban planning. The city-nation showcases innovative ways to achieve a sustainable future. Singapore is committed to solar as a renewable energy source to combat the country's year-round tropical climate. Singapore has the lofty goal of having its buildings achieve Green Mark Certification by 2030. A magnate for environmental thought-provokers creating new methods in urban planning and water solutions for a sustainable future.

Himalayan peaks tower above villagers walking the remote trails of Nepal.

AFRICA

Namibia: Located in southwestern Africa along the Atlantic Ocean, one of Africa's most natural and culturally diverse countries is Namibia. The untamed beauty of the beguiling Namib-Kalahari desert reaches all the way to the deserted and sand-swept Skeleton Coast. More than half of this eco-focused country is under conservation management, and nearly 40 percent of the land is preserved in national parks and animal sanctuaries. The world's largest populations of cheetahs and black rhinos inhabit this unique and captivating safari destination. Namibia was the first country to address conservation and habitat protection in its constitution. Today about one-eighth of the population work in tourism and conservation.

OCEANIA

New Zealand: Always a leader in global conservation with its 13 massive national parks and hundreds of miles of trekking trails, this South Pacific island nation is renowned for its attention to sustainable practices. Although it has only one native land animal (a prehistoric lizard called the tuatara), encountering New Zealand's marine and avian wildlife is an unforgettable experience. You can swim with a pod of playful dolphins, get up close and personal with colossal whales, watch baby blue penguins make a nightly march to their nests, or visit a wildlife park to see the national treasure, the small, flightless and nocturnal kiwi bird. (They're all but invisible in the wild).

   Palau: If diving or snorkeling with sharks and fishes is your passion, or exploring historic wrecks is your dream, the Republic of Palau in the western Pacific is a quintessential divers' paradise. Nicknamed "the underwater Serengeti," Palau comprises nearly 200 limestone and volcanic islands. Its famed Blue Holes offers some of the most diverse dive sites on the planet. And the nation is pioneering an essential model of sustainable tourism. In 2019, as Palau's 21,000 citizens welcomed more than 90,000 international travelers, it requested all visitors and its own residents to sign a pledge to act responsibly and ecologically within the trailblazing island chain.

Safeguarding the ocean's treasures by assuring newly hatched baby turtles make it to sea. It's estimated only 1 in 1,000 hatchlings will survive to adulthood.

SUSTAINABLE CITIES

In a world of increasing population pressures, the following cities lead the way towards more bikes and fewer cars, producing fewer harmful emissions while offsetting record levels of waste. These urban centers comply with the "eco-friendly" mantra demanded by its citizens, who seek to create a better environment for nature, visitors ... and themselves.

NORTH AMERICA

Portland, Oregon: Decades ago, the "Rose City" shaped an image as the most environmentally friendly city in the United States, thanks in large part to responsible city planning. Oregon's metropolis, stunning Mount Hood rising above evergreen forests to its east, embraces nearly 100,000 acres of green spaces and a well-planned grid of parks and trails that make it ideal for biking and walking. Environmentally progressive Portland is also a leader in the food-truck movement, in vegan restaurants and farm-to-table meals, with organic farms being a top priority for healthier living.

San Francisco, California: When it comes to sustainability, San Francisco is a global powerhouse in maintaining a pristine environment for its citizens and the crowds of tourists who visit. The City by the Bay was the first American city to mandate the use of plastic shopping bags, and citizens know to bring bags with them. San Francisco sends less trash to landfill than any other city in the United States, as 80 percent of the its waste is recycled, composted or reused. More than 1,000 hotels are ranked as eco-friendly. San Francisco is full of farmers markets offering fresh produce throughout the year. And the metropolis enjoys an abundance of bike lanes and one of the densest bike-share networks in the country.

Vancouver, Canada: The picturesque capital of British Columbia has been at the forefront of climate change since 21st Century began. Rated as the world's third greenest city, Vancouver maintains the lowest per-capita rate of greenhouse gas emissions in North America. The metropolis has planted early 130,000 trees since 2010; it has a goal of zero waste by 2040. Proving that a city can at once by ecologically progressive and economically sound, it has clean air and water and a surrounding natural environment of mountains, beaches and forests all within easy reach. Restaurants serve locally sourced food; many hotels have rooftop gardens; citizens regularly organize neighborhood cleanup parties.

EUROPE

Copenhagen, Denmark: The Danish capital, one of the world's most energy-efficient cities, has an ambitious plan to become the first carbon-neutral capital by 2025. It is a leader in recycling with less than 2 percent of the city's waste going to landfills. The streets are pedestrian-friendly, and it seems that no one is really in a rush. With its mantra of "more bikes, fewer cars," the green city has an impressive set of dedicated bike trails. Solar-powered buses and electric boats transport passengers around town and throughout the city's outskirts. One-quarter of city's total food sales, and 90 percent of food served in restaurants, is organic, and many establishments add food scraps to the soil in organic gardens.

ASIA

Bengaluru (Bangalore), India: One would expect nothing less from this progressive city of 8 million, the hub of India's answer to Silicon Valley. Although tech workers congest the mega-city, their forward thinking also envisions a a sustainable future, which is making considerable strides. A local scooter company, Bounce, leads the way with thousands of scooter rentals. Ergonomically designed Yulu e-bikes are reducing congestion, traffic and air pollution.

AFRICA

Cape Town, South Africa:

Cape Town is a perennial model for a brighter sustainability future for the entire continent of Africa. Ten percent of homes in Cape Town use solar power, and 10 percent of the municipality uses renewable energy. Wind farms have generated energy since 2008. Farmers and natural-foods markets have taken over the fertile landscape, growing locally sourced produce. Small leaps from plastic-free shopping to solar-powered coffee carts are changing people's perceptions. Sustainable wineries offer lessons in eco-friendly oenology. Cape Town boasts swelling waves for surfing and dramatic mountain scenery for hiking.

_ As polar routes become more popular and accessible, areas like emblematic Greenland need
to be protected. Expedition cruises.

VISITING INDIGENOUS SOCIETIES

On World Indigenous People Day, which falls annually on August 9, the United Nations brings attention to native peoples in countries around the world, praising their diverse cultural heritage while highlighting the challenges they face on a daily basis.

"Colonization, assimilation, globalization, industrial activities and tourism have often threatened indigenous identities and cultural practices," reports the United Nations World Tourism Organization (UNWTO). "While tourism can offer opportunities for economic development and cultural revitalization, it can also have negative impacts on indigenous communities."

Indigenous tourism — defined as owned and operated by native peoples with a connection and responsibility to their local community — is becoming an avenue of economic empowerment and sustainable development in many nations. "By engaging in tourism activities, indigenous communities can showcase their cultural expressions, traditional practices, and promote a sense of pride and identity," the UNWTO has said.

It's making giant steps in Canada, Australia and parts of Africa, where indigenous-led wildlife tours and community-based cultural experiences are becoming commonplace. In Canada, for example, more than 20 native organizations are members of the Indigenous Tourism Association of Canada. The UNTWO reports that this agency "spurs cultural interaction and revival, bolsters employment, empowers local communities, especially women and youth, encourages tourism product diversification, (and) allows people to retain their relationship with the land and nurtures a sense of pride."

Footloose Francis

Going Local queried Francis Tapon, a Silicon Valley marketing veteran, author, public speaker and modern-day Marco Polo, about his life as a nomad — particularly in Africa, where in eight years he set foot in all 54 countries — and his experiences with the indigenous populations. (He's also walked across Madagascar, Spain twice and the United States four times.)

Author, global nomad, public speaker Francis Tapon traveled to all 54 countries on Africa in eight years.

Q & A with Francis Tapon

GOING LOCAL: What were some of your early inspirations to travel? Were there individuals, books or broadcasts that encouraged you to step out of your comfort zone to explore the greater world?

TAPON: My dad inspired me. He left France when he was 17 to live in Argentina for seven years. He was an entrepreneur who traveled regularly to Latin America to buy merchandise to sell in the USA. His constant travel inspired me. Others who inspired me were (author) Bill Bryson, (climber) Reinhold Messner, and (hiker) Brian Robinson, the first to walk the Appalachian Trail, Pacific Crest Trail and Continental Divide Trail ("the Triple Crown") in a single calendar year.

GL: How were you influenced by your growing up in San Francisco?

TAPON: Cosmopolitan cities are healthy places to grow up because you're immersed in diversity. What sets San Francisco apart from other cosmopolitan cities is that it is unusually liberal. Until recently, that has meant that it is an extremely tolerant place, celebrating all manner of thought. Lately, however, extreme leftists have impeded the free flow of ideas so that conservative voices are not tolerated. That is a pity.

GL: How has travel broadened your mind or changed you?

TAPON: Funny you ask because my first TEDx Talk was on precisely that subject! Travel has increased my risk tolerance and my belief that most humans are good.

GL: Whenever we think of Africa, your intrepid travels to every country come to mind. What drew you to Africa, and what have the people taught you?

TAPON: Africans have taught me to be more tolerant, patient and forgiving. From a high-income world perspective, Africa is full of flaws: Few things work well. As a traveler, either you adapt or you suffer. You learn to forgive or you stay angry. Be patient or be miserable. Africa will either break you or make you a better person.

GL: What priceless, unforgettable moments with indigenous people come to mind?

TAPON: In my third TEDx talk, I talked about picking up 3,000 African hitchhikers. So often, they would invite me to their homes to spend the night. Unlike packaged tours, I got to live among Africans and get to know them.

GL: While I have briefly met and traveled with indigenous people, you've embraced many African tribes and cultures. What are some of your most cherished encounters with indigenous peoples of Africa?

TAPON: I told my couch-surfing host in Niamey, Niger, that I would stay with him for four days. He welcomed me. I ended up staying for four months because my car had problems! Living the day-to-day existence with his friends was fabulous and unforgettable. He lived in a city, not a village, but what made it special was that it was for so many months. I love sinking my teeth into travel.

GL: On recent travels to Australia, Canada and Mexico, we've noticed a push — or at least marketing efforts — to showcase the cultures of First Nations, Aboriginal people, and even indigenous cultures in Mexico, all of whom are traditional landowners. How can nations promote traditional culture yet keep locals unchanged?

TAPON: It's hard. Few locals remain unchanged. All human cultures change. Some evolve so slowly that they seem frozen in time (like the San Bushmen). However, even those cultures are changing, perhaps imperceptibly. They adopt phones and electricity. Even remote villages in the Sahara had satellite TV, which changes everything. We can lament the loss of diversity or celebrate the unifying power and benefits of globalization. I prefer the positive viewpoint.

GL: *Many top tour companies now attempt to connect curious travelers with indigenous communities. When done responsibly, we believe this can lift or better whole communities. Do you agree?*

TAPON: Yes. Wildlife safaris encourage Africans to preserve their wildlife. If they kill the beasts, they kill their main source of revenue. Similarly, our touring of exotic tribes encourages them to preserve and celebrate their exotic ways since they get valuable economic support when they do. There are downsides to such tourism, but the benefits outweigh the negatives.

GL: *What do you think are the biggest challenges that indigenous cultures face in their encounters with the modern world? How can they overcome, or at least assimilate, these challenges?*

TAPON: They face the same challenges that indigenous cultures have always faced — the seductiveness and comfort of modern living. European tribes gave up many of their exotic practices in exchange for supermarkets, central heating, A/C, electricity, plumbing, medicine and education.

People vote with their feet. If modern life sucked more than simple, indigenous life, you'd see massive migration to the hinterlands. But what do we see instead? Global urbanization. Why? Because most humans find urban environments better than rural, off-the-grid villages.

I'm unsure we must overcome these challenges. Just accept that humans like to live comfortable lives and for most humans that means living in an modern, urban environment. There will always be outliers, those on the edge of the bell curve, who feel the opposite. I understand them. I've spent years in the wilderness. But such people will always be anomalies. A dying breed.

GL: *As an expert in vibrant tribal cultures, what countries do you recommend travelers visit — whether or not off the beaten path?*

TAPON: Southern Ethiopia and anywhere deep in the Sahara.

GL: *What's next on your personal travel radar?*

TAPON: West and Central Asia! I hope to spend a year there!

In one of the Earth's last frontiers, travel and conservation must co-exist in fragile Antarctica.

The sustainability revolution will, hopefully, be the third major social and economic turning point in human history, following the Neolithic Revolution and the Industrial Revolution.
— King Charles III

Chapter Seven

SUSTAINABILITY

Choosing Travel Partners

In life, it's not where you go — it's who you travel with. — Charles M. Schulz, *Peanuts*

As we move in the aftermath of a once-a-century pandemic that stymied travel, protecting our environment has become a much more urgent mission than ever before. We must travel lightly, in an eco-friendly way.

Responsible tourism is about creating better places to live and visit. Travelers want to reduce their impact while traveling, so they seek organizations they can trust to positively impact the local economy, the landscapes and seascapes.

Whether you're traveling on safari and camping with an outfitter in Botswana, or on an expedition cruise to some of the most remote, tucked-away and pristine harbors on the planet, choose an operator who guides travelers responsibly, sustaining cultures and wildlife.

A tour operator's role is to positively contribute to the environment by furthering sustainable tourism goals. Protecting the local landscape and culture controls survival and growth. Travel companies must be at the forefront of giving back to the local societies they represent while treading lightly on our fragile planet.

"By traveling with a tour operator that's genuinely committed to operating responsibly, the fundamentals of supporting local communities and limiting your environmental footprint will have already been built into our trip," said James Thornton, CEO of Intrepid Travel, a small-group tour company and a leader in innovative and thoughtful tourism strategies. In 2014, the company was the first global company to remove elephant rides from its tours as inhumane.

For some companies, the social value of a travel experience is even more important to the provider than the profit it earns. "When we travel responsibly, we demonstrate respect for the people, culture and environment we're visiting," said Thornton. Responsible travel preserves local society and helps fund ecological and cultural conservation: Responsible tourism gives locals reasons to conserve, he said.

Justin Francis has long been a leader in the path to responsible tourism. "When you take a responsible holiday, you are ensuring that the money you spend benefits the local community," said the CEO of Britain's Responsible Travel, which sells tours from over 400 sustainable travel specialists worldwide. "One practice is staying in a family-owned lodge instead of a multinational chain, discovering local eateries which celebrate local cuisine as part of their culture, or going kayaking with a local guide," Francis said.

A responsible tourism policy should be at the heart of any action or decision by a company bringing tourism to a fragile land. Sustainability must be a part of its business strategy. Seeking responsible operators is an integral part of one's holiday, and one should always to book with companies with such a policy. If a company has no responsible tourism policy, it should be seen as a negative factor. As more companies incorporate such principles into their core values, more clients will recognize them as industry standards and become aware of their travel choices.

The goal of travel should be to meet, mingle and learn from local societies while traveling sustainably. Travel's impact upon local communities includes the economic implications involved in the journey and by travel operators.

A trusted operator, bringing tourists into new and old destinations, should believe in the development of responsible tourism — designed to fulfill the needs of host regions and present travelers, while at the same time sustaining the area for future visitors. Development conducted to enrich and enhance tourism's standing should have the values of respecting the cultural heritage, protecting the people, preserving nature and all flora and fauna of the region, especially including endangered wildlife species.

To ensure life-changing moments through encounters with local inhabitants, tourism must be responsible, while travelers must become conscious citizens of the world. The operator must instill these notions into its groups.

Travelers can positively contribute to their destination by choosing ethical travel companies. The operators listed below give back to the local community by providing adventures with missions based on conservation and sustainable-development operations. Whether a journey to the Arctic Circle or small-group adventure travel to the Andes, these tour companies share a deep love for the destinations they represent, sustaining cultures and landscapes and protecting flora and fauna.

Consequently, ethical travel companies offer a far richer experience because they remain based on knowledge, expertise, and passion for protecting people and fragile environments. This ethic is infused into every itinerary and experience, making each travel experience exclusive. From committed conservation and wildlife experiences to sequestered lodges and luxury safaris, bespoke itineraries and expedition sailings, here are some of the world's top eco-friendly travel companies and responsible travel leaders.

Tahitian locals enjoy water play with visitors to French Polynesia.

Operators Making a Positive Influence

Abercrombie & Kent

Providing local, sustainable travel experiences for over 40 years, Abercrombie & Kent strives at every turn to redefine the notion of what is possible on vacation, offering an award-winning combination of exclusivity, comfort and authenticity on all seven continents. The approach is one of a singular service — such as private passage by road and lake through the Andes or a maximum group size of only 12 guests on each Galapagos shore excursion — with insider-access opportunities unlike any available elsewhere.

A&K's luxury group journeys, led by experts at over 55 offices in more than 30 countries, ensure seamless and life-changing travels. Small-group tours, expedition cruises or tailor-made travel are escorted by a resident tour director. Each trip promises a unique experience, on-the-ground expertise supplemented by local guides every step of the way. You'll discover the culture, wildlife and history as Abercrombie & Kent uncloaks your destination with an authenticity beyond the reach of most other travel providers.

A&K formaliiized its first conservation efforts in the Masai Mara nearly half a century ago. Ever since, through education and sustainable tourism, philanthropy has been an integral part of the A&K philosophy and the company's commitment to giving back to local society has only grown. A&K's mission is to create long-standing partnerships with local communities that enable nature to thrive and cultures to leave a positive impact wherever the destination. *Abercrombieandkent.com*

Adventure Canada

Since 1987, when founders Bill and Matthew Swan began taking travelers to off-the-beaten- track destinations, Adventure Canada has been a leader in expedition travel. Curious global explorers traverse less-visited Atlantic and Arctic Canada regions, Newfoundland, Iceland, Greenland, Scotland, and the Faroe Islands on the purposely built *Ocean Endeavour.*

On board, a stellar team of naturalists, historians, musicians and other storytellers keep you enthralled as you seek out remote regions of the world, crossing passages inaccessible by larger ships. You learn about endemic wildlife and flora while docking in hidden locations. Sustainably exploring nature is the critical component of all Adventure Canada journeys. *Adventurecanada.com*

Amazon Nature Tours

For many global explorers, a trip to the world's largest rainforest is a once-in-a-lifetime experience. The Amazon is almost the size of the continental United States. In 2020, Nick was blissfully sailing the mighty jungle on the riverboat M/Y *Tucano* before COVID shut the world down.

Amazon Nature Tours offers small ship bespoke expeditions with a maximum capacity of 18 guests. Cruises begin in Manaus, Brazil, on the Grand Dame Motor Yacht *Tucano*, and venture up the mammoth river and into the vast jungle, nearly 100 miles further up-river than any other boat operator. Founder Mark Baker has been exploring the Amazon since 1988 in a quest for authenticity and sustainability. "Our goal has been threefold," said Baker: "To reduce our impacts on the rainforest, contribute to local communities of which we are a part, and promote rainforest conservation." *Amazon-nature-tours.com*

Aurora Expeditions

In 1991, co-founders Greg and Margaret Mortimer fulfilled their dream of exploring less-visited wild places with friends by creating Aurora Expeditions. For than three decades later, their passion for guiding curious explorers to remote regions of the world on small-group, up-close-and-personal expeditions has not faded.

Expedition cruises vary in length from 10 to 26 days. They are the perfect way to explore wild fringes that might only to accessible from the sea. The impressive route selection includes ice routes of Antarctica, the Arctic and Subarctic, Greenland, Iceland, Canada and Russia. In Europe, in-depth voyages include a deeper exploration of Ireland, Scotland and Norway's fiords. In Latin America, expeditions extend to biologically diverse Costa Rica and Panama, and wild and isolated Patagonia, shared by Argentina and Chile. Small-impact groups leaving a low carbon footprint also navigate Australian waters and the sublime isles of Raja Ampat off the coast of West Papua, Indonesia. *Auroraexpeditons.com*

Big Five Tours & Expeditions

Enriching lives through instinctive journeys, Big Five offers trips to destinations making an eco-difference, such as Namibia, which has sustainability written into its constitution, and Costa Rica, which aims to be the first carbon-neutral nation. African safaris with cultural immersion offer a new twist on classic destinations. As a leading operator, the company remains committed to the best practices of sustainable tourism that support cultural heritage, conservation, wildlife and educational initiatives. Knowing that children are our future, Big Five Tours & Expeditions is proud to announce a new partnership with the nonprofit group One More Generation (OMG).

Some of Big Five's journeys include meandering the vast western regions of China, the wilds of Tanzania, the rugged wilderness of Tasmania, the Andean landscapes of Chile and Bolivia, or isolated islands of eastern Indonesia. There are also visits to tiger sanctuaries in India and a noted wine estate, followed by a beach stay, in South Africa. *Bigfive.com*

Churchill Wild

Churchill Wild is the world's first and only company to offer polar bear safaris. These remote walking tours in northern Manitoba include stays at three handcrafted luxury eco-lodges, affording a chance to glimpse the famous beasts while gawking at the spectacle of the Northern Lights. Since 1993, the polar experts have had a 99 percent success rate in polar bear sightings between July and November near the Hudson Bay in Arctic Canada.

As stewards of the land it embraces, the company has developed a minimalist approach. Over the years, these leaders in polar sustainability have innovated techniques in water systems, waste management and lodge construction. Churchill Wild gives back to the community through philanthropic endowments to The Royal Canadian Geographical Society and Canadian Parks and Wilderness. *Churchillwild.com*

G Adventures

Since 1990, changing the world through travel has been the core value of Canadian operator G Adventures. The company works with social enterprises and NGOs while guiding small groups worldwide. G Adventures journeys build meaningful relationships with local communities, benefitting the inhabitants of the destinations where they lead travelers.

Tours share a love for life-altering adventures in various travel styles. These include tours geared to families, young adults, marine exploration, rail tours, active adventures, private groups and wellness. Its "Local Living" tours send you undercover into some of the most exciting places on the globe to discover life as it's lived by the locals every day. Unpack once at a central home base — a Tuscan farmhouse, an Icelandic home, a rustic lodge in the Amazon jungle — and discover the local culture with the help of an enlightened resident who knows the area best.

As the planet is the product, G Adventures changes lives in an eco-friendly way. Through its involvement in the Plateterra Foundation, the company aims to reduce poverty through community tourism. Whether staying in boutique hotels or farm-to-table Agrotourimo, G Adventures supports local projects with each trip. *Gadventures.com*

Hurtigruten

Sailing the entire coast of Norway, Hurtigruten is unique in the world. The crew is Norwegian, the sustainable food is traditional Norwegian, the experience is fully Norwegian. Unlike conventional cruise liners, Hurtigruten operates with a local's approach, a local's experience. The company annually transports close to 100,000 tourists throughout the fjords and waterways of Norway. Guests learn about the ports of call and immerse themselves in Norwegian traditions.

Adding value to destinations is Hurtigruten's mission, past and future. Geotourism incorporates the concept of sustainable tourism – that destinations should remain unspoiled for future generations, allowing growth while preserving and developing a place's distinctive character. As tourism provides steadily increasing revenues and jobs for Norway's economy, cooperation with National Geographic and a focus on sustainability become paramount. Hurtigruten strives to improve its skills and performance on all fronts, enhancing what it hopes will be the trip of a lifetime, whether viewing the Northern Lights or the Midnight Sun. *Hurtigruten.com*

Intrepid Travel

For 35 years, Intrepid Travel's small-group trips have guided adventure travelers to the earth's furthest corners and everywhere between. Intrepid's responsible; ethical journeys have trodden lightly on flora and fauna, sustaining communities since 1989. In these journeys, travelers experience real life, getting as close as possible to experiences and encounters. There are trips to more than 100 countries, including timeless Rajasthan, India; overland from Cape Town to Victoria Falls, Africa; or the Atlas Mountains on a Moroccan adventure. Local expert leaders take you far from the world of guidebooks and into a new world, waiting to be discovered.

Intrepid Travel promotes the notion that travelers, as citizens of the world, can be a real force of positive change globally. The nonprofit Intrepid Foundation assists in making the world a better place with some fantastic initiatives. The operators address the climate crisis, planting the first "travel-powered" forest in Kenya and funding a range of carbon-drawing seaweed regeneration programs. A leader in child protection and the human treatment of animals, Intrepid was the first tour company to cancel elephant rides from its itineraries. *Intrepidtravel.com*

Journey Mexico

Whether your passion is whale watching in Baja California or exploring the cultural epicenters of Mexico City and Guadalajara, Journey Mexico offers one-of-a-kind, sustainable tours. From a train ride through the Barancas del Cobre (Copper Canyon) to a boat ride in the jungles of Chiapas, Journey Mexico employs knowledgeable guides and trusted properties, immersing guests in the land of the Mayans and Aztecs and the birthplace of tequila.

Crafted journeys cater to various travel styles, whether the goal is adventure, culture, history, food, luxury, local markets, or spa and wellness. Custom-made itineraries are committed to environmentally responsible travel that promotes conservation, has low visitor impact, and provides for beneficially active socio-economic involvement of local populations. Immersive journeys facilitate understanding and promote cooperation among all the participants, from clients to guides to gracious Mexican hosts. *Journeyme xico.com*

Lindblad Expeditions

For over 50 years, Lindblad Expeditions has ben using the power of travel to make a positive impact. Small expedition ships travel to some of the most immaculate places on the planet — over 40 regions in all. Now Lindblad has joined forces with National Geographic to further inspire the world through expedition travel.

Lindblad is a 100 percent carbon-neutral company committed to green business operations and preserving the planet for future generations. Expedition leaders are deeply committed to remote wild places like Patagonia, South Georgia and the Falklands, and the Marquesas Islands of French Polynesia.

The Lindblad Expeditions-National Geographic Fund was created to support projects in the regions visited by the expeditions ... and beyond. These are fully funded by shipboard travelers, with Lindblad and the National Geographic Society contributing all operating costs. "We see ourselves as far more than a travel company," said CEO Sven Lindblad. "We are a conduit to exhilaration, to the feeling you get when you see something wild and unexpected, or rare and beautiful." *LindbladExpeditions.com*

Micato Safaris

To Micato Safaris founders Feliz and Jane Pinto, the African continent is more than simply a destination to view the planet's most extraordinary game. Africa is home. The Kenyan couple curate safaris whose memories linger long after you depart Africa. The Micato family includes some of the continent's most accomplished guides and astute trackers, who know the best locations to spot wildlife.

Escorted safaris venture out from luxurious, magnificently designed camps into the vast wilds. No two experiences are alike; each African nation provides a heart-stirringly unique gameland. Destinations include Kenya, Tanzania, Rwanda, Botswana, South Africa, Namibia and Zambia. The African experts also cover India.

This award-winning operator is dedicated to preserving the future of Africa. As a committed stewards of the land, Micato practices thoughtful and responsible adventure tourism. The company continuously engages with local communities to teach sustainability and maintain the authenticity of communities, while educating travelers on respecting cultures and ecological practices. *Micato.com*

Mir Corporation

One region that has eluded Nick, in his quest to visit every country on Earth, is Central Asia. In 2024, he'll check five more lands off his list when he joins Mir on a Silk Road journey through Uzbekistan, Kazakhstan, Tajikistan, Kyrgyzstan and Turkmenistan. His choice was well-considered: Mir is well invested in the people, lands and routes remote lands.

Curious travelers can adventure overland from Istanbul to Xian or from Beijing to Europe via Mongolia. In this breathtaking region, Mir is the unmatched leader of in-depth experience and expertise. For more than three decades, the company has catered to travelers with a wanderlust for a more distant world—those who seek new and unique destinations. At this writing, Russia (including the Trans-Siberian Railroad), Ukraine and Belarus are off limits. But you can still travel by Land Rover across most of Mir's 34 affiliated countries throughout Europe and Asia. *Mircorp.com*

Uzbekistani families pose at Itchan Kala, the 18th-century inner fortress of Khiva.

Mountain Travel Sobek

A pioneer of adventure travel since the early 1980s, Mountain Travel Sobek takes travelers on high-octane quests to remote destinations all over the world. Small groups embark on off-the-beaten-track adventures that may range from soft to arduous. The company's multilingual experts can help shape custom itineraries for exclusive tour options, which might include hiking Iceland's Eastern Fjords, going face-to-face with the matchless fauna of the Galapagos Islands, trekking between isolated Himalayan monasteries, or rambling overland through Africa's Sahara Desert. Its guides are flawless, hands-on field experts.

Commitment to sustainability is a mantra for MT Sobek, easily one of the most trusted and responsible of tour companies. It diligently works to preserve and sustain unique culture and fragile environments, doing everything it can to offset carbon emissions. MT Sobek goes the extra mile as a sponsor of the Alaska Conversation Foundation, the American Himalayan Foundation, The Fund for the Tiger, the Galapagos Conservancy, WildAid and The Wildlife Trust. Its guests are encouraged to donate to causes bettering the planet by sponsoring a student, donating funds to a local hospital or clinic, or contributing to wildlife projects. *Mtsobek.com*

National Geographic Expeditions

Possibly the most trusted brand in responsible and sustainable adventures is National Geographic Expeditions. The company was founded on the same belief in the importance of exploration that has distinguished the National Geographic Society's history of over 130 years. Launched in 1999, National Geographic Expeditions now operates hundreds of trips annually, spanning all seven continents and more than 80 destinations.

Since its earliest days, National Geographic has gone to great lengths to discover the unknown, immerse itself in extraordinary places, encounter new cultures, and investigate nature firsthand. These trips strive to create authentic and meaningful travel experiences that reveal wonders both hidden and celebrated around the globe. Its founders sought to understand "the world and all that's in it," inspiring journeys with a thirst for discovery and a passion for the wonders of our planet, creating eco-expeditions for the adventurous.

All proceeds from high-end eco-tours are directed to National Geographic research programs. The company supports sustainability initiatives in the fragile environments where many excursions begin. For example, one epic trip visits the Sabyinyo Silverback Lodge in Rwanda's Parc National des Volcans, habitat of the endangered mountain gorilla. A Rwandan community trust owns the lodge, and profits are used to finance local socio-economic and conservation initiatives. *Nationalgeographicexpeditions.com*

Quark Expeditions

Quart was established in 1991 to pioneer travel to the Arctic and Antarctica. Thousands of eager explorers now delve annually into these remote polar regions, where they experience lands whose environmental purity transcends political boundaries and whose beauty defies description. As an industry leader for exploring ice caps and penguins, Quark travels from the southernmost land masses, including South Georgia Island, to such Arctic destinations as Greenland, Iceland, Norway, Canada, even the North Pole. Polar travel is fascinating and out of reach to most travelers.

Quark remains passionate about ensuring that every passenger has the experience of a lifetime. Expedition cruises travel back in time to the heroic age of polar exploration, retracing the routes of such famed explorers as Roald Amundsen, Robert Peary and Ernest Shackleton. And as the invader of a fragile environment, Quark practices every possible sustainable initiative. These include carbon-neutral voyages, carbon offset, and vessels that burn Marine Gas Oil (MGO) – a clean-burning fuel with a low emission factor. Passengers are provided with reusable water bottles and the ship uses eco-friendly laundry chemicals in-cabin amenities. *Quarkexpeditions.com*

REI Adventures

If you thought REI only sells outdoor adventure gear, you'd be mistaken. Through the outdoor outfitters' stellar travel company, REI Adventures, you can branch out to almost anywhere in the world. REI offers more than 140 guided trips of all kinds for all skill levels of adventure and duration, led by expert guides worldwide.

Trips surrounded by nature include an 11-day trek on ancient Japanese trade and pilgrimage routes to an ascent of Kilimanjaro, Africa's highest mountain. You might explore picturesque backdrops of lavender, vineyards and olive groves on a hike through Provence in the south of France. REI also offers more trips in the U.S. national park system than any other company, including a winter snowshoe adventure in Yosemite.

The sustainable REI legacy always places the planet and people first. The responsible outfitter, while keeping lands pristine, dedicates a portion of its profits to help protect and restore the environment, make outdoor activities accessible for all, and inspire all travelers to participate in responsible outdoor recreation. *Rei.com*

Thompson Safaris

Thompson Safaris has welcomed travelers to Tanzania, a leading African safari destination, for more than four decades. Tanzania is a land with a staggering amount and variety of wildlife — a country with genuinely breathtaking landscapes like the iconic plains of the Serengeti, the lush green floor of the Ngorongoro Crater, and mesmerizing, snow-capped, equatorial Mount Kilimanjaro.

The company was founded by New Zealander Rick Thompson and his American wife, Judi Wineland, a singer whom he met in Southeast Asia in the 1970s when she was entertaining Vietnam War troops during a USO tour. In their subsequent travels, they settled in east Africa, establishing a safari company that partnered with and valued the people who knew the country best: the Tanzanians.

Over the years, Thompson Safaris has grown into a renowned small-group tour operator, styling trips to travelers' interests in culture, wildlife and trekking. "We believe that tourism can sustainably support a country and its people," said Thompson. "We meticulously review operations to ensure responsible practices are adhered to, from hiring and buying locally to operating camps with 'leave no trace' ethics and eco-friendly concepts in mind." *Thompsonsafaris.com*

UnCruise Adventures

Small-ship experts UnCruise Adventures started cruising 25 years ago in Alaska with just one yacht. Today, their fleet carries between 22 and 90 passengers. They guide travelers to far-flung waters in Alaska, Canada, the Aleutian Islands, the Sea of Cortez, Belize and Guatemala, the Galapagos Islands, the Columbia and Snake Rivers, the San Juan Islands, and the Hawaiian Islands. The company's fleet of smaller ships can enter closer to shorelines and waters where large vessels cannot reach.

The day's excursions, including hiking, snorkeling, kayaking, or guided shore tours with smaller groups, mean a more enriching adventure travel experience and an in-depth appreciation of local history, cultures and the natural world. Treading on fragile ecosystems, they actively promote environmental protection through education and initiatives calling for responsible travel. *Uncruise.com*

Variety Cruises

Greek small-ship experts Variety Cruises is a family-run business that has been in operation for an astounding 75 years. Its Aegean sailings vary from routes for first-time visitors to Greece, including the famous islands of Mykonos and Santorini, to itineraries designed for intrepid explorers. Smaller yachts venture to clandestine ports on off-the-beaten-path islands like Ikaria, Lipsi, Kefalonia and Amorgos.

Variety vessels also meander through the islands of Tahiti, Seychelles and Cape Verde, as well as Gambia and Senegal in West Africa. New in 2025 are Italy, Malta and Croatia. With a commitment to sustainability and a fleet of eight ships that carry no more than 49 passengers, Variety can promise unique experiences and personal encounters. "To travel is to immerse yourself," says Variety CEO Filippos Venetopoulos. *Varietycruises.com*

World Expeditions

In 1975, when small group tour operator World Expeditions guided its first explorers on a Himalaya trek in Nepal, it already adhered to a mantra of "leaving the world a better place." Still keenly aware of our planet's fragility, its immersive journeys still focus on sustainability — on preserving the natural environment, blending with remote cultures, and leaving a positive impact with a small footprint.

Popular journeys include cycling in Vietnam, trekking to Everest Base Camp and Africa's Mount Kilimanjaro, and walking in Patagonia, on Peru's Inca Trail and New Zealand's South Island. Overland journeys include the Silk Road through Central Asia, Madagascar, and the African continent.

The company creates carbon-neutral excursions, minimizes waste, uses local guides, protects women and children, and respects the natural habitat. *Worldexpeditions.com*

Yampu Tours

Considered South America's leading tour operator, Yampu Tours always looks for opportunities to give back to Latin American communities. Yampu's mantra is that responsible travel is a means not only of experiencing other cultures but also of supporting them, and sustaining their environments and communities. Tour destinations include the natural wonders and ancient civilizations of Central and South America. Yampu employs only local expert guides and other knowledgeable individuals who are equally committed to their communities and the quality of the client's experience.

Yampu clients are offered many opportunities to give back to the communities they visit, in ways most needed in that particular region. One option is a lifetime volunteer program, which creates a fulfilling journey for visitors to give back to local people. *Yampu.com*

Support local communities while obtaining a richer, deeper understanding of
the places we visit when using local guides.

Traveling in a post-pandemic world

In the world since the COVID pandemic, sustainable travel matters more than ever. That's our takeaway from Virtuoso Travel's interview with 10 industry experts, all of them passionate about travel's role in preserving the environment, protecting cultures and, perhaps most pressing in the wake of the coronavirus, supporting local economies.

In 2019, tourism accounted for one in 10 jobs around the globe. That's about 330 million. But in 2020, the COVID-19 pandemic forced the world to take a collective time out, pausing many of the economic opportunities that travel creates in the communities we visit. In September of that year, the travel-advisor magazine *Virtuoso Life* interviewed these notable experts on their response to the pandemic, the benefits of responsible tourism, and their hopes for the future.

Ashish Sanghrajka, president, Big Five Tours & Expeditions

We have much rebuilding to do. Once the pandemic took away our ability to travel, we saw tens of thousands of people become impoverished and an alarming rise in poaching. Sustainable travel represents the single most significant resistance to these issues. Employment opportunities created by tourism give locals a vital seat at the table. This is still the best way for travel dollars to reach indigenous communities directly.

Our company is built on this belief, from the hotels we visit (at least 85 percent of staff come from the local area) to providing entrepreneurship education to women weavers in Peru. With travel on hold, Big Five shifted its focus to raising funds for those in need. One silver lining of the pandemic: It's made the need to get off the beaten track all the more critical. The essence of a country is in the spaces between the prominent attractions and crowds, where life remains much the way it was 300 years ago. A bright future will await if we can maintain the need to travel with purpose and stay humble in seeing travel as a privilege.

Francesco Galli Zugaro, CEO and founder, Aqua Expeditions

The world's pause brought awareness to the impacts of over-tourism. Travelers are reevaluating their priorities. Moving forward, they'll seek out companies beyond comfort and luxury to provide meaningful experiences and show how their journeys support local economies. Aqua Expeditions has been committed to contributing to communities and protecting the environment from the beginning.

But the pandemic allowed us time to rethink our approach. One example is our support for the *paiche* project in the Peruvian Amazon, where we partner with local fishers working to nurse populations of this endangered species of native fish back to health. In addition to serving their sustainably caught fish on board *Aria Amazon,* we provide the tools to expand their business and sell to new markets throughout the country.

Kirsten Dixon, owner and chef, Within the Wild Adventure Company

Over the past few decades, travel has become the third most important industry in Alaska, behind oil and seafood. Oil is in decline and the seafood industry is in peril. Travel will save our state by providing a sustainable revenue source.

Over-tourism, we've known, is detrimental to nature. Now we know that crowding damages our health. In Alaska, there's been a trend toward bigger, bigger and more: more cruise ships with more people on board, more buses heading to Denali. Can we all take a step back and value quality over quantity?

My family owns two wilderness lodges – Winterlake and Tutka Bay – that accommodate only 12 people each. This is not a business-school model, but we have a tremendous quality of life. We must protect and preserve those places we wish to survive for future generations.

Marina Elsener, director, sustainable development and communications, North and Central America, Accor hotel group

The pandemic has demonstrated how interconnected our world is, and my hope is that this pause will lead to a heightened consciousness in the tourism industry. It's important that travel providers acknowledge and embrace their responsibility to the planet and people living and working in the places where they operate.

A few key areas of focus should include conserving water and limiting energy consumption; serving healthy and sustainable food; eliminating single-use plastics; promoting local hiring, development, diversity and inclusion — and protecting local communities, culture and heritage. Many companies have long been committed to addressing these issues, but there is always more that can be done.

Safari goers observe a cheetah—the world's fastest land animal—in Tanzania, Serengeti National Park.

John Roberts, group director of sustainability and conservation, Anantara Hotels, Resorts & Spas

The upside for sustainability is that destinations and hotels that provide space and privacy will now be the most in demand. And it's these smaller hotels that find it easier to implement sustainable best practices such as sourcing local foods, providing community-curated tours, and caring for the natural world.

With current concerns about long-haul travel, I hope travelers will seek new experiences in their home countries. I'd also like to see Anantara get more involved in nature-based tourism, similar to our camps in Cambodia and East Africa. This model has already shown how a socially distant, nature-immersive guest experience can protect the environment and fund broader conservation programs.

Gerald Lawless, ambassador, World Travel & Tourism Council; former president and CEO, Jumeirah Group

International travel provides a direct export contribution to the recipient country and ensures that local communities receive this economic benefit. This is particularly important in the developing world. We need to measure success in terms of the number of people taking trips and the value of such trips economically, socially and environmentally. I'd also like to see contributions to carbon-offset programs and initiatives — such as the

Emirates Airline Foundation, which supports education in developing countries — be encouraged through tax breaks.

Destinations that draw large crowds must work with nearby alternative attractions to ease demand. Ireland's introduction of the Wild Atlantic Way is an excellent example of how we can move visitors away from main centers such as Dublin. Economically, this has significantly affected small towns and villages along the seaboard, which helps the slowdown of population drift to larger cities.

Nick and his wife, Gaby, unfurl a Quark Expeditions flag upon visiting Antarctica.

Sherwin Banda, president, African Travel, Inc.

Tourism represents 7.1 percent of Africa's GDP and is a powerful tool for economic development and job creation on the continent. Before COVID-19, many parts of Africa saw incredible growth; for example, Rwanda's tourism GDP grew by 10.9 percent in 2019 due to its support for projects that promoted sustainability while benefiting the local people. Women are a driving force in Africa, so we look to support them on African Travel safaris. In South Africa's Sabi Sabi game reserve, we connect guests with female rangers, and in Tanzania, we give them beaded gifts made by women from the isolated Mkonoo Terrat village.

This income helps the women care for their elders and send their children to school. Africa is already a top destination for 2021, with more people now looking for the natural spaces that a safari provides. It will be necessary for governments to balance human needs to manage this growth and ensure everyone's well-being, and I hope they'll look to past successes in places like Botswana, Rwanda and Kenya. Travel matters, and when harnessed correctly, it will change the world.

Erin Green, Virtuoso travel advisor

Travel brings people together. It allows us to learn about different ways of life and appreciate the beautiful destinations we want to protect. As our world goes through this challenging time, we must continue to build these levels of understanding. And because climate change poses such a huge threat – both for travel and for life in general – it's critical that we continue to place pressure on the airline industry to research and develop new fuels and technologies to help reduce carbon emissions.

Sarah Taylor, Virtuoso travel advisor

When we travel, we're guests in another country, being welcomed into the cultural embrace of the place we're visiting. We need to treat that experience and the giver of that experience with utmost respect, honor and care. The "giver" is not only the hotel or tour guide but the airport employees, essential workers, neighborhoods, land and the entire ecosystem of the place we visit. Travel is a gift that enables us to experience other cultures, and we need to see it as such. My hope for the future is that more travelers adopt this perspective and not only "take" the experience, but give back to destinations positively.

Shannon Stowell, CEO, Adventure Travel Trade Association

The Adventure Travel Trade Association's mission is to empower the global travel community to protect natural and cultural resources while creating economic value that benefits trade members and destinations.

Whoever you are and whatever part of the industry you have a role in, I encourage you to pause and reflect, make room for big dreams and huge innovations, and imagine what as an industry and community we could do to affect change if we really take it seriously. Many reports in the near past suggest customers want more sustainable options but are not necessarily willing to pay for it. While it appears this trend is headed in the right direction, consider making sustainability a requirement, not an option.

Build for what you know is right. You, on the ground, can and should build for the betterment of the people and places that rely on responsible tourism. Don't only develop plans that are based on what the customer wants. Let's show them even greater possibilities and use tourism to effect real change. If the majority of travel companies only offer sustainable options, the entire industry has the potential to become a global leader in demonstrating the power of collective will.

I recently asked the head of a large travel operation: "When do you think it will be common for travel companies to include a climate surcharge with a travel purchase?: His response was: "Never." Let's prove this common assumption wrong.

Nick exchanges glances with a mountain gorilla in Rwanda.

Sustainability Matters to Travelers

The pandemic changed the attitudes of travelers toward sustainability. With climate change and environmental issues at the forefront of daily news, now more than ever, travelers have embraced the concept that we all must explore responsibly. That includes protecting people and the lands they visit with a commitment to experiences that support local communities.

In a survey with readers of the renowned *Rough Guides*, a whopping 96 percent of respondents declared sustainability as now at the forefront of their journeys. Interestingly, the results showed that it is as important to baby boomers and older adults as it is to young travelers. Over 30 percent said they would seek alternatives to flying, with train travel at the forefront — although they acknowledged that the high cost of travel by rail is also a deterrent.

Four out of 10 participants said that they would willingly pay an extra fee on their travels if it would help to reduce their carbon footprint. Ditching hotels to stay with locals is a common theme, with homestays gaining popularity. At least half the survey participants said that the cost of a trip would not outweigh ethical concerns. More than half said going local on their travels, supporting businesses that use sustainable tour operators, is an essential part of their trip.

"As soon as I saw you, I knew a grand adventure was about to happen." — A.A. Milne, Winnie The Pooh

Chapter Eight

VOLUNTEERING:

Another Way to Travel the World

Every person can make a difference and every person should try. — President John F. Kennedy

Travel changes us like nothing else. Volunteering during our travels fully immerses us in a new culture, giving us little choice but to become a contributing member of an unfamiliar society.

It's the opportunity of a lifetime to give back to a people, to share skills and knowledge and make a real difference in a foreign culture. Whether it's part of a vacation or a journey specifically designed to volunteer, the concept invariably helps local communities and their environments. The chance to partner with locals, while meeting other sustainable travelers with a like-minded mission, is the essence of volunteer travel. This is inherent in all of us.

You'll improve your travel experience as you learn new skills and make friendships that last a lifetime. You may even boost your career by helping a community overseas. Well-rounded travelers who give back are undeniably selfless leaders and team players.

Travelers can choose from among hundreds of volunteer projects. Whether teaching children in impoverished nations, helping construct and restore buildings in poverty-stricken communities, working with doctors, focusing on climate change, or helping protect leatherback turtles or dolphins, you're changing the world for the better. You can engage with local conservation projects aiming to protect the biodiversity of rainforests or other environments. Some programs offer the chance to care for children in orphanages. Others hire volunteers to teach at understaffed schools.

Even families can participate. When you make international volunteering a family event, young children become immersed in the lives of others through their culture. Teens learn the value of personal responsibility and commitment. The whole family is brought closer by expanding their horizons and becoming global citizens.

Many travelers want to be socially responsible and help others worldwide but feel they need more time or money for an extensive volunteer vacation. But even a short trip can make a difference and give back to others. Anyone can be part of the solution to protect our planet. Local experiences, saving the earth through sea-turtle rescue in Ecuador or working on a wildlife orphanage in Zimbabwe, have never been more accessible.

Aware travelers may simply volunteer for beach cleanup as opposed to sunbathing on the sand. Or carry an spare backpack of children's clothes or school supplies when they visit a destination. Schools and orphanages in every corner of the world desperately need help.

Volunteer Tamara Lowe bends to hear the words of young Latin Americans.

"Volunteering abroad not only allows you to travel to almost any destination in the world, it also provides you with the unique opportunity to explore, experience, and see the country you're in through the eyes of a local," says Jonathan Gilben, director of GoEco, a volunteer vacation and tour company. "You will truly become a traveler and not just a tourist."

Volunteer travel is not solely about what you give but also how you're changed for the better. After taking the plunge, you will never be the same. You will return home with a new outlook on life, a greater understanding of human interaction, and a greater tolerance for all people you encounter. By helping people, we can understand and learn from one another.

Some of the top budget-friendly countries for volunteering abroad are Bolivia, Guatemala and Peru in Latin America; Cambodia, India, Indonesia and Nepal in Asia; Ghana, Kenya and Uganda in Africa.

EMMI'S STORY

Emmi Mutanen was 20 when she left her native Finland to volunteer at Proyecto Kieu.

"A few years back," she wrote, "I went to Spain with the European Voluntary Service. I worked for a small organization, 40 kilometers from Madrid, in a village with only 5,000 inhabitants. My workplace was a youth center where I taught English, music and data processing. I worked at a local radio station and organized small events. I did anything they asked me to.

"When I went there, I spoke no Spanish and didn't know much about the culture, just what you see in movies. I had an apartment, and the program paid my rent and gave me 150 euros for food and 105 euros in pocket money, which was more than enough to get by. Once a week, I had Spanish language classes."

At first, wrote Emma, her Spanish inability made teaching difficult. "Everyone was very understanding and patient and wanted to help me learn and adjust to the culture," she recalled. "My very first month was filled with Spanish things. There were fiestas where they played traditional music, had a paella competition and an encierro, where the bulls ran on the streets. That wasn't the daily life in the village. I just arrived at a great moment!

"For a person that comes from a country where you don't touch even your family members without a good reason, it was peculiar that people were greeting me with kisses on the cheek and sometimes spontaneously slapping me on the back. Everybody also spoke much more loudly, even though they didn't always have anything to say. Over time, I got used to it and started acting more like them. Their freer way of life was very nice."

Emma said she learned to adjust her lifestyle to become more improvisational. "And the people of the village were amazing," she said. "Every time I went to have a drink, there was someone to speak with, someone wanting to show me something, tell me where I should travel, or wanting to hear about my country and culture."

And, oh, yes, she fell in love: "I still don't always understand my boyfriend because of language or cultural differences, but usually, he tries to explain," she said. "Sometimes he yells at me in super-fast Spanish and I answer in Finnish. The experience truly changed my life. Now I'm looking for a job in Spain to spend my future there, or at least until the travel fever hits me again."

ECO VOLUNTEERING

Volunteering to protect wildlife or marine life, or doing other ecological work, is a fantastic way to experience exotic locations while helping to conserve endangered species worldwide. From protecting wild orangutans in Borneo working in a rainforest in South America, from rehabilitating cheetahs in the African bush to protecting leatherback turtles in Costa Rica, there is a volunteer project for you on every continent. This is your chance to make a difference in the environment and assist in protecting many endangered species, while also learning about the local society and culture. You can create your own carbon footprint and make a positive impact.

As the world slowly emerges from two crippling years of international travel stoppage due to the Coronavirus, with COVID-19 restrictions still impacting programs especially in Africa, Central America has become a most-favored destination for volunteer travel. Sustainable travel is more valid than ever. Travelers increasingly know the need for an integrated, responsible approach to travel and tourism, including giving back on their journey.

With more than 10 million people volunteering abroad each year, and more than 1,000 different organizations offering volunteer trips, here are a few trusted organizations that provide enriching volunteer experiences with people, land management or animal and marine conservation.

Appalachian Trail Conservancy: The ATC would not survive without volunteers. Over 6,000 volunteers contribute more than 200,000 hours each year, keeping the Maine-to-Georgia trail available and accessible to all. Volunteers actively work all sections of the trail, from maintaining footpaths to assisting on major projects, such as building bridges and shelters or new sections of the ATC.

Although maintaining and monitoring the trail corridor is perhaps the most visible activity, volunteers also participate in wildlife and ecosystem protection, including removal of invasive species. As active partners in trail management, they provide support to nearby towns through the Appalachian Trail Communities program, support teachers in the Trail to Every Classroom program, offer hiker workshops and generally build ATC awareness. *Appalachiantrail.org*

Biosphere Expeditions: Founded in 1999, this citizen-funded nonprofit encourages travelers to make a difference on their holiday, assisting the award-winning, hands-on wildlife conservation group by contributing their time. Special skill sets are especially welcomed.

When you travel with Biosphere Expeditions, you'll meet a team of scientists and biologists, along with other like-minded responsible travelers who want to make a difference on our fragile planet. Spend a week or more volunteering to protect nature, not to make money. Some of the off-the-beaten-path destinations and projects include: Surveying whales, dolphins and turtles around the Azores archipelago, studying coral reefs and whale sharks in the Maldives, monitoring brown bears in Sweden, conserving elephants in northern Thailand, surveying snow leopards in the Tien Shan mountains of Kyrgyzstan, and work with wild cats, primates and parrots in the Peruvian Amazon. *Biosphereexpeditions.com*

Chipangali Wildlife Orphanage: If you love animals and want to spend time rehabilitating them, the Chipangali Wildlife Orphanage near Bushtick, Zimbabwe, cares for over 150 animals and birds with little hope for survival in the wild. It is a last refuge for creatures that have been orphaned, abandoned, born in captivity, or brought up unsuccessfully as pets. It is often the last refuge for the sick or injured, and increasingly a sanctuary for confiscated animals. Volunteering at Chipangali can only be described as a life-changing experience. From one month to the next, it's never the same. During your four, six or eight-week stay, volunteers may be involved in bathing a black rhino; hand-feeding leopards, lions and antelope; doing additional carnivore research, or contributing to other activities that save the lives of animals in the African wild. *Chipangali.com*

Conservation Volunteers, Australia and New Zealand: Conservation Volunteers recruits volunteers from Down Under and worldwide to join important environmental and wildlife conservation projects in Australia and New Zealand. You'll work in teams through various short-term projects to protect habitats and promote ecotourism. Volunteer opportunities range in duration and prices, but they typically include overnight stays and meals.

Visit the breathtakingly rugged West Coast of New Zealand's South Island and focus on coastal habitat restoration in the Paparoa National Park area. Volunteer projects with hands-on, practical, grassroots environmental action programs that support local environment and heritage conservation across Australia and New Zealand. *Conservationvol unteers.com.au*

Many popular volunteer jobs are in animal care, as at this Elephant Sanctuary.

Doctors without Borders: Chances are, you know about the fantastic healthcare work done by Doctors Without Border/Médecins Sans Frontieres (MSF) — helping the world by delivering emergency medical aid to people affected by conflict, epidemics, disaster or exclusion from healthcare.

MSF recruits medical, administrative and logistical support personnel to provide medical care to people in crisis in more than 60 countries worldwide. Every year, some 3,000 MSF field staff provide lifesaving medical assistance to people who would otherwise be denied access to even the most basic care. You can volunteer to work in-house in the New York headquarters, contribute to events around the United States or France, or apply to work in the field. as MSF regularly recruits medical and non-medical staff for field projects. *Doctorswithoutborders.com*

Earthwatch: This trusted environmental nonprofit needs volunteers everywhere — but nowhere so much as in the Arctic. Among 40 field expeditions around the world, one of the most fascinating is studying the global challenges of climate change in Churchill, Manitoba, a small town on Hudson Bay in northern Canada. While most famous for its population of polar bears, Churchill is at the front line of global warming. Expeditioners learn all they can about this fragile environment: its shrinking sea ice, retreating glaciers, a tree line that continues to migrate farther north as snowfall dwindles and melts earlier in the spring.

Summer and fall team members may don waist-high waders to take water samples while assessing the population of fish and frogs. They examine tree cores to reconstruct arboreal histories. In winter, team members experience the true power of the North, taking snow samples to assess the snowpack, traveling between research sites on a sled pulled by a snowmobile, perhaps building and sleeping in an igloo for a night. *Earthwatch.org*

Edge of Africa: Since 2007, this award-winning group has focused on restoring and protecting some of the world's most endangered plant and animal species. It is known for guiding positive change ethically and sustainably. The volunteer conservation programs in numerous African countries are as life-changing for the participants as they are for the wildlife itself.

Among Edge of Africa's projects are hands-on elephant and rhinoceros conservation, gorilla and chimpanzee protection, lemur research and biodiversity monitoring in Madagascar, dolphin and whale research and coastal conservation, and environmental restoration in a variety of ecosystems. *edgeofafrica.com*

Give A Day Global: "While traveling in South Africa, I volunteered for one day at a wonderful nonprofit in a township outside of Cape Town. The experience was transformational. This one day opened my eyes to the challenges that many poor communities face, and it was the most memorable day of my vacation," recalled Give A Day Global founder Kerry Rodgers.

The nonprofit is a platform that connects international travelers with one day of volunteering in developing countries. It helps travelers to get involved with a meaningful experience, even if they have only a single day of time to offer. They also aid community-based nonprofit organizations that are doing impactful work by feeding the poor, educating young people, economically empowering locals, and protecting the environment and wildlife, all by helping them expand their support networks. *giveadayglobal.org*

GIVE Volunteers: After volunteering worldwide, GIVE Volunteers founder Jake Allison discovered that there is real potential to foster sustainable change. "The GIVE promise is our commitment always to put people, projects, and principles above profit," says Allison.

Programs are one-of-a-kind — at a wildlife sanctuary in Luang Prabang, Laos, or at a hill-tribe village in Thailand. In Tanzania, volunteers empower a women's co-op on the slopes of Mount Kilimanjaro and support coastal villages on the tropical island of Zanzibar. On Nicaragua's isolated Emerald Coast, you will help build homes alongside local families or teach English in the rural fishing village of Jiquilillo. You can complete your dive certification in the vibrant Caribbean coral reefs through GIVE's Scuba Reef Conservation project. *Givevolunteers.org*

GoEco: Deciding to take a volunteer holiday is a heavyweight decision, so choosing a reputable organization is a paramount decision. Acting as a gateway to partnerships throughout the world, GoEco has provided more than 17,000 individuals with volunteer experiences — in 40 countries on five continents — in the 18 years since its launch. Its 150 international partnerships serve extraordinary community, wildlife and environmental initiatives worldwide.

Programs and activities include wildlife and animal conservation, marine and coral reef conservation, and community development, including humanitarian aid, healthcare and volunteering with children. One popular activity is cage-diving with great white sharks in South Africa, thereby contributing to marine conservation and eco-tourism efforts in the stunning Gansbaai area. *Goeco.org*

Grassroots Volunteering: Shannon O'Donnell left her Florida home in 2008 to travel the world. An award-winning travel writer, Shannon volunteered in sustainable projects at a grassroots level as she wandered. She founded Grassroot Volunteering in 2011 to assist service-minded travelers in finding meaningful ways to give back.

The site grew to help travelers access ethical and sustainable, service-minded projects. For some travelers, that means long-term volunteering. Others give their support to locally run initiatives, like restaurants or boutiques with underlying social missions. In either case, GV facilitates meaningful connections between travelers and local causes and communities. *grassrootsvolunteering.org*

A WOOFF volunteer, feeding a calf, gets room and board at an organic farm.

HelpX: Want to save money on your journey? Volunteer for free rooms and meals with HelpX, an online exchange site linking to a wide variety of accommodation types. Stay at working organic farms, ranches, homestays, bed-and-breakfasts, backpacker hostels, even sailing boats. Operating primarily in Australia, New Zealand, Canada and Europe, HelpX offers food and lodging to volunteers who typically work an average of four hours per day on short-term holidays.

This cultural exchange has grown steadily over the years, as hosts and helpers continually add new features and improvements. "What I like is the idea of sharing something with people," said Cedric from France. "We did it in 10 different places in Australia with 10 different hosts in cities and the Outback. You live like you're part of a family. It's a different way to travel. That's why we enjoyed this." *Helpx.net*

HOOP: The acronym means "Helping Overcome Obstacles Peru." Peru is a land of incredible contrast and diversity in both people and terrain. Volunteers who are fluent in Spanish enjoy helping children in the Peruvian Andes and around the country to overcome learning difficulties and assisting them in academic and social skills as well as formative thinking.

A holistic approach features numerous programs whose collective impact helps each member of a community, especially mothers and children. In Arequipa, the "White City" where the program is based, volunteers live in the city and travel to and from their workplace each afternoon. Free-time adventures include everything from canyoneering to urban nightlife. *Hoopperu.org*

International Volunteer HQ: Join the ranks of more than 135,000 volunteers from all walks of life who have chosen to spend a part of their holiday giving back, while immersing in a new culture. From as little as $20 per day, including accommodation, meals and 24/7 in-country support, International Volunteer HQ enables you to make a difference on a trip of a lifetime.

Locals operate impact-driven programs in over 50 destinations. Project themes include childcare, climate change, community development, conservation, construction, education, healthcare, social enterprise, wildlife, marine biology and more. A growing number of opportunities are available to seniors, for whom popular destinations include Cambodia, Sri Lanka, Costa Rica, Peru, Argentina and Ghana. "The reception of the children and support of the staff were certainly the high points of my experience," said Carol Head, who volunteered in Ghana at age 68. *volunteerhq.org*

Kibbutz Volunteer: A kibbutz is a communal agricultural settlement in Israel. The volunteer concept came about after the Six-Day War in 1967 when crowds of volunteers arrived in Israel to show solidarity by becoming kibbutz volunteers. Since the movement began, more than 400,000 Kibbutz volunteers have set foot in Israel.

Kibbutz Volunteer was founded by English backpacker John Carson, an English backpacker. "It's about living a sustainable life in Israel in a shared economy," he explained. This site offers tips, hints and information on volunteering and how to find the right program for you. There are more jobs to do on a kibbutz than there are people to do them. *Kibbutzvolunteer.org.il*

Naankuse Foundation: The nation's name, Namibia, derives from the surrounding Namib Desert, one of Africa's best-kept secrets. It's quite a spectacle to see its towering sand dunes plunging into the sea. The Naankuse Foundation is a conservation charity dedicated to preserving Namibian landscapes, cultures and wildlife. Beginning as a small bush sanctuary, it has become a leading preservation group, providing a haven for injured and orphaned animals.

Twenty-five percent of the world's threatened cheetah population live in Namibia. Of those, 90 percent live in the wild. Volunteer at Naankuse actively participate in the conservation and care of cheetahs and other African wildlife, including rehabilitation work. They join skilled trackers in monitoring free-roaming African dogs, lions, elephants and rhinos. *Naankuse.com*

Omprakash Foundation: Active in India, East Africa and in 58 countries across the globe, Omprakash creates transformative educational experiences. It connects pre-screened, grassroots social-impact organizations with an audience of volunteers, donors and classrooms that can learn from and support their work.

Search a database by location, area of focus or dates of availability. Reach out to the administrative team, fellow volunteers, interns and partners for suggestions or support then apply for positions that match your skills and interests. *omprakash.org*

Peace Corps: The Peace Corps has been a leader in international development and citizen diplomacy for more than 50 years across 140 countries. Although times have changed since its founding by the U.S. government in 1961, the agency's mission — to promote world peace and friendship — has not. With more than 200,000 current and returned volunteers, the Peace Corps changes the lives of its volunteers and people in communities around the world.

The Peace Corps forgest global citizens by teaching teaches leadership, ingenuity, self-reliance and relationship building. When you serve abroad, you'll work directly with communities to build capacity in education, health, youth development, community economic development, environment and agriculture. Each program has different time commitments and requirements, but all offer the opportunity to serve abroad and create change. *Peacecorps.gov*

Projects Abroad: When you join a Volunteer Abroad program, you become part of the solution to empower developing communities. You learn new skills and create positive changes around the world. Passionate travelers can support children's education, assist scientists in protecting endangered wildlife and ecosystems, and provide medical services to communities lacking proper healthcare.

The social-enterprise mantra is safety and hassle-free travel, all the while creating a real impact on local societies. Whether you're a high-school or college student or on your first adventure, a student on a gap year, traveling as a family, taking time off from work or retired, there is a volunteer project for you. *projects-abroad.org*

"That Lady from Europe," Rossana, enjoys volunteering in African schools.

Restoration Works International: This nonprofit uses volunteer tourism to restore cultural heritage sites worldwide. Volunteers assist communities in India, Nepal, Mongolia and elsewhere to prosper and reserve their heritage. An example is the Chhairo Gompa, a 17th-century Tibetan Buddhist monastery on the fabled Annapurna Trail, in the region known as Lower Mustang, once the religious center of the Takhali people.

When the Chinese government closed the Tibetan border in the 1960s, Nepali salt traders were forced to relocate their families. Villages along the trade route met with economic hardship and the Chhairo Gompa fell into poverty and disrepair. The last of Chhairo's resident monks left in the 1970s, leaving the fate of the gompa to the elements and a handful of villagers. Today, volunteers pay for the chance to work alongside local architects and artists to restore a hidden Himalayan treasure. *restorationworksinternatio nal.org*

2WayDevelopment: This UK-based social enterprise offers meaningful, tailor-made volunteer placements abroad in international development in Africa, Asia and Latin America. Individual placements are made after first understanding a volunteer's skills, background and goals, then matching them to the needs of one of over 150 partner charities—in the fields of health, education, human rights, economic development and environmental conservation.

A skilled team of placement advisors and managers help guide and support our volunteers so that their placements have the potential to change their lives and the lives of others. *2waydevelopment.com*

Volunteer Services Overseas: VSO is a British Organization that helps people in need worldwide. Your skills can make a difference in the communities where VSO works. As a volunteer, you'll live and work alongside experienced local professionals, improving the quality of life for people who need it most.

Furthermore, you'll become a part of a different culture in a way few people ever can. VSO volunteers work to fight poverty in the developing world, thus changing the lives of millions of people every year. "It was the most incredible 12 months of my life," VSO volunteer Olly Jeffries reflected. "Not only did I make a real difference, but I also developed professionally." *Vsointernational.org*

Working Abroad: Since 1997, Working Abroad has pioneered overseas volunteer work in more than 30 countries, with programs focused on sustainable community development, wildlife research and nature conservation. One such program involves protecting sea turtles. Of the seven species of sea turtle six are endangered. Fisheries, pollution, coastal area development, poaching and climate change are some of the culprits that threaten these graceful sea creatures. As most sea turtle efforts are underfunded, volunteering is of the utmost importance.

Professionally run conservation projects are located in some of the most breathtaking backdrops on earth. The program on the Caribbean island nation of Grenada focuses on leatherback turtles. Other venues include Costa Rica's Tortuguero National Park, nature reserves in the Seychelles Islands, Greece's Ionian island treasure of Kefalonia, Kenya's Lamu archipelago, Ecuador's Galapagos Islands, and the Maldives, where rehabilitation work includes repairing coral reefs. *workingabroad.com*

Worldpackers: Another stellar organization helping to make the world a better place is Worldpackers. With its mantra of "Travel, collaborate, make an impact," the organization offers thousands of volunteer positions for connecting, learning and immersing in the culture of more than 140 countries.

Local hosts provide accommodation (and sometimes meals and activities) in exchange for your volunteer time, teaching English or sharing skills. You might work in a farm or an eco-village, in a homestay or a hostel in a school or a holistic center. Worldpackers is a volunteer space leader. *Worldpackers.com*

WWOOF: If you love to dig your fingers in the earth, WWOOF might be for you. An acronym for Worldwide Opportunities on Organic Farms, this global movement links travelers with organic farmers, promoting cultural and educational exchange, and building an international community conscious of ecological farming and sustainability practices.

In exchange for your volunteer assistance, WWOOF hosts offer food, lodging and opportunities to gain practical skills in organic farming and gardening. Your tasks may include sowing seed, making compost, chopping wood, planting, weeding, harvesting, packing, milking, feeding animals, fencing, winemaking, cheese making, and bread making. The duration of your stay is negotiated ahead of time. WWOOF groups are available in 53 countries. *wwoof.net*

MAKING A DIFFERENCE: KEN FIRESTONE

In many cases, what might start as three- to six-week volunteer project can turn into a life-changing experience. Acts of random kindness and altruistic values will take you a long way in life. Dr. Ken Firestone discovered this as a social activist in Kenya's Maasailand. This is his story.

I was in a transition in my life professionally. I was a psychiatric social worker and academic with a doctorate in a sub-specialty of cultural anthropology and ethnicity. I found formal classroom teaching less impactful on students than informal experiential educational approaches. I had always been a social activist and had wanted to join the Peace Corps when I was younger, but I did not. Then I saw an opportunity to teach Maasai children in a village in southern Kenya in an area traditionally known as Maasailand."

I had traveled extensively and wanted to rough it while learning and living with a Maasai family. I was prepared to live in a manyatta, a traditional Maasai igloo-like hut without electricity, and to sleep on the ground. The traditional manyatta is usually one of many within a compound called a kraal, headed by a polygamous Maasai husband. Each of his wives builds their own manyatta for her children. The kraal is surrounded at night by acacia thorns to protect Maasai cattle from hyena and lion attacks.

My sponsoring organization dropped me off in the Maasai village of Kajiado. A woman was waiting for us. After she led me through a metal fence, we walked about 10 minutes to her spacious furnished home with lights on, a TV blasting the nightly news, a computer sitting on a table, and a New York Times on one of the chairs. I was both shocked and disappointed. Fatima was Muslim, spoke perfect English, and explained she provided space for volunteers now that her six children had grown up, gone to college, and lived in Nairobi. One was a doctor living in America. This was the beginning of my stereotypes about the Maasai warrior tribes people being shattered. It was just the beginning of many other stereotypes being broken.

The school where I would teach was about four miles away. Fatuma had arranged for a boda-boda driver (motorbike taxi) to pick me up to drive me to a private boys' school of 600 Maasai students the next day and for the next several months. I had expected this to be different. Private school tuition in East Africa is relatively expensive and very demanding for students and faculty. The curriculum is followed strictly, and the goal is for each student to pass an exam at the end of each term so they can move on to the next grade level. The Maasai children felt tremendous pressure to succeed as their father sold off valuable cattle to pay for school tuition in a culture in which one's value was based on the number of cattle owned. It also required the father needing to hire someone to take their son's place, herding the cattle to attend a school, when the father could not fully understand why such an education was necessary.

My first task was to figure out my role, as I needed more time to teach subjects I was most familiar with using multi-sensory teaching methods. After rotating to several topics and teachers, I located a social-studies teacher who seemed to know how to best use me as a resource. He called upon me when a social-studies topic came up where he felt I could add a perspective.

I sat on a small bench with six students in a classroom of 50 students, but designed for 20. Because of a shortage of books, four students shared one book, reading from all four directions. In other words, they were not only reading in English, but three students needed to read upside down or sideways. There was perfect classroom decorum. There was no side talk, and the students respectfully rose when the teacher entered the classroom, even though he was totally blind. I was thinking about how students in America would have taken advantage of such a teacher by fooling around to get a laugh. These students took their studies seriously and always behaved. No one took their education for granted. The children were delightful and full of curiosity and positive energy.

But what I got out of this school experience was surpassed by what I got out of my non-classroom experience. I was intrigued by my host. This Maasai woman rejected the lifestyle of traditional Maasai but fully identified as Maasai. She owned several businesses and rejected polygamous marriage and female circumcision. I had no idea there was a continuum of Maasai, from the traditional Maasai who lived in polygamous marriages and lived in manyattas within an acacia enclosure at night, to Maasai who were entrepreneurs living secular modern lives. She was intellectually curious, and we discussed various subjects, from politics to religion and culture.

I grew very attached to this wise woman. She had planned to run for parliament, representing the Maasai now that women were permitted to run for elected office. I returned a year after my assignment to visit Fatima, but this 56-year-old woman had died of cancer the day my plane touched down in Nairobi. So I never saw her again. In Africa, people die young, and life goes on.

I traveled throughout East Africa while I was there. I saw the social-service projects where other volunteers were working. These included orphanages for children whose parents had died (mainly from AIDS), medical and AIDS-education clinics, teaching, environmental conservation, construction and elder care. There were thousands of Western volunteers. Most were volunteering for three to six weeks. The extent of the need was massive in breadth and depth.

I left my assignment feeling that, while it felt good to help people, they were just about as vulnerable as the day I had arrived. My contribution was like a drop of kindness in a bucket of need. For the most part, we were addressing symptoms of poverty. The people needed access to quality education, healthcare and employment. My time would be better spent addressing the causes of poverty, not just its symptoms. I felt economic development would be the long-view approach to addressing these symptoms. I thought it was better to help the people of East Africa to build "fishing rods" rather than "catch their fish."

I went to Tanzania, just south of Kajiado, to the tourism center of Arusha, the co-called "Gateway to the Serengeti" between Mount Kilimanjaro and the Serengeti Plain. I went on safari and discovered that Western-owned companies dominate the lucrative tourism industry — so the major profits flowed overseas. I met an ambitious college-educated African woman who was knowledgeable about the safari industry but knew little about marketing to Westerners, how to use the internet, or what "customer service" meant to Western travelers. She needed seed money to get a business started. I trained her in these areas and provided seed money for a website, a computer and consultation.

Today she is a successful safari business owner, earning more money than she could have ever made as an employee of a foreign-owned tour company. She employs many safari guides and uses local vendors who benefit from her financial success. Tourists traveling through her company visit traditional indigenous peoples living in remote areas of the African bush who are compensated for their hospitality. This financially benefits these rural land-dependent peoples who are suffering from the effects of global warming. Economic self-sufficiency means empowerment.

I was getting to know the locals, creating productive relationships, and sharing practical knowledge. I was generating long-term relationships and commitments between Westerners, who could offer training and support, and the locals, who benefit through gaining access to quality education, healthcare and income-generating jobs. I would never have imagined my volunteer stint in Africa would lead to an entirely different approach to meeting the local people's needs. Merging with an indigenous family is something I will never forget.

LESSONS IN VOLUNTEERING: TAMARA LOWE

Tammy is an international development worker who left her stressful commuter life in London to explore the world with her husband, Chris. Since 2011, they have lived and worked in seven countries on five continents and visited dozens of others. Tammy documents her travels and expat life at tammyandchrisonthemove.com.

Q & A with Tamara Lowe

GOING LOCAL: *What does the expression "experiential travel" mean to you?*

LOWE: Experiential travel, to me, means not just touring a country in two weeks through an organized tour, rushing from place to place to tick off sights from your bucket list. You run the danger of only interacting with other tourists from your group rather than with locals. Experiential travel for me is to get away from organized tours, use local transport, eat in local restaurants, volunteer, live in homestays, or interact with local people.

GL: *How has volunteer travel changed your life?*

LOWE: Travel has taught me that the world is full of beauty crying out to be explored, but also full of injustice that needs to be fought. If not for my travels to developing countries where I witnessed poverty, human-rights abuses and other injustices, I may not have chosen to quit my civil-service career to work in international development. Travel taught me that I led a privileged life growing up in Germany, where I was able to say what

I want, do what I want, eat when I want, and attend school and university. Many people around the world can't enjoy those privileges. Witnessing that made me realize that I want to do my bit to help, no matter how small my contributions may be.

GL: What were some of your early experiences when you first volunteered?

LOWE: Volunteering has always been a big part of my life. Even while living in England, I volunteered for four different organizations, so when I left England in 2011, I carried on the theme and volunteered in Cambodia for six months. I have since volunteered in Peru and Ghana as well. I get more out of volunteering than just backpacking. I learned so much from volunteering, especially from the people I worked with. Often volunteer placements are portrayed as something where the volunteers teach local communities. But volunteering should be a two-way learning experience, where you teach something and in return get taught life lessons by the community you are working in.

GL: What volunteer projects or helpful websites do you recommend for travelers who have never volunteered?

LOWE: If you are looking for a long-term volunteer placement and already have some work experience. VSO (Voluntary Service Overseas) offers long-term placements for professionals in many sectors, such as education, marketing and healthcare. With VSO, you get substantive training before the placement, your flights and health insurance are covered, and you also get a small living allowance that will cover your rent and other living expenses. The US equivalent is Peace Corps, the Canadian CUSO, and the Australian AVI. United Nations Volunteers (UNV) also offer long-term volunteer placements to professionals. They also have online volunteer opportunities if you can't go on a long-term placement.

If you haven't got much work experience, but would like to get some in the field of international development, I can recommend 2WayDevelopment. They organized my six-month placement in Cambodia. It is a British organization that offers tailor-made volunteer placements based on your skills or interests. These placements are usually office-based. 2WayDevelopment charges a one-off fee, and they will offer volunteers three possible placements all over the world to choose from based on your criteria (i.e., area of interest and location). Volunteers have to cover all in-country expenses, flights, insurance, etc.

With so many dodgy volunteerism organizations around, you have to ensure that your placement is legitimate, doesn't exploit local beneficiaries, and benefits local communities and not just the organizations. The Omprakash Foundation is a grassroots organization network offering meaningful and responsible volunteering opportunities. HOOP, an NGO registered in Peru and Austria, works in a shantytown outside Peru's second-largest city of Arequipa. Volunteers teach English to children ages 3 to 18 in an after-school club. The minimum time volunteers have to commit to is one month.

GL: What life lessons have you learned from blending into local societies?

LOWE: To be grateful for what I have, to be more relaxed about life, and to understand that you don't need a lot of possessions to be happy. By merging into local society, I learned that all people are humans, regardless of their background. Seeing the poverty some people live in, I learned to be more humble and modest in my lifestyle. Back in England, I lived in a three-bedroom house. Since I left England in 2011, I have lived in modest apartments, hostels or shared accommodation. I no longer need many possessions to be happy; memories with local communities are far more valuable to me. No money in the world can buy those memories.

GL: What are some of the destinations that you are recommending to travelers nowadays?

LOWE: As I spent some enjoyable time in Cambodia and Peru, I highly recommend those two countries. They are both rich in history, have gorgeous landscapes, and the people are some of the friendliest I have ever met.

GL: Why should travelers seek out opportunities to be part of the local land-scape?

LOWE: Personally, I learn far more about a country by chatting to a local over a beer than listening to a tour guide rushing his group from one place to another. If you don't live, eat and travel like a local every now and then, and only travel in luxury transportation and live in 5-star hotels, how can you get a realistic picture of what a country is like?

One of my fondest travel memories was when I lived with an Ecuadorian family in a homestay for a few days. We could have easily stayed in a comfortable hotel. Still, instead, Chris and I shared a tiny bed, showered with buckets of cold water, and got to experience the incredible hospitality of an indigenous family. We cooked with them, we played games with them, we laughed together. I prefer that over having the same old conversation with other travelers in a noisy and overcrowded hostel any day.

Our prime purpose in this life is to help others. And if you can't help them at least don't hurt them. — His Holiness the Dalai Lama

Chapter Nine

TIME MANAGEMENT:

Making Room for Travel

There is no higher education than the school of travel. No classroom education could ever compare to what I learned exploring the world. — Anthony Bourdain

We were big advocates of moving and traveling when we were young. Wandering helped us decide what we wanted to do in our lives. Had we not explored the world in our twenties, who knows what we'd be doing now? And today, decades later, we still encourage young adults to travel, widely and often.

Both of us determined early on that our life's purpose was to work in the field of travel. Nick's entrepreneurial spirit led him to launch a travel agency that specialized in discount multi-stop travel. John, as an inquisitive journalist, traveled to write and wrote to travel. Those first steps led us to where we are now.

We weren't exactly pioneers, but more than 50 years have passed since John first blasted halfway across the Pacific on his first solo adventure. Nick wasn't far behind when he set out on his first unaccompanied exploit ... and just kept going.

Today, more and more people are taking time off — from their education, their jobs, their lives — and traveling the world. They may be students, between jobs, or baby-boomer retirees. Many of those bitten by the travel bug turn long-haul trips into multi-stop journeys. Some wanderers may travel Europe for three months, others for a year. An Australian or New Zealander, whose homelands are tucked away "Down Under" in the Southern Hemisphere, might tell you they need no less than a full year just to see the world.

Universities may have foreign exchange programs, but for young travelers, the class-rooms of international youth hostels are far more educational than institutional lecture halls. Serendipitous encounters with Americans, Canadians, French, Germans, Italians, Brits, Aussies, Brazilians, Argentinians, Israelis, South Africans, Japanese, Koreans, even Indians, are the fundamental building blocks of world citizenship.

While there is certainly nothing wrong with waiting to travel until later in life, we'll always insist that as a life-changing learning experience, travel is best begun at a younger age. Traditionally, and conservatively, it seems that too many young people look ahead to launching a career immediately after finishing their higher education.

It should be an essential rite of passage to wander the world after completing one's formal studies. *International Living* recently surveyed retirees about late-in-life decisions to sell their possessions and travel the world. Many said their only regret was not traveling in their 20s.

A trip around the world, or any travel that stretches one's personal boundaries, is a groundbreaking experience. Almost inevitably, there is a lifestyle break-through moment somewhere along the way. Indeed, if life is better understood when studied on the road, taking off on an extended journey is like studying for a doctorate. There should be a PhD awarded for the wisdom gained through the exploration of different cultures and societies, and for learning about the world through its local inhabitants. The knowledge one gains in navigating the globe can be applied to any profession.

Europe is a wonderful destination for North Americans to gently "get their feet wet" in international travel. Nick had deep family ties to Greece; John's grandparents all emigrated to North American from Scandinavia. It felt comfortable for our first extended overseas experiences to be in familiar places like these. But it was reaching beyond our comfort zones that our lives were, truly, forever changed.

In Nick's case, that happened in the unknown (to him) lands of the Indian subconti-nent, in Bangladesh, India and Nepal. For John, Southeast Asia — Indonesia, Malaysia, Thailand, Burma (now Myanmar) — was the catalyst. And once we had tasted the forbidden fruit, we could never really go back. You can read our stories in Chapter 12.

Anne and Mike Howard aka HoneyTrek hiking to Bhutan's Buddhist cliff monastery, Tiger's Nest.

WORLD'S LONGEST HONEYMOON

Digital nomads Mike and Anne Howard, who call themselves "HoneyTrek," left on their honeymoon in January 2012 and have yet to stop traveling. Inspired by other cultures, the great outdoors, and the endless education of the open road, they have no plans to make a home base. They created HoneyTrek.com to chronicle their journey across all seven continents and help people mobilize their travel dreams.

Their story of the World's Longest Honeymoon, savvy tips, and blog have been featured in hundreds of international media outlets — from *USA Today* to Lonely Planet. Firm believers that love and travel make the world a better place, they authored *Ultimate*

Journeys for Two — National Geographic's bestselling couples travel guide. To write their newest book, *Comfortably Wild,* they traveled 73,000 miles across nine countries to find the best glamping experiences in North America. Their current quest is to find the world's most romantic and sustainable destinations and share how rewarding responsible travel can be.

Having tried virtually every style of travel — from five-star luxury to hardcore back-packing, glamping, housesitting, RVing and volunteering — the Howards can speak to them all with authority and are a testament to the adage: Variety is the spice of life! (Just take a look at HoneyTrek's Instagram page.)

Q & A with HoneyTrek

GL: A 13-month backpacking trip around the world when he was 24 led Nick to a career in travel. At what point in your journey did you realize that your extended honeymoon trip would become your 9-to-5?

HONEYTREK: We were truly just going on our honeymoon without any intention of making travel a career, but a year in, our HoneyTrek articles and news of "The World's Longest Honeymoon" started to gain traction. In 2013, *Condé Nast Traveler* wrote a feature about our journey, followed by the *The Los Angeles Times*, then dozens more. All the while, our social media following and partnership opportunities were snowballing. In 2015, *National Geographic* asked us to write their first book on couples' adventure travel and we went all in.

GL: You must have fantastic travel tales from your first journey. What can you share about your initial honeymoon trip?

HONEYTREK: Leaving our lives in New York, we went headfirst into the Amazon jungle. With not much more than a dugout canoe, hammock and machete, we joined a local guide for a five-day trek and paddle. We learned how to make shelter from palm leaves, fish for piranha, and not get eaten by jaguars. It wasn't meant to be a survival workshop but, man, did we learn a lot — real fast. We proceeded to travel overland from northern Brazil to Tierra del Fuego. We fell in love with the journey itself — the chicken buses, the guesthouses, street food, and the changing of worlds from border to border — and continued to six more continents.

GL: In visiting more than 100 countries, we haven't had many negative experiences with locals. As you roam the planet, what have you learned about people?

HONEYTREK: It's amazing how many people ask us, "What's the scariest thing that's happened to you while traveling," and how shocked they are when we say, "Nothing, really." Aside from one pickpocket (who actually gave back our phone upon asking), we've never been robbed, hurt or threatened. Just like traveling in any big city in the USA, you need to have street smarts, move with confidence, and don't let little stuff ruffle you. But the bigger point is, the majority of people in the world are inherently nice, especially if you set that tone. When we walk into a situation with a smile and open mind, we find strangers are happy to help and be a friend.

GL: In Nick's 30s, he traveled overland from Nairobi to Cape Town, part of it as a hitchhiker. Family and friends thought he was insane. When you visit certain countries with so-called "unsafe" reputations and tell people about your travel plans, I imagine their responses are similar. How do you address their concerns?

HONEYTREK: Man, we are cut from the same cloth. We did that same Africa overland-meets-hitchhiking journey in reverse and it was one of our most memorable experiences! Not only did we successfully thumb rides on banana trucks and dhow boats, we got invited for dinner and stays in local homes along the way. When the Tanzania border patrol wouldn't accept our "old" $100 bill for our visa, our truck full of commuters pitched in to cover our fee. When we overslept because of a time change and exhaustion, a new friend woke us up to ensure we made the bus. The East African hospitality was incredible.

The news only reports the negative stories and is particularly unkind to certain parts of the world. We like to debunk those myths by getting out there and meeting the locals. One of the ways we explain travel to "unsafe" places is by sharing heartwarming stories that consistently ensue when we trust in the kindness of strangers.

GL: We thrive on mention serendipity, those out-of-nowhere chance encounters that happen as we travel. What are some of yours?

HONEYTREK: We were staying in a family-run guesthouse in Kerala, just laying low as we got our bearings in India. The owner looked up HoneyTrek and said: "Your 10-year honeymoon is quite the story. Mind if I pass along your contact to my reporter friend?" We gave him a business card and the phone started ringing. The local news station, magazine and the *Times of India* wanted interviews with us. It turned into a media blitz, we were honored, and the guesthouse owner couldn't have been more proud.

For the first two months of the pandemic (in 2020), we were trapped in Poland in a rented camper van. With hotels, campground and virtually all services closed and everyone weary of strangers, we were very much on our own. When our van ran out of water, we turned to our camping app and found that a farmer named Eva allowed RVers to fill up at her well. When this petite grandma opened the gate, we expected her to point us to a corner of the yard; instead, she greeted us with a big smile and insisted we join her for coffee and homemade sweets. Of course, we knew the social distancing guidelines, but how could we say no to such fearless generosity?

With the magical powers of Google Translate conservation-mode, we shared stories from our journey and learned about her farm-life and goat-cheese business, which she ran single-handedly. When we told her of Mike's Polish roots and pierogi Christmas dinners, she invited us back for a cooking lesson and bottle of wine. We spent five incredible days on Eva's farm, learning to milk goats, watching her newborn horse practice its trot, and gathering around the table for traditional Polish meals. Before we left, we translated our guest book entry about "Eva the Travel Angel" and, COVID be damned, it ended in a weepy-eyed hug.

GL: *Life-changing travel experiences pushed us toward a life of travel. Indeed, in your continuous movement, you must have had many such encounters. Might you name a few?*

HONEYTREK: Housesitting has been a rock in our nomadic lives. Whenever we feel the need to slow down and have a few comforts of home (namely strong Wi-Fi and a cute dog) while still satisfying our wanderlust, we find a housesit. (If you want to know more about how we score amazing free lodging around the world, check out HoneyTrek.com/Housesitting). We've house-sat a villa and lazy cat in Costa Rica, an East Village apartment and chihuahua, an award-winning retriever in Romania, and a four-acre farm in Portugal.

We've house-sat 28 times across eight countries, though Portugal really struck us. When we arrived, the homeowners threw us a party to introduce us to this close-knit community. When we harvested figs, we would pick extra for our neighbors, who would in turn shower us with tomatoes, spinach and plums. Every time we smelled her fresh bread in the stone oven, we'd visit Aurora, the 80-year-old baker, even though she'd sweet-talk us into buying too many loaves. We worked hard to keep the farm healthy and were rewarded with an honorary place in this special Portuguese farm community.

GL: You guys are prolific travelers and have been all over the world. Are there any countries you keep returning to again and again? Why?

HONEYTREK: With a vintage RV at our disposal and a love for road tripping, we keep zigzagging North America, as in 120,000 miles across all 50 states and 10 Canadian provinces. Having grown up in North America, we took our connecting countries for granted and never explored them thoroughly, until we got "Buddy the Camper." We're constantly amazed by the vast beauty of this continent, especially when you get into our public lands and little towns. And while we have RVed the length of the beautiful Baja peninsula, we find ourselves flying to Mexico again and again for neighborhood, getting to know our local markets, cantinas and neighbors. We've stayed in Baja, Guanajuato, Mazatlán and Mexico City for weeks at a time, and always extend our trip for more adventures in new Mexican states, now totaling 16. As fellow North Americans, we find we have so much in common with Mexicans, yet we're totally fascinated by how rich and varied their culture is. Between the food, music and sense of tradition, there is a real vibrancy and warmth that continually draws us back.

GL: "Perspective" is a word we hear quite a bit in travel. What sort of insights have you gained from your travels, especially from your visits to countries or regions that do not see many tourists?

HONEYTREK: We tend to gravitate toward developing countries. which often begs the question of "quality of life." Success is very material in the Western world, usually shown in the form of fancy houses, cars and clothes. In reality, so much of that is a facade and a total distraction from what matters. While it may seem like a village of simple bamboo houses with limited electricity is a "poor area," if basic needs are met and there is a strong sense of community, it's often a happy place.

Kids playing with a tire and stick are having just as much fun as they would on an i-pad (likely more). A ramen dinner cooked over the fire is plenty good when you're with friends. On our Indonesia trip, we remember going to a village a few hours' drive from the main tourist hub of Flores and saw kids playing soccer on a dirt field surrounded by thatch-roofed homes. We joined in the game, the parents invited us to dinner, and insisted we spend the night. The food and the accommodation by Western standards were pretty rough, but they were proud hosts and we felt like honored guests. Traveling has taught us to live more simply, and how fulfilling that can be.

GL: Have you participated in any volunteer work in your travels?

HONEYTREK: We wanted to volunteer from the get-go, so we became scouts for the Muskoka Foundation, which connected long-term travelers with do-good opportunities on their route. We helped vet nonprofits for them on three continents, and did a longer stint teaching English in a Red Dzao village in Vietnam. Our experience there was unforgettable, because upon seeing our commitment to the community, this insular hill tribe welcomed us with countless dinners and festivities around the Tet New Year. We've also done WWOOF, where we volunteered on a veggie farm in Japan, and loved our time harvesting produce, learning to cook traditional foods, chatting around the dinner table, and experiencing the Japanese way of life! Now that we work full-time in travel, we take 5 percent of what we make from every tourism campaign and give it back to local environmental and socially good nonprofits.

GL: What would you tell other couples or any travelers considering a nomadic lifestyle?

HONEYTREK: You need to be adaptable. Life on the road is unpredictable and poses challenges, but treat the bumps in the road as adventures and you'll grow stronger and have fun in the process. To find out if nomadic life is for you, do a practice run for a month or two. See if your boss will let you work remotely or challenge yourself to run your business in a new place. Then move again and see how you feel reestablishing your routine, or how you feel without a routine. No matter if this lifestyle is for you or not, you're clearly curious about it. So just stop wondering and give it a try!

OVERLAND AROUND THE WORLD

A global explorer who personifies the spirit of living and learning from locals is Tomislav Perko. Before 2008, Perko was a smartly dressed stockbroker in Zagreb, the capital of Croatia. The U.S. economy crashed, and the consequent recession hit Croatia hard. There's a saying that "When America sneezes, the world catches a cold," and Perko's lifestyle suddenly also crashed. "I decided to make a strange move," he recalled. "Instead of keeping at my job, I started traveling. ... It was not a typical or logical move, and I had little money in my pocket, so I started writing about my travels with little money."

After five years on the road, traveling in just about every imaginable way, including hitchhiking and by boat, Perko self-published his book *1000 Days of Spring*. Today he continues to be a global ambassador to globetrotters who search for the meaning of life on the road.

If there ever was an inspiration that it is possible to travel after college before hitting the job market, to travel while taking a break from work, or to simply quit your job to experience a new part of the world, Perko fits the bill. He epitomizes the concept that life's classroom is the open road. Whether sleeping in a local's home, breaking bread with new-found friends, or sharing travel tales during a drive, Perko has experienced more than even the most daring travelers.

All travelers have positive role models who influence them to hit the road running. Perko is one of ours. "I would never have started traveling if I hadn't heard so many inspiring stories from other travelers I met in my own city," he said. "It was different from watching documentaries and reading books: Chatting with live people made all the difference."

Perko can summarize his travel education in a single statement. "It all comes down to one major lesson," he said, "that people, no matter how much we try to point out the differences between them, are all the same. Traveling tore down my prejudices, opened my eyes to everyday wonders, and motivated me to enjoy my life to the fullest."

As for having a favorite nation or preferred countries, Perko insists, "I'm not sure I have favorite countries. It all depends on how much time I spend in any of them, which people I met, whether I was alone or with someone, and so on. I believe that 'experiencing' is the core of travel. Without it, traveling doesn't make much sense. You have to blend in with the locals, see their own country from their perspective, and understand that you came not to teach but to learn."

Why should travelers seek out opportunities to be part of the local landscape? "Because there is a façade of every country. Once you are there, you must dig deeper to see what lies underneath. That is the only way to experience a certain country. One learns that no matter where you travel, people are similar. And that traveling is not about the place you visit, but everything else that surrounds you."

An extended journey with little cash can be challenging. It requires creativity and flexibility, and finding new digs is a daunting task. "Many times I slept beside the road in parks or cars," Perko said. "I spent some time couch surfing and even using homeex change.com, sometimes sleeping on yachts or in beautiful homes with swimming pools, but also in caves and rock houses in Cappadocia, for example."

Perko traveled by just about every means possible. But he said his most life-changing encounters may come "with people that pick me up when I'm hitchhiking. Those random, time-limited encounters are amazing. Someone picks me up beside the road because they want to help me out, and we engage in honest conversation. These moments are always true, unique — and educational."

And the Croatian recalls other life lessons learned on the road. "The few times I stayed with indigenous people or tribes, they were always modernized versions of what I expected, with mobile phones and similar," he said. "Maasai warriors were great. I spent a few days with them and talked about Mother Nature and how most people forget to take care of her. We can learn so much from those people.

"Another way I found to meet local people was to volunteer. Those were great experiences and excellent ways to blend in with the locals. Also, most of the time, you can save some money working in exchange for food and accommodation."

Perko has many stories of eating with locals, but none so memorable as visiting developing countries and experiencing the hospitality of people through food. Being offered their last piece of bread will stand out in his mind forever. "I've learned that we are all the same, with similar wants and needs," he said

In his travels, Perko hitchhiked over 50,000 kilometers and visited 40 countries, with a daily budget of US $10. "I always tell people that it doesn't matter where you go," he said. "Focus on life experiences, on quality and not quantity. And it's much nicer to travel in a country where you can speak the language.

"I simply wish to find a place to settle down. I still haven't found the meaning of life, but I'm enjoying the search."

Most of us will not be as hard-core in our travels as Perko. But we can all learn from his experiences as we create our own around-the-world itineraries. It's never been as easy as today to travel safely on the road, to live, eat and play with local society. If our experiences are even half of Perko's, we all can make the world a better place on extended journeys away from our comfort zones. The nurturing qualities of knowledge and tolerance for our fellow man take us far in life, as we learn from other travelers and the local people we encounter.

Larissa & Michael Milne in Pyongyang, North Korea after they quite their jobs and sold their homes, opting to travel the world.

WOMEN'S EURO-ARABIAN NORTH POLE EXPEDITION

During Nick's first Arctic polar cruise with Poseidon Expeditions, he met Ida Olsson, a Swedish wilderness guide and kayak master in her early 30s. She told him about her intrepid overland expedition to the geographical North Pole on skis.

Conceived by renowned British explorer Felicity Aston, an author, research scientist and the first woman to ski across Antarctica alone, an international team of 11 remarkable women from Europe and the Middle East showed their cultural solidarity in overcoming countless challenges — ranging from shifting sheets of ice to temperatures that fell to -38º C.

At its core, the objective was to nurture peace and understanding between Western and Arab women, creating a more sublime dialogue between the two groups. Mark Twain's mantra, "Travel is fatal to prejudice, bigotry, and narrow-mindedness," was on full display.

As she recounted the experience, Olsson told Nick that she had been chosen from among nearly 1,000 applicants. The team of 11 came from all walks of life, representing a diverse range of ages, cultures and life experiences. They came from Saudi Arabia, Qatar, Oman, Kuwait, Slovenia, Sweden, France, Cyprus, Russia, and the United Kingdom. Several had never seen snow, and some of the Arabic women had to ask permission from their husbands to join the quest. Two years of preparation included training in Iceland and Oman.

The expedition began on April 14, 2019, with an early-morning flight from the northernmost commercial airport in the world at Longyearbyen, Svalbard, to a floating ice station at 89 degrees North. From there, the female-only group, which included three film crews, set off on their 100-km trek on cross-country skis. They slept in tents and used sleds to haul the supplies they needed to survive the harsh conditions. After seven days of skiing over the shifting pack ice of the Arctic Ocean, the brave women reached their goal at the top of the world, 90 degrees North Latitude.

Nikolai Saveliev, the founder of Poseidon Expeditions, sponsored Olsson, helping her to raise the $40,000 each woman needed to join the expedition to the North Pole. "By doing it the hard way, I will inspire more people to care about the polar wilderness we cherish," Olsson said.

"I'm extremely proud to have been part of this exciting expedition, bringing together women from all over the world to experience the challenging yet fragile environment of the Arctic Ocean. Being from Sweden and now living in Svalbard, I've traveled all over the Arctic for many years. I have seen how precious this ecosystem is and the importance of protecting it. We aim to highlight these polar regions' conservation and preservation efforts."

Kiwi travelers Leanne and Michael Young surprised Nick in San Blas, Mexico.

SMASHING THE MYTHS OF TRAVEL

As you travel the world and wander the diverse continents, you will see the myths of travel and humanity crumble to sand. Of course, there's risk involved. You may return home transformed — well-informed, wise, understanding, tolerant, insightful, and with a keen sense of humor to carry into whatever road you later forge.

One of the emotions associated with extended travel is, inevitably, fear. We are taught to believe that our home is the safest place in the world, at least for us. But in fact, we're far more likely to encounter harm at our home base than on the road.

Are you doomed if your trip is shorter than a life-altering long haul? Famed travel author Pico Iyer mentioned that no matter how far or near you travel, it can be life-changing if you use it as a launchpad for reflection and learning. "It's only when you get back home that you can really begin to understand a trip and implement the changes it may have set into motion inside you," he insists.

Nick who spends a large part of his year in Mexico, says he can't count the number of times he's been asked, by friends living in large metropolitan cities like Los Angeles or New York, "Is it safe living in Mexico?" He has learned not to listen to his couch-sitting friends whose only travels have been within their comfort zones, nor to the American media, which rants that you are only safe in the United States.

The chances are quite minuscule that you'll be traveling to the five or 10 countries on the planet that are truly unsafe. John has spent the past five years in Vietnam and Cambodia, both of them nations where Westerners weren't widely accepted two generations ago. No matter where you go, you will find that 90 percent of people you encounter are good people, just like yourself. Sure, the world is not a perfect place. There may be bad people anywhere, including North America. But as a whole, just as you would never harm another human being, a local in the world's most remote regions has zero interest in hurting you.

Your connection with the people whom you encounter and befriend will far outweigh any fear of the unknown. You will return home well-rounded and with a better perspective on life. Whatever quest or endeavor you plan, your resume will inspire you to teach others that travel makes you tolerant, likable, and better adapted to any further goals you may have.

There's no truth to the myth that traveling worldwide for an extended period will make you less employable. The knowledge that one absorbs on travel is priceless. Jobs will always be there when you return. Indeed, the concept of a gap year between diploma and career is gaining more and more traction. And many travelers have made a career from their travel experiences.

A potential employer can weigh the value of your travel resume. Certainly, travel may inspire you to shoot for the stars in whatever venture you choose. You might become a writer or photographer, or learn a new money-making method from the locals you meet as you travel. As has happened through the annals of civilization, you may absorb new ideas and bring them back to your home country.

Some long-haul travelers have gone on to help change the world by forging a volunteer life. Others have chosen to work in conservation or with the National Park Service. Some travelers followed a passion for teaching, or marine biology, or adventure sports. Numerous female travelers have launched clothing or custom-jewelry lines in Bali. The import-export business is filled with traveling entrepreneurs who began collecting on their first worldwide adventure. What do these wanderers have in common? They all took a chance to see the world.

Travel teaches us to break down false barriers and dismiss false myths. Being intoxicated by humanity is a powerful lesson. The sights, sounds and smells; the personal inquiries into what makes a society tick; and getting captured by the allure of travel make us all better world citizens. We trust that all people have similar needs of food and shelter, of getting a better education for their children, and people do not let us down.

The seduction of traveling for an extended period is mind-altering. No money in the world will buy you the knowledge gained from personal insight and exploration and getting away from your comfort zone. Nothing else approaches climbing in the Himalayas or Andes, teaching English to children in Peru or Laos, spending New Year's Eve with locals dressed in traditional white on Copacabana Beach, discovering how to make fresh pasta and pizza in Tuscany, plunging into the undersea world of SCUBA diving in the Red Sea or Great Barrier Reef, traveling overland through Europe or Australia, or volunteering in Africa or Asia. There's no better way to "go local" than traveling the world.

Swedish polar guide Ida Olsson led an all-women's expedition to the North Pole.

THEY QUIT THEIR JOBS TO TRAVEL

We're going back more than a dozen years here, but the story is still compelling and instructive. In 2011, Pennsylvanians Larissa and Michael Milne were in their 50s when they quit their jobs, sold their home, gave away most of their remaining possessions, and took off to travel the world.

They thought they might be gone for a year. Five years later, after learning to live much more cheaply than they had, they were still traveling. The Milnes have demonstrated that at almost any age, it's possible to leave the comfort of one's home and depart on a very long journey.

They started a blog, changesinlongitude.com, that won the 2013 Lowell Thomas Travel Journalism Silver Award for best travel blog. They began selling stories to their hometown Philadelphia Inquirer and other media outlets. The Milnes found that by living more simply and earning a living along the way, they could enjoy a nomadic lifestyle.

"Travel can be expensive, or it can be cheap," Milnes said. "We fall somewhere in the middle. We collect experiences, not things: Experiences last forever." Social media sites such as TripAdvisor and Yelp were often their best friends. "We're not in the backpacking and hostel phase of our life," they said. "We've done most of our traveling by plane and train."

Among their favorite countries to visit was Vietnam, "for its friendly people, favorite foods and cheap prices." At My Lai, site of an infamous massacre of civilians during the Vietnam War, they were asked by a multi-generational Vietnamese family where they came from. "Considering where we were standing, it was an uncomfortable question," Larissa confessed. "Our response, 'America,' and what happened next surprised us. The family surrounded me, shaking my hand, hugging me and saying, 'US-Vietnam friends now.' I was shocked at this outpouring of goodwill." Life experiences such as this provide the best education they've ever had.

Another memorable moment came in Malaysia: "We witnessed a Hindu infant head-shaving ceremony known as Mundan," Michael recalled. "We were visiting Batu Caves, a large Hindu temple built atop a hillside outside of Kuala Lumpur."

Peer-to-peer travel has helped the Milnes to "go local" by merging into the society. "We usually rent from Airbnb, which places us in local neighborhoods well off the tourist path," they said. "That has us shopping at local markets where we encounter language barriers and foods we don't know. This immersive travel is the best way to learn about local culture."

They've traveled to every continent but Antarctica, from France to Australia to North Korea. "We travel slowly, staying in apartments and immersing ourselves in the local culture," they said. "As global nomads with no fixed address, we call the world our home." And some of their accommodation choices have been quirky, to say the least.

"From a kitschy throwback hotel in North Korea to a nudist B&B in Portugal, we found a few unique places to stay," Michael said. "Shichachai Shadow Art Hotel, in Beijing, had shadow puppet shows on its walls. The Belar Homestead, on a 3,000-acre ranch in Australia's bush country, is owned by fourth-generation cattle farmer Rob Wright and his wife, Deb. Ai Aiba is a rock painting lodge where we stayed in Namibia; it sits within a 12,000-acre reserve boasting over 150 of these paintings.

"The Munduk Moding Coffee Plantation was an interesting one. If you've dreamed of waking up to a view of a coffee plantation on the island of Bali, this is the place. True coffee addicts can hike the plantation then retire to the lodge for a fresh cup of Kopi Luwak. Made famous as the java of choice for Jack Nicholson in *The Bucket List*, it's brewed from beans that have first been eaten and shat out by the civet cat. As an added bonus, you can visit the civets in cages and watch them prepare the beans for roasting." Larissa tried it. Michael is not a coffee drinker.

Inevitably, food and drink are an indelible part of their travel memories. "We spent a day working at the last Polish bakery in Buffalo, New York, which was a great way to meet locals," Larissa remembered. "We arrived at 5:30 a.m. to start making the donuts!"

Of course, travelers also discover cultural faux pas, as the Milnes did in Dublin, Ireland. "In America, a Black and Tan is a popular drink poured with equal parts dark Guinness and lighter-colored Harp beers," Michael explained. "Since the two liquids have different weights, they don't blend and form an eye-catching display in the mug. In Ireland, though, Black and Tan has a different, more sensitive connotation. That was the color of the uniforms worn by the British paramilitary troops formed around 1920 to put down the Irish after their failed Easter Uprising. These soldiers had fought in the bloodiest trench battles of World War I and were not about to be put off by rebels wielding rusty hunting rifles and pitchforks. Ordering a Black and Tan was a mistake we learned never to make again."

Perhaps their best dining experience was in the southwest African nation of Namibia. "During two weeks in the countryside, we had feasted on all types of game meat — oryx, impala, springbok, even wildebeest. So I was ready for some good old-fashioned beef when we returned to the capital city of Windhoek. Our friend Jim took us to the Soweto market in Katutura, a village dating from the apartheid era. to try some kapana, the famous Namibian street barbecue."

They were in Namibia, Larissa said, "because we wanted to see the animals of Africa but were not interested in a group safari. It is not recommended to drive on your own in Kenya and Tanzania, but Namibia is a safe country bordering the Atlantic Ocean. We drove around the country independently for three weeks, which really enhanced our experience.

Sharing food is a great way to break down barriers between individuals and cultures. Larissa took cooking classes worldwide, with unique encounters in Malaysia and in a pasta-making course in Italy. It's easy to find opportunities on local tourism websites or on apps such as meetup.com, where they have connected with locals around the world.

So: What's next? "We are heading to Romania, which I understand has the third fastest internet in the world," Milnes said. "As digital nomads, that is important to us."

On assignment for CBS, Peter Greenberg beats his own drum in Belize.

'YOU DON'T HAVE TO BE RICH TO TRAVEL'

San Blas, Mexico, is not the hub of Mexico tourism, but the historical port town is home to a handful of American and Canadian expats who fled south to a warmer climate.

Among them is Nick. If you're traveling the Pacific Coast between Mazatlán and Puerto Vallarta, you might find him some Saturday night, *cerveza* in hand, at the La Familia Hotel and Restaurant.

That's where Nick met Michael and Leanne Young, a Kiwi couple from New Plymouth, New Zealand, passing through on an extended motorcycle journey through Latin America. If all goes according to plan, they'll eventually arrive in Ushuaia, Argentina, the southernmost city in the Americas. But the itinerary? Plan? There is none. What inspired this trip? Nick wondered.

"We went out for a walk one night after work," said Mike, 63. "Leanne had a bad day at the office. I said I felt like quitting my job and just going ... anywhere! Next it was, 'Why don't we just go?' Then it was, 'Where should we go?'" With New Zealand passports, we can travel almost anywhere. We thought about sending our motorbike to London and driving north to Scandinavia but decided to stay away from Europe with the current political climate in Ukraine. In the end, we chose southern Africa and the Americas."

Serendipity plays a role in all great journeys. "Before we could travel, we had to rent out our home," said Leanne, 56. "We met a couple in one of our favorite restaurants, a Brazilian guy and a Dutch woman. We struck up a conversation. We mentioned that we're going traveling and will be in Brazil. They noted that they were looking to rent a house for a year, and we rented them our home. Wow, no rental app is needed! All done through meeting other travelers."

As wanderlust set in, the gutsy couple shipped their Husqvarna Norden 901 adventure touring motorcycle by cargo ship from New Zealand to Los Angeles. Biding their time, the Youngs found new exploits. On the recommendation of fellow Kiwi bikers, they booked a 22-day tour through southern Africa with SAMA Motorcycle Tours, a tour operator out of Pretoria.

"We joined a group of 10 extraordinary people for a ride from South Africa to Botswana, Zimbabwe and Namibia, finishing in Cape Town," Mike told Nick. "These are densely populated countries. There were some long days as distances between towns or settlements are far, sometimes eight- to 12-hour days with nothing to see but African bush and desert." They went on safari in Botswana's Chobe National Park. "To see elephants and more African game in the wild is something we've never experienced and is unforgettable," Leanne recalled.

From Cape Town, the Youngs flew Swissair to Europe, making a brief stopover in Zurich before continuing to New York. There they stayed as guests of a Greenwich

Village couple whom they had met through an online global community of motorcycle enthusiasts called Adventure Riders (advrider.com). "It's bikers helping bikers," Mike explained. "This lovely couple offered us a room in their home. Not sure if we were imposing, we gave them so many chances to back out and not host us, thinking that in the end they might change their minds about hosting us. They didn't, and we had a great time.

Modern day hitchhiker Tomi Perko left Croatia and traveled the world mostly over land.

Highlights of their New York sojourn included visits to the Empire State Building and the 9/11 Memorial. "We also went to a Yankees game," Mike said. "I asked a guy next to me about some of the rules of baseball, and he was so kind, teaching me the game. A guy even proposed to his girlfriend during the game. Our hosts introduced us to their friends and took us to a bar where we met a friend of a friend who had played (at the famous rock festival) in Woodstock. The hospitality and generosity of our new friends was special."

Finally, it was time to pick up their touring motorcycles in Los Angeles to begin the planned moto-journey. The generosity of travelers prevailed again. "We met a guy on the Adventure Riders website who offered to assist us in getting our bikes," Mike said. "Los Angeles, we learned, is difficult to manage. It's so big compared to New York, with so many freeways. This kind fellow took us to Long Beach to get our bikes from customs and even assisted us with some assembly. We offered to buy him lunch, but he did not accept."

After four nights, the couple left for Las Vegas and later visited the Grand Canyon before finally entering Mexico, where they connected with other bikers in Sonora and Chihuahua states.

Nick asked about safety. "Of course, you have to use common sense, but most people are good in the world," Leanne said. "Part of our travel is to avoid tourist towns. Here we are sitting in this square in a small town in Mexico at a local expat bar, talking to you. We found San Blas because other travelers mentioned this place to stop between Mazatlán and Puerto Vallarta. We've met generous people throughout our journey through Mexico."

The Youngs said they planned to get to Ushuaia by Christmas, but with six-month visas to Mexico, the dates were not set. "We're are not on a trip to sit by a pool in Cancún drinking," Mike said. "Our home is rented until next April. All we know for sure is the length of our Mexico visa is for six months and that Belize will be after Mexico.

"Tourist destinations aren't important. The experiences and the memories are. Just like we're doing today. We met you in a small town and now we're having a beer together in a town square. We've been given kindness from people on our travels; our home is open to other travelers that we meet along the way. You learn to listen to people more, see how they live, and talk and ask about their experiences.

"Tolerance and patience are two important words on our travels. Open your mouth and talk to people; don't judge based on their appearance. Everyone is just a person and has a story. You get people talking; the next moment, they guide you around their city or country."

I ask the Youngs about weight: You can only carry so much on a motorcycle. "As we're on a motorbike, we travel with next to nothing," Mike said. "I tell Leanne that you can buy anything you want as long as it fits on the motorbike. We have small items in our home that bring back memories of the people and places we encountered along the way."

Travel doesn't have to be expensive. "People think that we must be rich to travel, but that's not the case. Nevertheless, not everybody has the opportunity to travel. We remember that we're very fortunate. We do feel blessed to travel the world," said Leanne.

You may say I'm a dreamer, but I'm not the only one. I hope that someday you'll us and the world will be as one. — John Lennon

Chapter Ten

LIVING OVERSEAS:

A Better Life for Half the Price

When you move from one country to another, you have to accept that there are some things that are better and some things that are worse, and there is nothing you can do about it. —
Bill Bryson

There is no substitute for living in another country. Once you take the plunge, your life will be changed forever. So, too, will be the lives of your new friends. One can only truly understand the world by experiencing different cultures, by becoming a stranger in a strange land. This is how to exit your comfort zone.

Living, eating and making friends with the local inhabitants opens your mind to a wealth of knowledge while dispelling any myths that may have been hung upon your door. Perceptions regarding people and cultures change when you find yourself living in a new society. When you immerse yourself in an alien language and force yourself to think in it, you will discover limitless new ways to think and perceive the world.

But don't worry about speaking (or not speaking) the local tongue. In a matter of weeks, you'll absorb the basics almost without trying; and even if you don't, no language is more universally spoken than English. Many expatriates worry that the foreign infrastructure may not be up to the standards they're used to in their homeland; indeed, some may need help with healthcare, safety, corruption or the ability to make local friends. But as they become more accustomed to their new home, they may very well find that levels of health and safety are an improvement over what they had before.

Packaging up, departing your comfortable home, and moving to a foreign land is a big decision. The website "Best Places on Earth to Retire" asked nearly 400 expats from the

U.S. and Canada, who moved to Mexico and Central America, about their fears and how later they were demystified. A whopping 45 percent of respondents said they were dead wrong in their presumptions. And once they were acclimated, most respondents' fears dropped by 80 percent. As for making new friends, the reality is that if you make even the slightest effort, locals will want to learn as much about you as you do about them.

John visits a "longneck" mother and child in a Kayan village near Chiang Mai, Thailand.

Cultural immersion

As you travel, you can immerse yourself in the language and learn about a culture's traditions and foods. Perhaps you studied French in school or wanted to learn Spanish. Maybe you had a fascination with the Maasai tribal culture of Kenya and considered learning Swahili. Now is the time to learn and use it! And even if you choose to settle in another English-speaking country, you may be amazed to discover the contrasts between two cultures with the same basic language. You immediately gain a new perspective on your home country and realize that all the things you took for granted as being "normal" were only normal in your country.

Simple things like the architecture of a building, the cobblestone paving of the streets, or the way the sun rises over certain neighborhoods and sets over the sea, might be your fondest recollections of your time in a new land. Or study the history, the music and the arts for a whole new perspective on a culture. Adopt the food as your preferred diet, get to know neighborhood haunts, engage locals in chance encounters at the market. Watch local television and read the beloved books of a new society, even in translation. You'll finally come to understand the references you've been hearing in everyday conversation.

These days, Nick spends more time living in Mexico than in California. Only a three-hour flight from San Francisco, he has discovered a perfect blend of magical towns, exquisite cuisine, year-round festivals and sundrenched beaches. Each of Mexico's 32 states features a unique culture and cuisine. Its proximity to the U.S. and Canada makes Mexico a no-brainer for many Norte Americanos.

As of this writing, John hasn't set foot in North America since he left five years ago, having sold almost everything he owned. (The purging, he said, was the hardest part.) Enamored of Southeast Asian culture for decades, he wanders between coffee-cloaked mountains and golden sands, exotic modern cities and ancient temple complexes. Sometimes he even snacks on fried tarantulas — which are delicious, he insists, when eaten with the right chili sauce.

John arrived in Vietnam shortly before the COVID pandemic struck. He hasn't looked back. He describes the experience in his award-winning blog, *travelsinvietnam.com*. Unquenchable curiosity, which led him to a career in journalism, has been both a blessing and a curse. It has manifested not only in learning new languages, but also in understanding and accepting the histories, political systems, and systems of religious thought of the societies where he's lived. Perhaps most difficult was learning how, or how not to, fall in love according to cultural mores. But he wouldn't have it any other way.

Mikaku Doliveck from California married a Balinese women and moved to Bali. Shown here with his wife, son, and Barong Dancers

Better lives, longer lives

There are many reasons why people move to another country. Some people relocate overseas to study, for love, for work, to learn a new culture, for warmer weather. Whatever the reason, you need a plan for a job that allows you to make your living, and in today's internet age, this is more realistic than ever. There are many jobs one can do from a computer. Many entrepreneurs can even work remotely from the beach in e-commerce. Many travel writers and bloggers choose to work entirely from the road.

According to the Nomad Capitalist, "The sudden rise in the remote working trend, the introduction of digital nomad visas, and ever-increasing conversations about the digital nomad lifestyle have made people believe that digital nomadism is a fairly new concept. That's not true, though." Indeed, people have had jobs allowing them to travel the world since well before 1997, when the term was coined.

In the past two decades, people who retired overseas have not only seen their life expectancy rise but also have been much healthier in their later years. Many older Norte

Americanos are now retiring in Belize, Mexico, Panama, Costa Rica, and Ecuador. Your money goes further in Thailand, Vietnam, Cambodia, the Philippines, and most parts of Asia. Australians have long migrated to Bali. At the same time, Europeans who wish to stay closer to home might relocate to Greece, Portugal, Italy or Spain — nations with warm climates, historic cultures, and a more relaxed way of life—or even to Armenia and Georgia. Many New Zealanders migrate to Fiji or the Cook Islands, and their dollar goes 33 percent further in Greece and Portugal.

Medical advances and better diets are helping people to live longer. According to Harvard professor David Cutler, who conducted studies on longevity: "Except the year or two just before death, people are healthier than they used to be. ... Effectively, the period in which we're in poor health is being compressed until just before the end of life. So where we used to see people who are very sick for the final six or seven years of their lives, that's far less common. People live to older ages, and we are adding healthy years, not debilitated ones."

Over the past decade, medical tourism has been on the rise. Simple procedures such as having a cavity filled can cost a small fortune in the Western world. Now, almost all doctors and dentists worldwide are fully trained to do the same work for less than half the price at home. Most countries on your list of "suitable nations" have excellent practitioners.

If you've spent most of your life in cold European or North American winters, living abroad on a fixed income can allow you not only to live a better life — but as you move to a warmer climate, the chances are also that you might live much longer. Where do you want to be in January: Shoveling snow from your driveway in Toronto, Frankfurt or Boston? Or sipping an umbrella drink in Jamaica, Mexico or Phuket?

As we live longer, people want to travel, explore new lands, interact with local people, take cooking classes, learn a new language, or learn a craft like making pottery. And imagine how your life would change if you had more money to spend. What if you woke up every day and the temperature was warm enough to swim in the ocean or relax by the pool? And with increased buying power, you could order a drink on the beach, dine at the best restaurant in town, travel to explore your new homeland, and still have money left over.

Take it from an expat, living in Thailand, quoted in Tim Leffel's "Cheap Living Abroad": "I make a whole lot less than I did in

New York City, but here my rent is only one-fifth of my income instead of taking half of it." Another expat who moved from San Francisco to Kerala, India, to teach English, said: "In California, I was living in a one-bedroom apartment with a tiny little living room for $2,500 a month. Once you add in power, internet, etc., it was $2,800. In Kerala, my rent is $247 for a nicer place, and I'm within walking distance of work. I couldn't get a cab in San Francisco for less than $20. Here I seldom pay more than $1.50."

Nick with the local Gutierrez brothers in his expat world in San Blas, Nayarit, Mexico.

The Inca Trail

Maureen Santucci has carved a stellar life of encounters and experiences since moving from Denver to the Andes of Cuzco, Peru. "It was a total fluke that I ended up in Peru," she said. "It was probably more like fate, but either way, it wasn't planned ... not by me, at least.

"I'd gotten divorced a couple of years before and had decided it was time to see more of the world. I was living in L.A., had many Latino friends, and was inspired to go someplace south of the border. Honestly, I didn't care where. A friend had wanted to go to Peru for years and was planning her trip for January 2008. I decided to join her on her four-week odyssey without knowing it would change my life completely.

"Almost from the moment I landed, I felt at home here, a feeling that expanded exponentially when sleeping in the mountains while hiking the Inca Trail. Through another 'fluke,' I ended up back in May 2008, confirming that I would move here in a couple of ... oh, hell no, I can't wait two years! When I returned in October 2008, I was looking for work to sustain me while I built a massage and acupuncture practice, thinking that March or April the next year would be the perfect time for me to move. But when my new employer said she was looking for someone to start that November or December, I just said ... OK!

"I think one of the things that has helped me tremendously in my immersion into local culture is just that: I wanted to immerse myself. I never saw myself as 'other,' even though I am easily recognized as non-Peruvian. But I think of myself as a person first and foremost, rather than Caucasian or American. And I think that comes across to the people here as I get treated more like another human rather than a 'gringa' or foreigner, as many do."

Maureen said the ability to make friends easily was key to her ability to settle in:

"When I first came here, I met a few people I kept in contact with and visited again. The person we rented horses from in January became the person I went to the jungle with in May. We didn't have a hostel reservation because he thought there were enough lodgings. When we couldn't find a place, we spent the night in sleeping bags on someone's floor.

"That night, I listened to my friend talking to the man who owned the rustic house as best as I could, with my limited Spanish. This man was dressed in ratty sweatpants with rips and tears. It turned out that he had sold a fair amount of the surrounding land. I wondered how much money he had in the bank, despite being dressed as he was. I repeatedly saw that you could not predict how much money someone had by what they wore. You will often see a *campesino,* a country farmer, enter the bank in old clothes and pull out a wad of cash to deposit."

"Another time, I visited a friend's parents in an out-of-the-way high-jungle town. They are humble, hard-working folk, the salt of the earth. They kept piling my plate with food each meal, and I just couldn't eat that much. They asked if I liked *cuy* (guinea pig), a delicacy in Peru. The truth is, if it's cooked well, I like it ok. But what went through my mind was ... crap. If I say no, I'm the 'gringa'; if I say yes and don't eat it all, I'm still the 'gringa.' I ate as much as possible, and, thankfully, they are very gracious people."

Moving from place to place with a local, Maureen said, is "like having a pass to an underground club. If you are introduced as a friend, you can enter a world that you wouldn't be able to otherwise, or at least not at the same level. From adult birthday parties with clowns to yearly festivals with endless costumed dancing and crates of beer, to ceviche and cerveza on the beach at dawn, to impromptu house parties — this is a country where people, by and large, put the value of spending time with people they love above other more fleeting matters, however important they may be by 'first-world' standards.

"Time and again, what's been proven to me is that you must approach each new situation without expectations. It also helps you if you can live in the moment. Sometimes you may not want to be where you are, or do what you're doing, but it's amazing how much fun you can have if you lighten up and leave your judgment at home. And often, these memories will stick with you most for years to come."

'Bali high' found him

Michael (Mik) Doliveck began traveling back and forth between his home in Cleveland, Ohio, and the Indonesian island of Bali in 1990. He married a Balinese woman in 2006 and soon thereafter began offering tours to highlight the island's unique culture, rituals and a hidden side of Bali that most visitors miss.

In 2013, the couple moved to Bali full-time to open a wellness resort. Today the luxurious, award-winning Floating Leaf Eco-Luxury Retreat *(balifloatingleaf.com)* facilitates wellness and healing through yoga, spa and detox treatments while immersing guests in Balinese culture.

Mik immediately fell in love with Bali. He embraced the culture, spirituality, art forms, healthy lifestyle, and passion for life as seen through its people, even connecting with local surf culture. To Doliveck, there is no place in the world like Bali. "I've never experienced such graceful, open, compassionate and welcoming people," he said.

In his experience, Mik said, he has seen more artisans — more paintings, dancing, singing, carving, craftsmanship and drawing — per capita in Bali than anywhere else in the world. They are helping him to seek out authentic experiences and create life-changing moments.

One of his first encounters with locals, he said, occurred many years ago as he was photographing Bali. When he stumbled upon a cremation ceremony, he was uncertain if he would be welcomed to observe the traditional ritual. But as it turned out, Mik not only was encouraged to film the sacred event; villagers helped him climb upon a platform for a closer look at the last rites and final prayers, including a blessing with holy water just before cremation.

The world over, locals often are thrilled to share their culture with a stranger, a foreigner. On Bali, Mik said, he experienced a series of seemingly magical, mystical, healing encounters. He melted into Balinese life and culture as a specialty tour operator running the eco-retreat. Now the Dolivecks have started donation programs to subsidize organic farming, and a cleanup and recycling project that teaches locals how to make money through recycling.

When you move overseas, you quickly learn to love the culture and its children.

A Better Life for Half the Price

Like Nick, travel author, blogger and web entrepreneur Tim Leffel has chosen Mexico, the land of tequila and mariachis, as his home base outside the U.S. He lives in the mountain town of Guanajuato when he's not at his American home in Tampa Bay, Florida.

In his book, *A Better Life for Half the Price,* Leffel tells readers they can cut their expenses by 50 percent living abroad. Nowadays, many travelers can work remotely. Imagine if you could keep or make the same salary you make in the U.S., Canada, Northern Europe or Australia, but double your buying power. You could spend less while living a more fulfilling life. Depending on your choice of country, your disposable income and lifestyle will change dramatically. In most countries where travelers relocate, goods and services cost much less. Your dollar will go much further.

In warmer, expat-friendly nations like those of Central and South America, Southeast Asia, southern Europe and Mexico, you can live in a condo overlooking the sea for no more than $500 a month. A maid might clean your place for as little as $5 daily. A freshly squeezed vegetable and fruit juice combo costs $1, a filling lunch entrée around $5, and cleaning your car with some detailing costs $7. A bus or tuktuk ride into town is only 50 cents.

As Leffel mentions, the average median salary in the United States is around $58,000. That money goes a lot further in Mexico than it does in the U.S. In such expat-favored nations as Armenia and Georgia, Vietnam and Cambodia, Nepal, Ecuador and Belize, your pension might elevate you to upper middle class. Take that money to Nicaragua, "the next Costa Rica," and your money even stretches further.

Besides the second edition of *A Better Life for Half the Price,* Leffel is the author of *The World's Cheapest Destinations*, *Travel Writing 2.0*, and *Make Your Travel Dollars Worth a Fortune: The Contrarian Traveler's Guide to Getting More Less. A Better Life* has stories and pointers from more than 50 expatriates worldwide, plus rundowns for the best values of international living. For more information: *cheaplivingabroad.com.*

Going Local spoke with Leffel about living overseas.

Travel writer Tim Leffel, shown traveling in Patagonia, has found "a better life for half the price" in Mexico.

Q & A WITH Tim Leffel

GOING LOCAL: Tim, how did you get your start in the field of travel?

LEFFEL: After working in the music business for many years as a marketing guy, my then-girlfriend and I chucked all that and went backpacking around the world. I already had a lot of writing experience, so I started working on travel articles and getting things published in magazines.

GL: Who were positive role models or who influenced you to a path of travel?

LEFFEL: I got a late start, so my girlfriend, now my wife, gave me the shove I needed to get out of my rut. After that, just a lot of books were read on the road.

GL: What are a few of your favorite countries for a local experience, and what do you love about these destinations?

LEFFEL: I drift back to mountainous places with fascinating local cultures, so Nepal, Peru, the mountainous areas of Europe, Guatemala and central Mexico. But I've been to a lot of places I've loved.

GL: While no longer a new buzzword, "experiential travel" or "peer-to-peer travel" is what we preach. What does this mean to you?

LEFFEL: It means doing more than snapping selfies in front of a monument and moving on. It's digging deeper, going slower, and experiencing what makes a place and its people unique.

GL: You're a big proponent of living overseas. Why should people live abroad?

LEFFEL: You can only learn so much about a place in a few days or even a few weeks. It's hard to go beyond a surface impression. But when you live somewhere, you become immersed in the place and the people, the language and the food, on a much deeper level.

GL: What's your biggest challenge living in a foreign land?

LEFFEL: It tries your patience sometimes, especially dealing with government bureaucracy, but my home country is no picnic either, so it's all a wash. Most problems we encounter on the road can be solved by money, time or kindness. Patience can accomplish a lot so I try not to be too tightly scheduled, cutting things too close.

GL: What misconceptions have you discovered living in Mexico?

LEFFEL: The biggest one is that Mexicans are lazy. They'll work their asses off when they're working. They just aren't going to work crazy hours just to impress someone, or work Sundays because the crazy gringo wants his kitchen renovation finished faster. And there's the misconception that Mexico is violent and dangerous everywhere, when in fact someone moving south from the USA will generally be moving into an area with a much lower crime rate, especially for gun homicides.

GL: What off-the-beat encounters or out-of-the-blue moments have you experienced while living overseas?

LEFFEL: The most memorable was in Morocco, when we went against all the prevailing advice and trusted a stranger who was going our direction. He ended up showing us Fez like an insider, inviting us to his home for lunch, and giving us terrific ideas for where else to go in the country. He didn't want anything but the company and to show off his country.

GL: Never before has food been such a large part of one's travel experience. Can you recall some encounters with food or over a meal?

LEFFEL: Everywhere I go I try to dive in and order what's unique to eat and drink in that country, trying the street food and the local joints. Only to a point, though — I'm not trying to impress anyone by downing things that are nasty just to prove something. I do like to go on market tours and food tours in a city; these give a lot of insight into the culture.

GL: Have you taken any cooking classes while living in Mexico or anywhere else on your travels?

LEFFEL: I've taken cooking classes in Puebla, San Miguel de Allende and Oaxaca, so I know Mexican food and cooking styles well. All those were with my family and we also did one together in Bangkok. It's a great way to dive into the cuisine and learn more about how it's prepared.

GL: Have you ever worked on an ecological project such as marine, animal conservation, or other eco-volunteering?

LEFFEL: I experienced the RED Travel turtle-tagging program in Baja Sur, near Magdalena Bay in Baja California. They have a terrific ecosystem there. I worked with the Sierra Gorda Biosphere project in Queretaro, another great project that has really tried to elevate the local communities as well as preserving the environment.

GL: Can you tell us about your experiences with home exchange? What is the concept in exchanging homes?

LEFFEL: We used to rent our Guanajuato house out through Airbnb, but we've been much happier doing home exchanges: The people in that closed community are more respectful and need less hand-holding. Homeexchange.com has opened options to live like a local in places we've done exchanges, instead of just being hotel guests or renters. For far less money, too, of course.

To travel is to discover that everyone is wrong about other countries. — Aldous Huxley

Chapter Eleven

TRAVEL INDUSTRY ICONS SPEAK

When you come to a fork in the road — take it. — Yogi Berra

When Gen Xers, millennials – and yes, even baby boomers – speak of those who motivated them to travel, a handful of names inevitably rise to the top of the list. They include Tony Wheeler, who together with his wife Maureen founded Lonely Planet Publications in 1973 to share budget travel advice about crossing Asia overland; Rick Steves, who launched Europe Through the Back Door in 1976 and grew it into a mega-tour and public broadcasting network; Richard Bangs, the "father of modern adventure travel," a prolific river adventurer, book author and pioneer of online travel publishing; Don George, a San Francisco-based travel editor and author most recently at *National Geographic Traveler;* and broadcast journalist Peter Greenberg, a multiple Emmy Award-winning investigative reporter and travel editor for CBS News.

We are gratified that each of these five gentlemen, when approached them about sharing some of their knowledge with our readers, replied with a hearty "Yes!" And why not? Every one of them has been preaching the gospels of collaborative cultural exchange and peer-to-peer travel for half a century. At least three generations of vagabonds know the world (and themselves) better because of the road paved by this Mount Rushmore of travel pioneers.

No less influential are five other professional travelers who have likewise been leaders in raising the consciousness of modern travelers: Patricia Schultz, author of *1,000 Places to See Before You Die;* author James Michael Dorsey, whose works focus on marine biology and remote tribal cultures; journalist Judith Fein, author of *Life Is a Trip: The Transformative Magic of Travel;* Jeff Greenwald, author of nine books and co-founder of EthicalTraveler.org; and the late David Noyes, a famed photographer who started Innocent Eyes Project to support childhood education in the developing world. We are privileged to be able to publish their reflections here from lifetimes of travel.

TONY WHEELER: Lonely Planet

No other world travelers have changed more lives, including our own, and altered the way we travel like Tony and Maureen Wheeler, who established the Lonely Planet guidebook series in 1973.

Born in England in late 1946, Tony grew up with an aviation industry family in Pakistan, the Caribbean and Canada, and spent his high school years in the USA. He returned to England to earn an engineering degree at Warwick University, work for a couple of years as an automotive engineer for Chrysler, then return to university for an MBA at London Business School.

Days after graduating in 1972, Tony and his new wife, Maureen, set off on an overland trip from London across Asia to Australia. They intended to be away for a year, get travel out of their systems, and settle down. They drove a beat-up minivan to Afghanistan and eventually arrived in Sydney with 27 cents between them. By this time, they had jettisoned their plan to return to London. Continual questioning from people they met — How did you travel? What did you see? What did it cost? — inspired them to turn their diaries into the first Lonely Planet book, *Across Asia on the Cheap* (1973), followed quickly by *South-East Asia on a Shoestring* (1975). John, in fact, purchased the first thin edition of *Shoestring* in Australia in early 1976 and immediately used it to guide him from Bali to Bangkok.

In the early Lonely Planet years, Tony personally worked on numerous titles including the award-winning guide to India and the best-selling Australia guide. The Wheelers helmed the company until its sale in 2011. He continues to write, including *Bad Lands: A Tourist on the Axis of Evil* (2007) and the compact *On Travel* (2018); and, with Maureen, *The Lonely Planet Story: Once While Travelling* (2008).

Tony Wheeler at Admiral Yamamoto's crash site in Papua New Guinea

Q & A with Tony Wheeler

GOING LOCAL: Tony, how did you come up with the name "Lonely Planet"?

WHEELER: It's an interesting story. We had done the first book and were just about to get it printed and did not yet have a name for the business. We had just seen a movie, a concert film, called *Mad Dogs and Englishmen*. It was about a rock'n'roll band on the road in the late '60s: You can still find the CD in shops. In this film, Joe Cocker sings a song called "Space Captain." There is a line that says, "Lovely planet caught my eye," so we altered it! "Lonely Planet caught my eye."

GL: South-East Asia on a Shoestring changed our lives. We carried it around like a bible. How did you come up with the concept?

WHEELER: After we arrived in Australia with 27 cents in our pockets, we decided to write about our trip. Our first book was titled *Across Asia on the Cheap,* but shortly, a lot of Asia went wrong. The Russians invaded Afghanistan. Iran was in turmoil. We carried on to our second book, which was *South-East Asia on a Shoestring.* A new edition comes out every two years. Now it has sold well over a million copies. One book led to another. In 1981 we came out with the India book. Suddenly, we had a bigger book, selling for more money. Lonely Planet grew slowly, but like a snowball gained momentum, and we created more books. Now, the young Chinese are allowed to travel and a new generation is using *South-East Asia on a Shoestring.*

GL: *How were you influenced to travel the world?*

WHEELER: From an early love for stamp collections and a wanderlust through geography

GL: *One of the things that you mention when traveling is that people should be knowledgeable and respectful. Can you elaborate?*

WHEELER: Don't violate customs or taboos. If you admire and respect a destination, if you make an effort to know about the destination, you're a more appreciative and better traveler. If you go to Munich, learn about beer. Writing guidebooks prompts you to learn things you might not otherwise learn, making them much more interesting. You're a better traveler when you get under the surface of a place. You discover more enriching experiences.

GL: *You often mention that besides Maureen being the love of your life, clearly travel is your other true love.*

WHEELER: By the time I co-founded Lonely Planet Publications in 1973, I already had the travel bug. It's done wonderful things for me. I've been to lots of interesting places. It's been a life, a career, a business and an enjoyment. I really have always enjoyed it. There was a 10-year period at Lonely Planet — not when it was a baby learning to walk, but when it was a teenager growing really fast, excited at everything — when it was a wonderful time to be doing it. People often say those years working for us were brilliant. It was exciting. Really the whole of it was good, but there were periods that were wonderful.

GL: *As the founder of the world's most prolific travel series, you must get asked frequently for travel advice. What do you tell travelers?*

WHEELER: Just go, do it. I've also been given lots of little bits of good advice — try that restaurant, that museum, that sort of thing. For example, I remember once being on an overnight boat from India to Sri Lanka, a service that's been closed for about 30 years now. Some young Tamils on the boat told us that when we got there everyone was going to run to the booking office for the overnight train to Colombo. "Don't do that," they said. "Instead, go round the back of the office to the berth reservations counter. If you do that quickly, while everyone else is booking tickets, you can get a sleeping berth." It was terrific advice because instead of spending another sleepless night standing on a train, we had this really comfortable sleeping berth. I remember the next morning we woke up feeling wonderful. We pushed the blind up and it was sunny with palm trees and rice paddies. Sri Lanka, what a beautiful place.

GL: *During our travels, we've had a couple of near-death experiences. Have you ever felt close to death?*

WHEELER: You don't know, do you? You've come out of the taxi, and then 100 meters down the road, it's had an accident. Once when Maureen and I were in Belfast when things weren't good there, we were walking and came to a crossroads where we could go one of two ways. We chose one direction, and a bomb went off in a street the other way. They had cleared the street but nonetheless we heard this big boom, and dust started flying up above the rooftops. That was close.

A few years back, I was in the Congo. I did three flights there, and the last two were with the same airline in the same aircraft — the only 727 they had. I remember looking over the door of the aircraft as I got on the plane: There's usually a sign there, saying when the plane rolled out, and this one was going to have its 50th birthday in two years. I flew from Kinshasa to Kisangani, and a few days later flew on the same plane to Goma. Precisely a week later it crashed and it killed nearly everybody on board. It was the worst crash in the world anywhere that year. It was the same flight number, same airline, same aircraft, just seven days later.

GL: *We are all old enough to have hitchhiked when it was somewhat the norm. To us, it was the ultimate way to "go local." Going overland is just a better way to travel.*

WHEELER: It's a shame it has pretty much disappeared in the Western world. I think New Zealand and Ireland were the last hitchhiking places. I have hitched rides in Saudi Arabia and Iran in recent years. I've consider myself fortunate enough to have traveled by foot, car, train, bus, boat, anything that moves at surface level. As for traveling overland, the only other way is to fly across border, isn't it?

I commend Graham Hughes' effort to visit every country on earth without flying to any of them, i.e., all at surface level. You can read the story on my website: *tonywheeler.c om.au/every-country-on-earth-at-ground-level/*. I think China has more land borders than any other country on earth and I've crossed seven of them: Pakistan, Mongolia, North Korea, Hong Kong, Macau, Vietnam, Nepal.

GL: *Is there a place that you go back to personally or in your mind that you especially love?*

WHEELER: Every place is interesting and unique. Kathmandu still is a terrific place to go. I like to go walking and hiking. It's not the same place that it was, but getting lost in the back streets and seeing the mountains is still wonderful. Burma, now Myanmar, for the longest time was politically incorrect to travel to, but now it seems like everyone is going there. There are also places that I have never been. For some reason, I have never been to the Yemen.

GL: We are intrigued by your most recent project, Tony Wheeler's Dark Lands. Can you tell us what the book is about?

WHEELER: *Dark Lands* is about my travels to some of the darkest corners of the world, my exploration into troubled nations. Every country has its problems, but some problems seem so vexed, so intractable, so absurd, you can only shake your head. I delve into some of these places and attempt to understand how things got so messed up. Along the way, I get stoned (with the thrown variety) in Palestine, score a speeding ticket in Zimbabwe, and get arrested for photographing a bar in the Congo. Plus I visit Osama bin Laden's Abbottabad in Pakistan. It is being translated into other languages. I called it "Dark Lands," after the Badlands of the Dakotas and Nebraska in the States. I could have called it "Evil Countries" or "Naughty Nations."

GL: What would you say to a first-time traveler?

WHEELER: Simply, "Go."

GL: Any places that you would not recommend to visit?

WHEELER: Home?

GL: In the end, what has travel taught you?

WHEELER: That people are the same everywhere.

RICK STEVES: European travel guru

Guidebook author and TV travel host Rick Steves is one of the world's most respected authorities on European travel. Rick took his first trip to Europe in 1969, visiting piano factories with his father, a piano importer. When he was 18, Steves began traveling independently, funding his trips by teaching piano lessons. In 1976, he started his business, Europe Through the Back Door, now Rick Steves' Europe. It has grown from a one-man operation to a company with a full-time staff of 80 well-traveled employees at his hometown headquarters in Edmonds, Washington, a Seattle suburb. From the window of his office — where he and our own John Gottberg co-authored several editions of *Asia*

Through the Back Door (now out of print) back in the 1980s — he can look out at his old junior high school.

Today, in addition to more than 50 guidebooks on European travel, *Rick Steves' Europe* has become America's most popular travel series onpublic television. Rick also hosts a weekly one-hour national public radio show and writes a weekly syndicated column. Through a travel center and website (*ricksteveseurope.com*), Rick Steves Europe operates 46 separate guided tour itineraries.

Author and TV personality Rick Steves visits with Persian students in Tehran.

Q & A with Rick Steves

GOING LOCAL: Rick, as perhaps the foremost authority in North America on European travel, you advise people to: "Become a temporary European." Can you explain what you mean by this?

STEVES: Many travelers tramp through Europe like they're visiting a cultural zoo. "Ooh, that guy in lederhosen yodeled! Excuse me, could you do that again in the sunshine so I can get a good picture?" It's important to stow your camera, roll up your sleeves, and enjoy the real thing. By developing a knack for connecting with locals and their culture, we become temporary Europeans, members of the family — approaching Europe on its level, accepting and enjoying its unique ways of life. When I'm in Europe, I become the best German or Spaniard or Italian I can be. I consume wine in France, beer in Germany, and small breakfasts in Italy. While I never drink tea at home, after a long day of sightseeing in England, "a spot of tea" really does feel right. Find ways to really connect with locals.

GL: *Do you recommend getting off the beaten path?*

STEVES: Yes, hit the back streets. Many people energetically jockey themselves into the most crowded square of the most crowded city in the most crowded month (St. Mark's Square, Venice, July) — and then complain about the crowds. If you're in Venice in July, walk six blocks behind St.Mark's Basilica, step into a café, and be greeted by Venetians who act as though they've never seen a tourist.

GL: *What do you mean when you tell travelers to "Play where locals play"?*

STEVES: A city's popular fairgrounds and parks are filled with families, lovers and old-timers enjoying a cheap afternoon or evening out. European communities provide their heavily taxed citizens with wonderful athletic facilities. In Britain, check out a public swimming pool, called a "leisure centre." While tourists outnumber locals 5 to 1 at the world-famous Tivoli Gardens, Copenhagen's other amusement park, Bakken, is enjoyed purely by Danes. Disneyland Paris is great, but Paris' ParcAstérix is more French.

GL: *What are some other ways to mingle with the locals?*

STEVES: In Southern Europe relax with a paseo, a stroll, in the early evening. Join a Volksmarch in Bavaria to spend a day on the trails with people singing "I love to go a-wandering" in its original language. Mountain huts across Europe are filled mostly with local hikers. Most hiking centers have alpine clubs that welcome foreigners and offer organized hikes.

Get up early. Throughout Europe — on medieval ramparts, in churches, produce markets, alpine farmsteads and seaside villages — the local culture thrives while tourists sleep. In Germany, walk around Rothenburg's fortified wall at breakfast time, before the tour buses arrive to turn the town into a theme park. Crack-of-dawn joggers and walkers enjoy a special look at wonderfully medieval cities as they yawn and stretch and prepare for the daily onslaught of the 21st century. By waking up with the locals on the Italian Riviera in the off-season, you can catch the morning sun as it greets a sleepy village. Breathe in the damp, cool air and experience a rare Italiansilence. Among travelers, the early bird gets the memories.

Or go to church. Many regular churchgoers never even consider a European worship service. But any church would welcome a traveling American. And an hour in a small-town church provides an unbeatable peek into the community, especially if you join the congregation for coffee and cookies afterward. I'll never forget going to a small church on the south coast of Portugal one Easter Sunday. A tourist stood at the door videotaping the "colorful natives" (including me) who were shaking hands with the priest after the service.

GL: *What are some other ways to immerse in a local society?*

STEVES: For many Europeans, the top religion is soccer. Getting caught up in a sporting event is going local. Whether enjoying soccer in small-town Italy or hurling in Ireland, you'll be surrounded by a stadium crammed with devout fans. Buy something to wear or wave with the hometown colors to help you remember whose side you're on. In Dublin, I joined 60,000 locals to watch a hurling match at Croke Park. Taking my seat, I was among new Irish friends. They gave me a flag to wave and taught me who to root for, the rules of the game ... and lots of creative ways to swear.

In Greece or Turkey, drop into a teahouse or taverna and challenge anyone to a game of backgammon. You're instantly a part (or even a star) of the café or bar scene. Normally the gang will gather around, and what starts out as a simple game becomes a fun duel of international significance. If you're a member of a service club, bridge club, professional association or international organization, make a point to connect with your foreign mates.

GL: *You urge travelers to "join in" to local society. Can you elaborate?*

STEVES: When you visit the town market in the morning, you're just another hungry shopper, picking up your daily produce. Traveling through the wine country of France during harvest time, you can be a tourist taking photos — or you can pitch in and become a grape-picker. Get more than a photo op. Get dirty. That night at the festival, it's just grape-pickers dancing — and their circle could include you.

Richard Bangs is known as the "Father of Adventure Travel." The travel pioneer produced the first internet travel site www.mtsobek.com.

RICHARD BANGS: Adventure travel

Often called "the father of modern adventure travel," Richard Bangs has spent more than 40 years exploring the world. Among his achievements was leading first descents of 35 rivers worldwide, including the Yangtze in China and the Zambezi in Zambia and Zimbabwe.

Richard's 18 books include *The Lost River: A Memoir of Life, Death and the Transformation of Wild Water,* which was honored with a National Outdoor Book Award in literature. He has written hundreds of magazine articles, including semi-regular features for the *Huffington Post*. He has produced a score of documentary films and several CD-ROMs and has lectured at the Smithsonian Institution, the National Geographic Society and the Explorers Club.

Bangs was the co-founder of Sobek Expeditions, which in the early 1990s merged with Mountain Travel to become Mountain Travel Sobek, and president of Outward Bound. He was a pioneer in online travel publishing as a founder and editor-in-chief for Microsoft (Mungo Park and Great Escapes), Expedia.com (including Expedia Travels,

Expedia Radio and Expedia Cafes), and ventures with Slate, MSN, Yahoo and American Public Television.

Q & A with Richard Bangs

GL: What fueled your passion for adventure travel?

BANGS: I think I ended up in a life of adventure travel due to inspiration from my father. He was a career officer in the CIA, part of the first class that came from Yale, and he truly believed he could change the world for the better, as the OSS did before him. He later found disillusionment with The Company, and returned to school to finish his doctorate. Next he became a sex therapist, even had a radio show, "Ask Dr. Bangs." So he inspired me in a number of ways.

GL: What would you tell the next generation of explorers seeking out to blaze new trails seeking to explore the world?

BANGS: Simply stated, follow your passion. It is the only way.

GL: You spent the majority of your life as a voice of ecotourism. How do you think you've made a difference?

BANGS: The tension will always exist between the short-term economics of extraction and the long view of sustainability. I'd like to think emotional currency is part of the equation, and hope I can bring a voice to wildlife and wild places, a song of romance that comes with knowing and embracing. I'm a sucker for any organization that works to sanctuary our wildness. I was president of Outward Bound; several of my books were published by Sierra Club; I have served on the boards of International Rivers Network, Four Corners School of Outdoor Education, and others.

GL: You were raised in Maryland. As a child or young man, what was your first river adventure?

BANGS: Here's a story of my first adventure: My father never really cared much for the outdoors. He preferred a cozy chair and a fat book, a night at the movies, maybe a ball game on TV, certainly restaurant food. But one weekend when I was a small boy he took me camping. I don't remember where he took me, but it was by a river, a swift-flowing stream, clear and crisp. I have a faint memory now that my dad had a difficult time setting up the tent, but somehow worked it out and he was proud of the task. With some soda pop and our fishing poles, we went down to the river to have one of those seminal father-son bonding experiences.

The air told me first that we were someplace special. It whooshed, delivering the cool message of a fast river on a hot summer day. Then a muffled sound came from behind, back at camp, and we turned around and could see through the trees that the tent had collapsed. My dad said something under his breath and started up the hill, then turned back to me and said, "Don't go in the river!" They were the wrong words.

At first I put my hand in the water to swish it around and was fascinated by the vitality, the power that coursed through my arm, into my chest, and up into my brain. I looked in the middle of the stream, where tiny waves burst into a million gems and then disappeared. It was magic, pure magic. I stepped into the river to my waist and felt the water wrap around and hug me and then tug at me like a dog pulling a blanket. Another step and the water reached my chest and pulled me down wholly into its vigorous embrace. I was being washed downstream. Effortlessly, the current was carrying me away from confinement, toward new and unknown adventures. I looked down and watched as a color wheel of pebbles passed beneath me like a cascade of hard candy.

After a few seconds, I kicked my way to shore perhaps a hundred yards downstream. When I crawled back to the land I had changed. My little trip down the river had been the most exhilarating experience of my life. I felt charged with energy, giddy, cleaned, and fresh, more alive than I could remember. I practically skipped back to the fishing poles and sat down with a whole new attitude, and secret.

When my father came back, he never noticed anything different. And I didn't volunteer anything. The August sun had dried my shorts and hair, and I was holding my pole as though it had grown as an extension of my arm since he left. Only my smile was different — larger, knowing. I grew in that little trip, like corn in the night.

GL: *You probably have too many adventures to count. But tell us one of your favorites.*

BANGS: It was the attempt to make the first descent of the Baro River in Ethiopia. A young man drowned, and it haunted me to the degree I almost left the field. But then I recognized a hard truth — that it is better to go forward and be in the ring and perhaps suffer the consequences than to never step at all and die on the inside.

In Edmund Burke's 1757 essay, "Of the Sublime and Beautiful," he posits that terror is a source of the sublime, that is, it is productive of the strongest emotion which the mind is capable of feeling. If there is a common element to the code of adventure it is the frisson that comes from touching the maw. At the moment of plunge into a giant rapid we are febrile but also unlocked in a way that never happens in the comfort zone, so that the slightest tap makes us shiver to the bottom of our beings.

In Hemingway's classic story, "The Short Happy Life of Francis Macomber," a milquetoast of a man finds an instant of bliss as he fearlessly (and fatally) faces a charging buffalo. I would like to believe that the day of the drowning there [in Ethiopia] allowed a lifetime deep and rich and connected, if only for a flash, and that it was better than a dull and deadly senectitude.

GL: I've never been to Cuba. I see that you visited been there. What are your impressions about the isolated nation?

BANGS: I had the privilege of experiencing Cuba the way millions of Cubans did in the '90s — by bike. On two wheels, I explored the country's landscape and encountered the oddities and eccentricities of local life that often get passed by when you are in the enclosed comfort of a car, taxi, bus, etc. With my then-7-year-old son and some close friends, two of whom claim Cuba as their favorite place to cycle, we pedaled through the island country marveling at the crumbling yet vibrant buildings and a culture both steeped in history and alive with the tinkering of innovative individuals and the excitement of new beginnings. At times, the cycling could be challenging — traversing rocky roads, swerving between trucks, avoiding ditches — but all of this added to the enjoyment of raw experience. Cuba was a Class V adventure, and I'd go back in a heartbeat.

GL: For well over a decade now, we've been hearing about experiential travel. What does this travel style mean to you?

BANGS: Every destination has an infinitely deep well of cultural experiences, from the rich backgrounds and variety of your block to the souks, bodegas and bazaars on the other side of the world. The trick is to be curious, open-minded, to turn over the rock, and to ask questions wherever you are. Proust famously said, "The real voyage of discovery consists not in seeking new landscapes, but in having new eyes," and I couldn't agree more.

GL: What destinations do you keep going back to and why?

BANGS: To me, travel is not so much about departing and returning to destinations as much as it is the constant thirst, or you could say obsession, to move. There is no place unworthy of re-visitation and there is an infinity of places yet to explore. I never know where I'll end up. My goal is only to continue the quest—to distant lands, or perhaps my own hometown, to uncharted territories, or perhaps familiar ones. All I know is that I will go, I will explore, and, no matter the destination or the circumstances, I will leave with weary legs and a spirit brimming with new adventures.

GL: *Are there any travel providers you recommend for providing a sustainable and local experience?*

BANGS: Mountain Travel Sobek (*mtsobek.com*) is a company I co-founded and, if you're looking for adventure, I can't recommend them enough. With these guys, I helped lead 35 first descents down some of the world's wildest rivers. MTS are dedicated to providing an up-close, interactive experience for travelers while supporting a number of organizations whose ethos is rooted in sustainability and low-impact involvement in the communities and environments they are exploring.

DON GEORGE: Travel editor

Don George found his passion in life, combining his devotion to both travel and writing, after living on fellowships in Athens for a year and in Tokyo for two years. His first regular job was as a travel writer for the *San Francisco Examiner*. From there, he would become the travel editor of the San Francisco *Examiner & Chronicle*.

Over the years, George received dozens of awards for his writing and editing, including the prestigious Society of American Travel Writers' Lowell Thomas Travel Journalist of the Year Award. Tempted by the irresistible allure of cyberspace, Don then founded the groundbreaking travel site, Wanderlust, on Salon.com.

George has also been editor-at-large for National Geographic Traveler; global travel editor for Lonely Planet Publications; special features editor for BBC Travel; and editor of Geographic Expedition's online magazine, Wanderlust: Literary Journeys for the Discerning Travel. He is the author of *The Way of Wanderlust: The Best Travel Writing of Don George* and *Lonely Planet's Guide to Travel Writing*. He continues to visit new destinations and inspire others to travel.

Travel writer Don George, is an editor-at-large for National Geographic Traveler, and is shown here in Delos, Greece.

Q & A with Don George

GOING LOCAL: How did you start traveling?

GEORGE: My family used to take a car trip somewhere every summer from our Connecticut home — North Carolina, upstate New York, Nova Scotia. My parents loved to travel and passed their love on to me. The summer between my sophomore and junior years in college, my family took my brother and me to London and Paris.

The following summer, I went to Paris on my own on the Princeton Summer Work Abroad program. I lived with a family in the 16th arrondissement, bumbled and stumbled through daily life using my college French, and had many wonderful adventures with many wonderful new French friends. That was just the beginning. The next summer, after graduation, I lived again in Paris on the same program, then moved to Athens, Greece, for a year on an Athens College Teaching Fellowship. The rest is wanderlust.

GL: As more travelers seek out local experiences, what inspires you when you travel the world?

GEORGE: Encountering and absorbing newness inspires me. I love meeting new people, experiencing new places, and learning about history, arts, traditions, foods and beliefs — the whole patchwork of humanity. Essentially, my quest is to learn, to experience, as much of the globe as I can. And within that, the goodness and kindness of people everywhere inspire me greatly. I have always found that if you approach the world with an open heart and mind, you will be welcomed and embraced the same way.

GL: What are some of your favorite destinations?

GEORGE: The three places where I have lived abroad — France and Greece, because they opened me up to the wonders of the world right out of college, when I was trying to decide what to do with my life. And Japan, because it showed me that the life assumptions I grew up with are not necessarily shared by the rest of the world, and because I met my wife there. She has been an integral part of my life's adventures ever since.

GL: Let's say you've just won the lottery and have a pile of cash you can use to travel wherever you want in the world, with whomever you want to take along. Where would you go and why?

GEORGE: This is a mind-boggling question. Let's say that pile of cash is so big that, not simply can I go wherever I want in the world with whomever I want to take along, but that I can take a year off from all the monthly writing and editing responsibilities that support me. In that case, I would travel slowly around the world, visiting a mixture of the places that have changed my life — France, Greece, Japan, Bali, Australia — and places that entice me and that I haven't yet visited: Bhutan, Tibet, Vietnam, Laos, South Africa, Brazil and the Amazon. I would have a constantly changing caravansary of family and friends with me: It would be a magical moveable feast!

GL: Paris is arguably the most beautiful and intoxicating city in the world, but your love for the City of Light runs deeper. Can you explain?

GEORGE: I first moved to Paris as a French literature undergraduate on a Princeton summer work-abroad program. Living with an aristocratic French family in shabby 16th-arrondissement splendor, I sipped the simultaneous thrills of inhabiting the past, surrounded by 18th-century family portraits, armoires and settees, and rewriting the present in a foreign tongue. My providential presence provided the 20-something heir of the family and his exuberant fiancée with the perfect excuse to concoct elaborate picnics and parties, and by the middle of the summer, I had a new answer when people asked me what I was doing in Paris: "J'étudie la bonne vie française," or, "I'm studying the good life, French-style."

When I moved back for a second summer on the same program, everything was different. This time I had the confidence to tackle the city on my own, Having just graduated, I felt exhilaratingly untethered; life stretched before me like a grand boulevard of possibilities, all intriguing alleys and archways. After a withering week looking for lodging, I discovered a dream place on the fashionable Rue de Rivoli, just opposite the glorious green Jardin des Tuileries. I was supposed to stay confined to the former maid's rooms in the interior of this sprawling apartment, but after a few days the owners left for a month on the Mediterranean, and that evening I found a way to unlock the door into the main salon. Towering French windows opened onto the Tuileries deepening into twilight, and as I gazed in wonder, the summer Ferris wheel's lights began to blink like fireflies and the majestic sounds of an open-air orchestra swelled on the breeze.

GL: Any amazing encounters or out-of-the-moment exchanges?

GEORGE: One evening in Paris, I was walking home from work and came upon two college students from Alabama who were clearly lost. I helped the young women find their way back to their hotel, which turned out to be the hallowed Ritz. In gratitude their, parents invited me to join them the next two nights, first for the famous duck dinner at the opulent Tour d'Argent—"one of the most expensive restaurants in Paris," my envious colleagues told me the next day—and then for the flashy, fleshy fête at the Moulin Rouge, which somehow led to a Champagne-fueled soirée back at the Ritz, until the bells rang in the rosy dawn.

GL: Do you have a least-favorite traveled country?

GEORGE: I've truly never been to a country haven't liked. I realize how saccharin that may sound, but even in the most challenging places, I've always found someone to connect with and something valuable to learn. And the more we travel, the bigger we become.

GL: What is a mistake that you made in your travels, or an embarrassing travel moment?

GEORGE: I think the worst travel moment was the time I just missed a connecting train from Greece to Turkey and was abandoned in a truly middle-of-nowhere border town called Python for about eight hours, until the next train came through. All I had for diversion was my journal — but as it turned out, that was more than enough.

GL: What travel authors or books might you recommend and/or have influenced you?

GEORGE: First of all, I think a thorough grounding in English, American and French literature has been a great help to me, so before focusing on travel writers, I would very strongly recommend that budding travel writers read, read, read and read some more — not just travel writers, but great fiction writers and poets too. In some ways, my most profound influences were James Joyce and William Butler Yeats, TS Eliot and Charles Baudelaire, Hemingway and Fitzgerald.

But as for travel writers: My favorite book of all is *The Snow Leopard* by Peter Matthiessen, a masterful combination of intensely personal exploration and intensely vivid description, infused with a searing, soaring humanity, spirituality and intelligence. Also on the list, in no particular order: Paul Theroux, especially *The Great Railway Bazaar*; Bruce Chatwin, *In Patagonia*; John McPhee, *Coming into the Country*; Annie Dillard, *Pilgrim at Tinker Creek*; Pico Iyer, *Video Night in Kathmandu*; Tim Cahill, *Pass the Butterworms*; and Jan Morris, *Journeys*. Just about anything by Jan Morris is transcendent, but *Journeys* is a good place to start.

GL: Do you have any inspiration for travelers wishing to jump start a career in travel media?

GEORGE: If you want to launch yourself as a travel writer today, it's essential to create a portfolio website. This is a digital billboard where you can showcase your biography, your published articles, essays and books, your photos, your past and upcoming travels, and your social media feeds. In the ever-more-congested world of travel content creators, a portfolio site is a great place for readers/viewers — and editors — to find you. So: Build your portfolio platform now!

PETER GREENBERG: Broadcast journalist

Peter Greenberg describes himself as "a curious global explorer" — a multiple Emmy Award-winning investigative reporter and travel editor for CBS News. Peter has been fortunate to visit some of the world's astonishing places and has been touched by both the beauty and tragedy of the human condition.

Peter Greenberg, on location at Elephant Rock at Al Ula, Saudie Arabia.

Q & A with Peter Greenberg

GOING LOCAL: Peter, you've had quite an illustrious career in travel. Who were some of your early influencers?

GREENBERG: My influencers were the legendary journalists and writers who traveled, ranging from (Ernest) Hemingway to (Paul) Theroux; and my grandfather, one of the original "front page" reporters for William Randolph Hearst in Los Angeles in the 1930s. And then, believe it or not, Mark Twain. Read his book, *Innocents Abroad,* and you'll quickly discover why.

GL: Success comes in many forms, and you've accomplished so much as a travel insider, including your leading role as "the Travel Detective." What do you consider your greatest accomplishment?

GREENBERG: It gets down to a definition of travel journalism itself. For me, it's not about pretty destinations, lovely London or beautiful Bermuda. It's about the process of travel, and my work as an investigative reporter in aviation accidents and aviation safety.

GL: Who are some of the memorable people you've met in your travels?

GREENBERG: It ranges from heads of state — the King of Jordan, the presidents of. Peru and Ecuador, the prime ministers of Israel, Poland and New Zealand (come of whom have been part of my Royal Tour series on PBS) — to the people who really make a difference. I think of William Magalla, an Egyptian cab driver working in New York; Rocky Talese, who helps run the ramp at JFK for Delta; boat captains in Bangkok and on the Nile River and at Long Island, New York; the housekeepers at hotels and the skycaps at the airport, just to name a few. These are some of the folks who are great storytellers and who enlighten me every day with the real truth in travel.

GL: Is there a place or time on your travels where you've been afraid?

GREENBERG: Once in Guatemala, I asked the president about torturing civilians. I was then immediately hustled out of the palace and deported. Once in Port Said, I was arrested as a spy for taking pictures of sunken Egyptian warships after the 1973 war. Then there was the Israel/Syria border in 1970, targeted with mortar fire and nowhere to run; in Khartoum, during the civil war in Sudan; in Kuwait, during Gulf War One. And let's not forget waiting for the 6 train in New York.

GL: While I (Nick) was in Istanbul right after the October 2016 bombing, you interviewed me on your radio show, Peter Greenberg Worldwide. What do you say to people who ask if travel is safe?

GREENBERG: I always ask people, when it comes to travel safety: Are you talking about terrorism or car traffic? With exceedingly few exceptions, I worry more about being hit by the Madison Avenue bus than any act of terrorism. I have always believed that, even though they may be well-intentioned, most U.S. State Department advisories are misleading and ignite misguided, fear-based decisions.

My criteria for where I wouldn't go, based on safety, are locations where no one is in control. Would I go to Iran tomorrow? Yes, I know who is in control. North Korea? Yes, for the same reasons. But what about parts of Yemen, Chechnya, Syria, Ukraine? No, because I don't know who's in control. Of the roughly 196 countries in the world, I'd go to about 188 of them tomorrow.

GL: *What has travel taught you about people?*

GREENBERG: That in the end, it creates essential common ground, the basis for great conversation and learning. Shared experiences bring different people, cultures and politics together, whether they like it or not, and build unanticipated and unexpected bridges of understanding.

GL: *What advice would you give to a college graduate or any young person contemplating traveling the world versus beginning a career?*

GREENBERG: I don't separate the two. As a journalist, I began my career by traveling! Pick an area of expertise and specialize in it, then travel to pursue those stories. I'm an investigative reporter who loves to travel. I simply combined the two.

GL: *You speak of two kinds of airline baggage: carry-on and lost. Are you still shipping your luggage within the U.S. and attempting to travel with carry-on bags only on international flights?*

GREENBERG: In recent years, I've gotten even smarter: On domestic flights, just carry-on. On international flights, I do check bags but I do whatever I can to not book connecting flights.

GL: *As much as we love to travel, we're not big fans of the travel process: TSA, airports, long lines and delays. As you fly over 300,000 miles a year, what advice do you give travelers to ease the process?*

GREENBERG: Actually, I now fly over 420,000 miles a year. But one thing hasn't changed: There are 47 points of abuse that await every traveler, from the moment they make reservations to the time they stumble back home hoping their luggage was on the same flight they were. My job, as I define it, is not just to identify those 47 points of abuse, but to work to mitigate them before I ever leave home. My one piece of advice, which is also my mantra, is to never take a "no" from someone not empowered to give you a "yes" in the first place.

GL: How do you respond when, as a traveler, you find yourself in a potentially dangerous or uncomfortable situation? Can you give an example?

GREENBERG: The first thing you need to do is to park your ego. Find the person in control and then don't talk about the situation or yourself. Talk about them; put yourself in their shoes. For me, navigating dangerous situations requires the same principles used in hostage negotiations. It doesn't have to be adversarial. And in the end, if you're lucky, you'll work with that person in control together as a team to figure it out.

PATRICIA SCHULTZ: 1,000 Places to See

Patricia Schultz is the author of the #1 New York Times bestsellers *1,000 Places to See Before You Die* and *1,000 Places to See in the United States and Canada Before You Die.* A veteran travel journalist with more than 25 years' experience, she has written for guidebook publishers Frommer's and Berlitz and periodicals including *The Wall Street Journal* and *Travel Weekly.* She also executive-produced a Travel Channel television show based on *1,000 Places to See.* Her home base is New York City.

Ten beautiful women surround prolific author Patricia Schultz in Malawi, Africa.

Q & A with Patricia Schultz

GOING LOCAL: People speak different languages and they do crazy weird things, different from us; but at the end of the day, how very similar we are. Travel opens your head to all of these things then reduces it to the very simple and very fundamental. How has travel changed your life?

SCHULTZ: I'm a better person. I'm less prejudiced, I'm more accepting, I'm more tolerant, I'm humbled, I'm less arrogant. I see other ways, peoples, traditions, customs, and other people's histories. If you stay at home and merely study it from a book or a flat screen (most people don't even do that), that's a start and it's a very admirable start; but I think when you get up and out there and see it in the three-dimensional and in the here-and-now versus just a more static way, it affects you, only then, in ways huge and subtle.

GL: Since today's traveler is seeking out local experiences. What advice would you give unseasoned travelers seeking unique and unforgettable encounters?

SCHULTZ: Ask yourself, what are your interests? Then choose destinations that make you sit up and listen. What people do you want to meet? What culture is calling you? How will you experience the destination?

Sit down and have a conversation with yourself or your other half. What has always piqued your interest? What strikes you on a personal level for reasons you don't know? For instance, why have you always dreamed of going to, say, Fiji? Why has Italy always had you salivate? (That's a good word for Italy!) Why has the culture of England, with which America shares so much, always fascinated you? And also, what is it generally that interests you? Food, natural beauty, design, culture, music? Would you get on a plane and go to Austin for the music or to Vienna for the music? And if so, does that interest your other half?

With a couple, there is always some degree of compromise — if not for the destination, then how you experience the destination or what kind of budget you're going to blow. The more you know about your other half, the less conflict and disagreement there will be, because you know what makes the other one happy and you know what makes you happy. Mark Twain had this wonderful quote about how you never really know someone until you travel with them. So the first trip can be a real eye-opener. Ideally, you'd take from that and plan the next trip accordingly, so that you don't go to someplace you know is not going to be met with a lot of enthusiasm. How often do we travel? Do you want strife? Do you want to spend all of that money and effort and energy to go someplace that the other 50 percent of the team is just not into?

GL: As travel is all about experiences, and the new buzzword is "experiential travel," one way to immerse in the local landscape is to attend festivals. What are some of your favorite international festivals

SCHULTZ: I've been to the Salzburg Festival in Austria, the Montreux Jazz Festival in Switzerland, and Carnival in Rio, which is pretty remarkable. If you don't like crowds, you just don't go to some of these festivals. I've been to some lesser festivals, too, which can be just as enthusiastically celebrated, such as Carnival in Barranquilla, Colombia, and the biggest in the Caribbean, in Trinidad and Tobago. The Carnival before Mardi Gras in New Orleans is just hysterical because those people are serious. It's always fun when you see the local people as well as the travelers and tourists.

All throughout Europe in the summertime there are music festivals; and there's a big Inca Festival in Cusco, which is the jumping-off point for Machu Picchu in Peru. My book is filled with these kinds of quirky, lesser-known festivals. ... Argentina has a really interesting Gaucho Festival right outside of Buenos Aires, and in Buenos Aires they have this huge international Tango Festival where some of the best talent is not from Argentina but from Russia and China and from all over the world.

GL: If you had to choose one destination the keeps calling you back, where would it be?

SCHULTZ: Although my list of favorites is a long one, since you ask for only one, I must admit that it is Italy to which I return most frequently. For a country of its size, the number and variety of highlights — many of them unique to Italy — know few rivals. Italy, for example, has more UNESCO World Heritage Sites than any other country. Much of its magic is found in small medieval hamlets and stuck-in-time hill towns.

But its principal cities of monumental palazzos and world-class museums are what lure me to come and explore. Florence flourished as the cradle of the Renaissance, while Rome boasts 25 centuries of unparalleled history. Venice stands apart. "La Repubblica Serenissima" was a ruling city and maritime republic built on the water in a way that still stumps historians and engineers. It confuses and enchants, and bids you to throw away the map (or turn off your GPS) and let yourself wander back through time. You could spend a lifetime in Venice, but other adventures call: neighboring cities that in their heyday were some of Europe's most important, still worth visiting today for their artistic and historical legacies: Verona, Padua, Bologna, Varenna. Each is a precious gem in Northern Italy's crown.

GL: *Patricia, much has been said about Cuba, ever since President Obama's 2015 phone call with Raul Castro made history and stunned the world. Is Cuba high on your World Travel List?*

SCHULTZ: Cuba is on everyone's lips these days, although there remain infrastructure issues with the limited number of hotels in Cuba. But should you go now? My answer is a resounding "Yes!" While Cuba may not be for everyone, my trip with International Expeditions was an experience simply not to be found elsewhere. Just 90 miles from our shores (and a hard-to-believe 45-minute flight from Miami), it offers an experience that feels light years away. It is a place of romance and intrigue, at once elegant and downtrodden, uplifting and at times heartbreaking. It is important to note that Cuba is not for the average traveler, and an adjustment of expectations is important.

GL: *What is a destination that adventurers might not know but which should be on the traveler's radar?*

SCHULTZ: The "Stans" — that is, Kazakhstan, Kyrgyzstan, Tajikistan, Uzbekistan, and Turkmenistan — are the heartland of Central Asia. I doubt most travelers could place the five in order on a map. Uzbekistan has always been the region's heart and cradle of culture. Its top-three destinations are spectacular: Samarkand, Bukhara and Khiva, whose Old Towns (all impressively restored, although at times overzealously so) are an incredible maze of exotic architecture, covered bazaars and gorgeous decorative arts that are a glorious blur in my memory. Now is the time to visit these countries as, surely, change is on the way.

GL: *What about elsewhere in Asia? Where do you recommend travelers keep in mind?*

SCHULTZ: Taiwan remains Asia's best-kept secret. Today only around 65,000 tourists from North America visit Taiwan each year. The island nation has much to be desired. Taipei has long enjoyed a reputation as having the finest food in northeast Asia — most say more delicious and varied than its mainland counterpart, Beijing. Another must-visit in Taipei is the recently renovated National Palace Museum. There are over 15,000 temples in Taiwan.

It's a scenic three-hour drive through the breathtaking beauty of the island's east coast to the steeply chiseled Taroko Gorge. The 12-mile-long road that cuts through the national park (one of eight on the island) is an engineering marvel, involving 38 tunnels and a procession of bridges through the dramatic marble-walled landscape. A network of easy hiking trails allows you to enjoy it up close and personal. Taiwan's most famous natural wonder is named for the aboriginal Taroko people who still live there.

A week barely gave me time to skim the island's highlights. They were mighty impressive. I learned a lot about the incredibly friendly people and life in the shadow of the giant neighbor just 100 miles west across the Strait of Taiwan. As Taiwan pursues its separate identity, it is resigned to being unrecognized by the major powers of the world. Yet it carries on with homeland pride — and I, for one, was won over.

GL: Can you mention a few other nations that travelers should not miss that are on your World Travel List?

SCHULTZ: Myanmar (the former Burma) is one. See it while time still stands still. If you really want to get away from tourists, Papua New Guinea is a must-see destination. If you feel the world is shrinking and there are few places left where tourism has yet to leave its imprint, head to this island nation. There is really nothing quite like it in the world.

Scotland is another nation I love. With warm and inviting people, it's well worth getting in a car, driving the whiskey trail and getting lost in its miles of lochs.

Colombia may have once been an unsafe travel destination, but in the past 10 years it has cleaned up its image. My stay in the "Coffee Triangle," which immersed me in the rich agricultural life of a lush landscape, was an unforgettable experience. Cartagena, with its vibrant art and music scene, is a low-key Caribbean gem.

I am admittedly enthralled by all things African: A safari is something you simply must do before you die. But I'm also fascinated by Ethiopia. Africa's oldest independent country boasts a unique culture and heritage, and it holds a place as one of the oldest locations of human life known to scientists.

JAMES MICHAEL DORSEY: Global explorer

James Michael Dorsey is an award-winning author, marine biologist, photographer, and lecturer who has traveled extensively through 56 countries. When he is not on the water interacting with whales, he visits remote tribal cultures to write personal narratives about his travels.

His articles and essays about marine wildlife strive to enlighten and entertain those who may not have the same access to remote areas or who prefer to travel from the confines of

their easy chair. He is an active fellow of the Explorers Club and member emeritus of the
Adventurers Club of Los Angeles.

Cultural explorer James Dorsey has visited the remotest parts of Africa and Asia.
Here, Dorsey immerses with Voodoo priest, in the Taneka region of Benin.

Q & A with James Michael Dorsey

GOING LOCAL: Tell us where you grew up and who were some of your role models in taking on a life of travel?

DORSEY: I grew up in Los Angeles watching the great travel shows on early television. Never missed an episode of Lowell Thomas, "Seven League Boots" or "Travel with the Linker Family." I also watched "This Is Your Life" with the late great John Goddard, who later became both a friend and mentor. There are probably not many people reading this who will remember those days.

GL: While you are traveling, what inspires you?

DORSEY: Meeting people who by my country's standards are dirt poor, living every day without bitterness, jealousy or a desire for a different way of life. People who would not trade their life for mine because they know that no one way of living is any better than another. People who find happiness in the smallest of pleasures and are grateful for what they have, no matter how little.

GL: As our book takes on the theme of "Going Local," blending into local society and becoming a better traveler, can you tell us about an epic immersion with inhabitants while on the road?

DORSEY: I spent a month crossing the lower Sahara of Mali with Tuareg nomads. We rode from Arouane to Timbuktu. They were so honored that I wanted to immerse myself in their way of life that they dressed me as one of them, gave me a camel, invited me to their ceremonies, and treated me as a brother. We lived on goat and rice, rode 10 hours a day, and spent our evenings under a silver moon trading stories of each other's very different lives.

GL: To us, there's nothing like sharing a meal. Food, people and culture blend harmoniously. It changes a traveler's perspective on people. You learn a lot about society when you break bread in new surroundings. What was one of your favorite encounters sharing a meal with locals?

DORSEY: I was invited to a dinner in Xiangxing province, China, by the head of the local Communist party. It was on a Chinese air force base overrun with feral cats. I could not eat many of the dishes being served, like eyeballs and boiled rabbit embryos. To not eat would have been an insult to my hosts but the food made my stomach turn. I was saved when one of the stray cats stationed itself under the table where I could pass scraps from my plate and make it look as though I were eating the meal. I thought I was busted when the cat belched, but everyone thought it was me, and belching after a meal in that part of China is a compliment to good food, so that cat gave me great face that night.

GL: You are a prolific traveler and have certainly been all over the world. Are there any countries you keep returning to again and again? Why?

DORSEY: I have covered much of West Africa to investigate voodoo, especially in Benin, where it supposedly originated and where it is still the official national religion. Also, Baja California in Mexico, where I have worked in a gray whale sanctuary as the resident naturalist for 22 seasons. I have always felt more at home in remote places than in large cities.

GL: If you had to decide which destination has been the most influential in your life outside of the United States, where would you choose and why?

DORSEY: Ethiopia, because it probably has the oldest selection of cultures on the planet, many unchanged since the time of Christ. They believe they have the original Arc of the Covenant in a church vault in Axum. I have visited eight different tribal cultures in Ethiopia and found each of them to be uniquely fascinating.

GL: Like you, we are fascinated by what we've seen of Africa, including over-land travel from Nairobi to Cape Town. We want to delve deeper into Africa. Tell us some of your favorite encounters in some of the more remote regions of the continent or about encounters with tribes of Africa.

DORSEY: I underwent an exorcism in a voodoo ceremony in Benin, was shot at by bandits on the summit of a volcano in Ethiopia, and was used as bait during a baboon hunt by a hunter-gatherer clan in Tanzania. Also, I attended a very different wedding in Ethiopia's Omo Valley where the women were voluntarily scourged as a way to show their love for their clan. I have also smoked local ganja with numerous witch doctors and medicine men. That is besides riding with nomads in the Sahara.

GL: In recent years, I have been astonished by the whales I've seen on expedition sailings in the Sea of Cortez, Greenland and Antarctica. As you are a cetacean specialist, tell us about your love for these mostly gentle giants and where you have spotted them.

DORSEY: Twenty-seven years ago on a sea kayaking trip, I encountered my first killer whale when it came right up to me. I was so intrigued that I began to study cetaceans and have spent the subsequent 2½ decades working on the water on and off as a cetacean naturalist. I have chased whales all along the rim of fire from Alaska to the tip of Baja, Mexico. My latest book, *The Lagoon*, is a memoir of those years.

GL: What advice would you give younger travelers, or even older empty nester explorers, on starting a career or second career in travel writing?

DORSEY: I find it hard to be encouraging about that since everyone with an iPhone 14 now seems to lay claim to being a "travel writer." If you want to stand out, you need to immerse yourself in the subject, and not just join a tour group that spends two hours taking photos before returning to happy hour at the hotel. Do your homework before going, learn as much as you can about the people and place before you get there, and be ready for things to be radically different from your familiar. It is embarrassing to hear people constantly comparing where they are to what it is like at home. Experiencing the difference is the essence of going in the first place. More than anything, show your hosts respect, because their culture was probably thriving for thousands of years before your own.

GL: Please briefly explain the Explorers Club and Adventurers Club of Los Angeles, of which you fondly mention your association.

DORSEY: The Explorers Club was established in 1904 and membership is based primarily on field work. It is about true exploration, from which you learn and teach through publication, as opposed to simple adventure. The Adventurers Club was established in 1921 and is oriented to those who simply wish to live a less mundane life off the beaten path. We like to say we are the only club whose members have nothing in common, as we have no set criteria for membership. We have astronauts, mountaineers, divers, etcetera — you name them and you can meet them at the Adventurers Club.

JUDITH FEIN: Travel journalist

Judith Fein is a multiple award-winning travel journalist who has contributed to over 100 publications. With her photojournalist husband, Paul Ross, Judith gives keynote talks, leads workshops, teaches travel writing, and takes people on immersive trips. She is the author of award-winning books *The Spoon from Minkowitz* (about emotional genealogy and ancestral travel), and *Life Is a Trip: The Transformative Magic of Travel.*

Judith lived in Europe and North Africa for about a decade, helmed an experimental theater troupe, and was a Hollywood screenwriter for 13 years. She was a regular on public radio as "The Savvy Traveler" for six years. She resides in Santa Fe, New Mexico. To join her blog list or learn about workshops and trips, go to *GlobalAdventure.us.*

Award-winning storyteller Judith Fein relaxes with Sikh companions in India.

Q & A with Judith Fein

GOING LOCAL: I always marvel when I read that you've been publishing since the age of 6. I'd like to know more about the early days of your life and your positive role models.

FEIN: I grew up in a middle-class family. Money was spent on books, travel and theater. It was as natural as eating and breathing. The question was never *if* we would travel. It was *where*.

GL: When did you first discover that you had a a lust for travel?

FEIN: Probably in utero.

GL: How has traveled changed your life?

FEIN: I wouldn't say that travel has changed my life. I would say that travel *IS* my life. I try to face every day, whether at home or on the road, with a traveler's mentality. That means saying yes to new things, enjoying and seeking out people who are different from me, asking questions, being really interested in anything I don't know about, appreciating culture in all its quirky and fascinating manifestations, listening deeply, keeping an open heart.

GL: What are a few of your favorite countries, for local experiences, and what do you love about these destinations?

FEIN: Portugal, Tunisia, Georgia, Colombia, Mexico, Turkey, Guatemala, Vanuatu, Micronesia ... and anywhere else that retains authenticity.

GL: Like you, we have been traveling our entire lives, seeking authentic travel moments. Now, it's even a buzzword: "Experiential travel" is even on the minds of luxury travelers. What does it mean to you?

FEIN: A buzzword? Well, maybe it is a buzzword, but it has always, to me, been the only way to travel. It is a mindset. A heart set. I edit a website for experiential travel stories, *yourlifeisatrip.com*. There are about 170 writers. They write about experiences that have changed, inspired, taught, amused, challenged, frightened and touched them. Again, travel is not separate from life. The way you live is the way you travel. Jetlag is not a prerequisite for experiential living and travel; an open heart and curiosity are. When my husband and I teach travel writing and photography, we include how to have significant travel experiences so you have something to write about.

GL: We like how you attempt to guide travelers to jump into local society. Most locals are kind and wonderful people — just like us!

FEIN: Yes, seek out locals and talk to them. Ask them where they go to eat, drink, party, relax and get inspired. Once you are engaged in a conversation, you may find that you get an invitation to join them. Go. Say "yes"! Unless it is dangerous, always say yes. If language barriers are stopping you, don't worry; you will always find someone who can communicate in decent English. And it's a chance to dust off your high school French or Spanish and not be afraid of making a thousand errors.

Don't be competitive. Don't try to find the most expensive this or the hottest that so you can go home and practice one-upmanship with your friends. The trip is for *you,* not to impress others. Be curious. Ask questions. People love to talk about themselves and their culture and lives. Really listen.

GL: *Why should travelers seek out opportunities to be part of the local landscape?*

FEIN: Because being separate from people and places impoverishes life. Engaging enriches life. It is that simple. Also, when you engage, you are an ambassador for peace. You leave behind a good impression of the country you come from. You would never want to go to war with a country you have visited.

GL: *We like to use the term "going local." What life lessons have you learned by merging into local society?*

FEIN: I wrote a book, *Life Is a Trip: The Transformative Magic of Travel*, about 14 life lessons I learned from 14 different cultures. I think your questions are wonderful. As for truly merging, I think the merging is temporary. Then you go back home, and carry a piece of the country with you in your heart and mind.

I focus on the people and the cultures I encounter around the world. I think that learning from and connecting to others is good for the soul and good for world peace. You and I share a similar mantra, telling travelers to "go outside your comfort zone." Indeed, one must go outside. Stretch. Try things that are new and unfamiliar. If you are a little uncomfortable, stick with it. It can yield great results. Everything I say about traveling pertains to life itself. You are a traveler in life. Your life is a trip. You do not have to wait to go to Peru to live like a traveler, to remember what is important, to focus on what matters. That is the biggest secret I can share. You, your life and your travels are all one.

GL: *What are some of your favorite encounters or interactions on your travels?*

FEIN: Teaching kids to count to 10 in English. Becoming foolish by trying something I am not good at. Experiencing local healers. Communicating in a language I do not speak. Learning from elders about their lives, how they grew up and how things have changed.

GL: *What misconceptions did you discover by visiting a destination and seeing life firsthand?*

FEIN: I seldom have preconceptions when I travel. I leave in ignorance, do little preparation, and arrive ready to learn.

GL: *What is a unique or strange accommodation where you have stayed?*

FEIN: I have stayed in hotels that cost thousands of dollars a night. I have slept in primitive huts, in a tent at temple ruins in Cambodia, and on the floor of a Maori meeting house in New Zealand. I stayed at wine estates in Portugal's Douro valley and the music-themed Aria Hotel in Prague. On a remote island in Vanuatu, I dodged bugs the size of baseballs and showered with a hose slung over a piece of cement. On the deck of a dangerously overcrowded boat headed to the outer islands of Yap, in Micronesia, I slept miserably. I confess that I enjoy comfort and hot water.

GL: What are some off-the-beat encounters or blue moments that you have had?

FEIN: The blue moments fade, they really do. I shudder for a moment when I think back on them, and then they are quickly replaced in my mind by silver memories.

GL: Have you encountered or lived with indigenous people or tribes? How was your experience?

FEIN: My heart sings when I encounter people whose traditions and customs and food go way back. I love that they have that deep connection. It makes me connect more to my own traditions and my own ancestors.

GL: Before travel and cooking shows, food might not have been a primary reason to visit a destination. Never before has cuisine become such a large part of one's travel experience. Can you name encounters you've had with local food culture?

FEIN: I am a bit dismayed that so much of the Travel Channel is about food. Food is a great way of engaging with a culture. It is a way of exciting your taste buds, trying new foods, getting a window into a culture — but it has become too obsessive for my taste. I loved learning about vodka culture in Russia, experiencing toasts in Georgia, eating at a Maori hangi, eating four hour meals at Michelin-starred restaurants in Portugal, making hot chocolate with Zapotec people in Mexico, hearing the sound of hands slapping tortillas in Guatemala, having the neck of a pottery vessel sliced open and watching the food pour out in Tunisia.

GL: Have you taken any classes, such as language or cooking classes, in your travels?

FEIN: I studied Spanish for two days in Antigua, Guatemala. I was a winemaker for a day in the Douro Valley in Portugal. I took cooking classes in Thailand and Mexico. But all of travel is like being in a fabulous school.

GL: What are some of the destinations that you are recommending to travelers nowadays?

FEIN: Whatever I say will change by the time your book comes out. So my answer is: Go anywhere that calls to you or anywhere you know nothing about.

GL: Even well-established globetrotters have a bucket list. What's on yours?

FEIN: Anywhere I haven't been, period.

GL: In this post-COVID world, never before have travelers sought sustainable travel options, choosing operators treading lightly on pristine lands and local people. Can you comment?

FEIN: In Tokyo, I was surprised to see no graffiti, no trash in the streets — and no trash cans. Millions of people and no detritus? It turns out they take their trash home with them. "Why would I want someone else to pick up after me?" a woman said. Take care of the earth we rent space from, care for other people, use what you need, buy what you like or desire and not to impress others, respect ancient traditions, be generous with others, stop taking selfies, walk as much as you can, take local transportation unless it's not safe, be in awe of and protect pristine lands, and radiate love. It's not just about how you are when you travel. It's about how you are in life.

JEFF GREENWALD: Author and activist

Jeff Greenwald is the author of nine books, including *Shopping for Buddhas* (now in its 25th anniversary edition) , *The Size of the World* (for which he created the first internet travel blog) and *Snake Lake*. His features, profiles and essays have appeared in such publications as *Wired, Smithsonian, Afar, Outside* and the *New York Times Magazine.* Jeff's latest book — *108 Beloved Objects* — was published in 2021 in a limited edition of 108 hardcover copies. It is now available print-on-demand from Amazon.

Adventures at home and in more than 100 foreign lands provided Jeff with rich material for storytelling, and his narrative tales have been featured at "The Moth" and on NPR's "Snap Judgment." His critically acclaimed solo show, "Strange Travel Suggestions," premiered in San Francisco in 2003. In addition, Jeff is the co-founder of *EthicalTraveler.org,* an alliance of travelers supporting human rights, environmental protection and social welfare.

Author Jeff Greenwald's books include Shopping for Buddhas, set in Nepal.

Q & A with Jeff Greenwald

GOING LOCAL: Jeff, you're from the Bronx and now call Oakland, California, home. Many of my New Yorker friends have ultimately ended up in California. How did you end up in the San Francisco Bay Area?

GREENWALD: I was drawn west by a number of books that hinted at literary and artistic opportunities far beyond the ken of my New York life. Especially influential were *On the Road* (Jack Kerouac), *The Electric Kool-Aid Acid Test* (Tom Wolfe), *Sometimes a Great Notion* (Ken Kesey), and a Sierra Club book called *Navaho Wildlands*. All of them ignited my sense of adventure.

GL: What attracted you to become a travel writer?

GREENWALD: Travel invited me to change my focus as a writer. I transitioned gradually from self-involved journal entries to storytelling. After my first trip to Asia in 1979, I published a few stories to *Westways,* and began writing for *Santa Barbara Magazine* and the *Santa Barbara News & Review.* But all this changed in 1983, when I was awarded a Rotary Foundation Fellowship to study journalism in Kathmandu, Nepal. This was the pivotal event in my professional career, as I began writing for international publications like *GEO* and *Islands* and began assembling my first book, *Mr. Raja's Neighborhood*.

GL: Which travel writers and which books should every traveler read?

GREENWALD: There isn't room here for an adequate list, as there are so many! We're all familiar with the big names, including Bill Bryson, Elizabeth Gilbert, Tim Cahill, Beryl Markham, Jan Morris and Pico Iyer. But here are eight lesser-known travel-ish books that brought me a lot of pleasure:

The Devil's Cup by Stewart Lee Allen. *To the Elephant Graveyard* by Tarkin Hall. *Red Mars* by Kim Stanley Robinson. *Last Chance to See* by Douglas Adams. *Meeting Faith* by Faith Adiele. *Invisible Cities* by Italo Calvino. *Not Where I Started From* by Kate Wheeler. *Magic and Mystery in Tibet* by Alexandra David-Neel.

GL: We consider *Shopping for Buddhas* a must-read for global explorers. In our earliest world travels, both of us made Nepal one of the first countries we visited. What makes Nepal such a popular destination?

GREENWALD: I wouldn't say every traveler should visit Nepal, but it does have an unusually rich culture where Hinduism, Buddhism, Islam and animism are marbled together — blended, yet distinct. There's stunning architecture, beautiful wood carvings and metalwork, good food, welcoming people ... and an infinity of microclimates! For the physically adventurous, there's the opportunity to get out of the Kathmandu Valley and explore the Himalaya, for the incomparable scenery and its mix of mountain cultures. Nepal felt deeply familiar from the first time I visited, nearly 45 years ago. But other travelers may find their own spiritual home(s) elsewhere.

GL: We agree that giving back on our travels is intrinsic to our nature. You have a deep history of volunteering in Asia. Please delve into some of your volunteer work in Asia and how it changed you.

GREENWALD: In 1979, during the Cambodian civil war and the rise of Pol Pot, I volunteered with the United Nations High Commissioner for Refugees (UNHCR) and helped build the largest of the refugee camps along the Thai-Cambodian border. And in Nepal, after the 2015 earthquake, I led a photography project that included giving cameras to children in one of the large tent camps in Kathmandu. But to be honest, I haven't done much volunteering in Asia. My work for Mercy Corps in Sri Lanka after the 2005 tsunami was paid, as was my reporting on projects in Fiji and Indonesia sponsored by the wonderful NGO Seacology.

That said, both paid and volunteer work have a profound impact on one's worldview and sense of place. Interacting with local people and helping to meet their needs — whether during life-threatening crises or on community building projects — creates friendships and bonds rarely experienced by casual travelers. One of the obvious perks of travel is bringing back stories, and the best thing about volunteering is hearing the stories of people from completely different geographic and cultural backgrounds.

GL: *Tell us about your global community, Ethical Traveler, and how it empowers travelers to change the world.*

GREENWALD: Ethical Traveler was founded in 2003, taking a page from John Muir's work with the Sierra Club. That was focused on the wilderness. We decided to work globally. "Who better to help change the world," we reasoned, "than those who love to explore it?" While our early work focused on letter-writing campaigns and even boycotts — protesting logging, mining, oil extraction, human-rights violations, and animal cruelty — we later replaced the stick with the carrot.

For the past 12 years or so, our main contribution has been our annual "Ten Best Ethical Destinations" list. To create this list, we gather information about the most attractive and travel-friendly countries in the developing world, and determine which are showing the most commitment to, and progress in, four categories: social welfare, human rights, environmental protection and animal welfare. We announce the winners, often with a public ceremony, in early spring. The idea is that, by visiting these place, travelers can "vote with our wings," supporting nations and governments who are doing the right thing in terms of social justice and sustainability. Our 2023 report, for example, celebrated these 10 countries: Barbados, Belize, Botswana, Cabo Verde, Chile, Costa Rica, Mongolia, Palau, Seychelles and Timor-Leste. A link to the full report can be found on our website *(ethicaltraveler.org)*. Ethical Traveler is a project of the Earth Island Institute, based in Berkeley, California, and founded by the late David Brower, past president of the Sierra Club.

GL: *I was clueless about a career when I was young, in my early 20s. I traveled the world and ultimately created a job for myself in the field of travel. Why should college kids, before or after university, take the time to explore the world?*

GREENWALD: There are many reasons why travel should precede university. For one thing, it gives a context for so many things we choose to study, from archeology and economics to psychology and engineering. It gives us a sense of the global community, and how things like climate change, religion and even revolution shape the world. And the world is ever-changing. The surge in international travel — combined with the fore-mentioned issues related to global warming, over-tourism and political unrest — may make some places, like Israel, Macchu Picchu or the Colorado River Canyon—difficult or impossible to visit in the future.

Finally, there's the unknowable question of our own future. A few years ago, to my astonishment, I was diagnosed with a progressive disease which will drastically limit my own ability to travel. I'm so grateful I traveled the world as early in my life as I did. So seize the day, and embrace the world while you can. Don't wait for some unpredictable future opportunity.

GL: Travel changes us like nothing else. When we share a meal in our host country, the lives of both host and guest change for the better. Name some of your favorite meal-sharing tales.

GREENWALD: My favorite shared-meal activities included attending a Passover seder in Havana; enjoying an incredibly spicy dinner with my Tamil hosts in Sri Lanka; attending an informal kava ceremony with new friends in Fiji; and a lavish Shabbat dinner with a rabbi in Jerusalem, followed a few days later by a simple but delicious meal with a Palestinian family in Hebron. But the experience I've shared the most was not exactly my favorite. I was the guest of honor in a very remote Nepali village, and served an impossibly generous meal of rice, vegetables, lentils, a fried egg, and a roasted chicken leg — all on a polished brass tray, which I accidentally knocked over onto the dirt floor.

GL: We are big believers in "just winging it." We tend not to overprepare, instead leaving our journey, in part, to chance encounters. What are your thoughts on this?

GREENWALD: I'm in complete agreement. Using the food and lodging recommendations in a guidebook is often the best way to meet fellow travelers — but experiences with locals require an invitation to serendipity. My whole life in travel has been inspired by a sentiment expressed in Kurt Vonnegut Jr.'s book *Cat's Cradle:* "Strange travel suggestions are dancing lessons from God."

GL: We all have places that we have missed. We can name Easter Island, Papua New Guinea, and the "-stans" of Central Asia as places that we have yet to visit. What are some of yours?

GREENWALD: I totally recommend Rapa Nui (Easter Island), it's one of the most surprisingly lovely places I've visited! Personally, I do have a few regrets. I wish I'd gone on safari to witness a big wildlife migration in South Africa (I've only ever been to north and west Africa); that I'd make my way to the South Pole (or at least to Antarctica); and that I had spent some time exploring Ireland before the tech revolution changed so much of its character (or so I've heard).

Mainly, though, I wish I'd been able to experience the advent of affordable space tourism. And not just Earth orbit, but a return loop around the Moon, as Apollo 11 astronaut Buzz Aldrin has suggested. Seeing planet Earth from a distance, as a glowing blue marble against the blackness of space, must be one of the most transformational experiences a human being can have. But who knows? We're not dead yet!

We shall not cease from exploration, and the end of all our exploring will be to arrive where we started and know the place for the first time. — T.S. Eliot

Chapter Twelve

OUR STORIES:

Nick and John Reflect

"If you're 22, physically fit, hungry to learn and be better, I urge you to travel as far and as widely as possible. Sleep on floors if you have to. Find out how other people live and eat and cook. Learn from them wherever you go." — Anthony Bourdain

When you travel in your "comfort zone," your life is not so different than it might be back in your hometown. Oh, sure, you may have sand and sea beyond the balcony of your resort hotel, but the supermarkets are selling the same soft drinks and frozen dinners, the taxi drivers speak your language, and the restaurants still serve hamburgers and fried chicken.

Perhaps you'll extend yourself a bit and take a trip somewhere like Mexico or Greece, where you may be forced to learn a few words of a foreign language, or chow down on tortillas or souvlaki. You may be pushing the boundaries of that comfort zone. But the basic way of life isn't so different from Hoboken.

The next step, into your *discomfort* zone, is a big one. And that's where we want you to go next. Fear — of the unknown — is always an inhibiting factor. Traveling "light" is a state of mind, and we're not talking about limiting our physical baggage. Go to a hotel, or a hostel, or a guest house, without a reservation. Eat with someone you've never met before. Or eat alone. Take a daylight walk along a street with no map to follow.

This is much less frightening now than it was in past generations when there was no internet, no Wi-fi, no cell phones. Our families and friends may not have expected to hear from us more than once a month, and then by mail if at all. But it was reaching beyond our comfort zones for extended periods that we — that's Nick and John — found our lives truly, forever, changed.

These experiences were more than life-changing. They were life-*defining*. In Nick's case, that happened in the unknown–to-him lands of the Indian subcontinent, in Bangladesh, India and Nepal. For John, Southeast Asia — Indonesia, Malaysia, Thailand, Burma (now Myanmar) — was the catalyst. And once we had tasted the forbidden fruit, we could never really go back.

Nick shows off his catch of piranha while fishing from an Amazon river-boat.

NICK: 13 MONTHS AROUND THE WORLD

I was 24, and had been traveling through Europe since I was 16, taking ferries from Greece to Italy to board trains to traipse around Western Europe. Most of my California friends had already capitulated to the 9-to-5 grind, taking jobs in sales or investment banking or graphic design. I toiled away at side jobs, like selling souvenirs and beer at concerts and sporting events at San Francisco's Candlestick Park in San Francisco while living in my parents' basement.

As I paid no rent, I could stockpile a bit of money to allow me to travel. Greek parents from my generation would seldom kick a kid out of the house. Perhaps at 24, I could have frittered away the hours behind a desk; but I recall telling my friends, "I'm going to keep the dream alive," at least for one more summer. My parents were excited that at least I was returning to my motherland of Greece.

I quickly headed to an old stomping ground. Ios remains today one of the largest party islands in the Mediterranean. If you're 18 to 29, it's the place to be for raucous nightlife, drinking and mingling with like-minded revelers, a great many of them Scandinavians.

Little did I know, as I nursed a Fix beer at the legendary Blue Bar in Chora town, that my life was about to change forever. The facilitators were an offbeat couple from Stockholm, Sven and Maria. With nowhere else to go and nothing better to do, the three of us pounded shot after shot of ouzo, a chalky, milk-like Greek liquor with a mild licorice flavor. Our travels often are not logical; we indulge in the beauty of serendipity.

"Nicky!" Maria suddenly exclaimed. "Why don't you come with us to India and Nepal? It will be great fun!" Dizzy-headed, I first tried to dismiss the thought. "I can't," I said. "I have a return ticket back to San Francisco." But as my buzz kicked in, I found myself mentally, at least, on my way to Bangladesh, the former East Pakistan.

"We bought this great ticket at a bucket shop in Athens," Maria said. "For $280, we fly Biman Bangladesh from Athens to Dhaka, then from Kathmandu to Rangoon to Bangkok."

I barely knew that Bangladesh was the capital of Dhaka — or was it the other way around? I asked Maria, "How do we get from Dhaka to Kathmandu?" "Silly boy," she chided me, more than slightly sloshed. "Through India! You've been overland through Europe many times before. It's the same thing with buses and trains. You'll love it!" I hoped she was right.

The next day I called my dear Greek parents to give them the mindblowing news: "Mom, Dad, I'm not coming home. I'm going to Bangladesh." I worried that my Greek immigrant parents might drop dead on the spot. Much to my surprise, they were at peace with my decision to travel the world. It wasn't as if companies were breaking down the door to hire me. "Just be safe," they said. "Call home and tell us you are well."

In a state of shock, I found my way to a small travel agency, Intertrust Travel, in Athens' Plaka district. Travelers' cheque in hand; I took the plunge into a world previously unknown to me. Dhaka, here I come.

Go with the flow

I could not have chosen a more challenging destination for my first journey outside of North America or Europe. The Indian subcontinent became my classroom. My home-work assignment would be to discover how to navigate this labyrinth of humanity in one of the most densely populated regions of the world.

Coming from San Francisco, a city of fewer than a million people, I had never experi-enced urban hustle and bustle greater than that of hectic, chaotic New York. But nothing in my wildest dreams could have prepared me for Dhaka. I silently reflected: Is this how all of Asia will be? Dhaka was New York on steroids. It was pure bedlam. The blaring snarl of tuk-tuks in the streets, traffic congestion everywhere, a humid nightmare of concrete. I remember saying to Sven: "How does anyone get around here? And how does one get out of here?"

But I soon began to adjust to my new surroundings, meet local people, and even blend in a bit. I adapted to the omnipresent odors of cement and burning rubber. The smells of aromatic Bangladeshi street curries were strangely intoxicating.

Crossing the land border from Bangladesh into India, a burly patrolman insisted that I offer him a drink from the bottle of Finlandia vodka that I had lugged from Athens. A German traveler counseled me: "Stay calm and be content, no matter what India throws at you. It's the only way to survive in India. Any attempt to change India is futile."

I had learned to go with the flow in Bangladesh. In India, I learned more life lessons and graduated with flying colors. I traversed the country from Kashmir to Kerala, even trekking to the Annapurna and Everest base camps in Nepal. Immersion learning was my classroom. I traveled the length of India in every conceivable way, even sharing third-class trains with pigs, chickens, snakes and other assorted animals. I experienced kindness everywhere, even high in the Himalayas, where Nepali children would murmur *"Na-maste!"* ("I bow to you!") as I trekked past. This extended around-the-world trip would teach me more about life, about myself, about spirituality, than four years of college ever could. And I had an epiphany: I realized that I would continue to explore the world for as long as I was able.

Unquenched wanderlust

From India, with Tony Wheeler's Lonely Planet travel bible, *South East Asia on a Shoestring*, in hand, I forged to the peaceful Buddhist lands of Burma and Thailand, polar opposites of the frenzy of India. In Bangkok I joined the hippie backpacker route, making my way by train to Singapore, by air to Jakarta, and overland to Bali with a pair of Dutch women who had been on the road for two years.

I flew from Bali to Darwin in Australia's Northern Territory, where I met Aussies Colin and Michael and their German friend Hans. Our ensuing three-week safari across Queensland to Sydney was an adventure in itself, a nonstop beer binge in Michael's VW Combi hippie bus. When we finally arrived in Sydney, I marveled at how Sydney reminded me of San Francisco home, and how Sydneysiders were so friendly.

The final leg of my journey, I traveled on France's former UTA airline via New Caledonia and Tahiti to Los Angeles. Then it was a short commuter hop to my City by the Bay.

Little had changed in San Francisco during the 13 months I was away. The city had not fallen into the ocean. Two good friends had found "real" jobs. But I felt like a fish out of water. I wanted to tell whoever would listen about my life-changing journey. I guess I was now a travel bore.

My well-intended parents had decided that I should now become a schoolteacher. Perhaps I would be happy in some tedious desk job, to retire with a pension after 40 years. But I had other ideas. After a trip to New Zealand — a more beautiful place on earth I could not imagine — I was back in San Francisco for good. But my wanderlust was unquenched. I was ill-suited for an office job.

I interned at a travel agency, then joined some friends in our own agency on Haight Street. Soon I branched out on my own, taking the connections I had made around the world to open the first American travel agency specializing in discount around-the-world airfares. It was the first of its kind in the United States. The media even bestowed upon me a nickname: "the Lonely Planet of Airfare."

John at Angkor's Bayon temple

JOHN: AROUND THE WORLD IN 33 MONTHS

"I saw the world. I learnt of new cultures. I flew across an ocean. I wore women's clothing. I made a friend. I fell in love. Who cares if I lost a wager?" — Steve Coogan as Phileas Fogg in "Around the World in 80 Days" (2004)

I began my travels a few years earlier than Nick. I knew before I entered my teens in Oregon that I would become a journalist. My initial career arc would have led me to become a big-city sportswriter covering major-league baseball. But college summers in Hawaii and a post-university circuit of western Europe — including a snowy winter in the family woodworking business in rural Sweden, where my grandmother was raised — whetted my appetite for further travel. Yes, sir, please, I'll have some more!

I didn't experience an OMG "You're going to Bangladesh!" moment in an Aegean taverna. But even before Nick began to offer one-stop fare shopping, I had booked my own round-the-world ticket, inspired by Kiwi and Aussie journalists I had met in Honolulu. It would be valid for a year. Together with my travel agent, I created an itinerary with multiple stops that would keep me moving in the same general direction, through Australasia, Asia and Europe, finally returning to North America.

After a year on the road, I had crossed the Pacific but not much further. I renewed the ticket. A year later, I renewed again, paying only the price increase. I could ill afford to continue to travel without an income; I counted upon finding jobs along the way. An awkward balance of blind confidence and naiveté somehow carried me through 31 months as a dishwasher, cook, bartender, hotel porter, musician, door-to-door salesman, sheep shearer, ski instructor, carpenter, translator, and, oh yeah, journalist, which had been my actual profession when I began this crazy escapade. The ability to bullshit can carry you a long way.

I was 24 years old when I boarded the flight to Pago Pago, my first stop. Although earlier European travels had smoothed some of my anxieties about solo adventures, I knew that the cultural challenges I would face in the Pacific and especially Asia were far different than what I had encountered in western Europe.

The first year

I landed in New Zealand after dreaming of a White Christmas with transvestites in Samoa (thinking of you, Bing Crosby) and engaging in a traditional kava-drinking ceremony on the beach in Fiji. I learned to drive on the wrong side of the road in Auckland, tinkled the ivories at Chateau Tongariro, took a ferry through the Marlborough Sounds to the South Island, and found my way to the Christchurch home of Flash McBride, a fellow journo whom I had introduced to baseball two years earlier. His family had a vacation home in Queenstown, a resort community on Lake Wakatipu in the Southern Alps. I went there with him for a weekend. I wound up staying six months.

O'Connell's Hotel had a job for me washing dishes, then carrying luggage, then cooking bacon and eggs for Australian tour groups. I took time to hike the legendary Milford Track. But once ski season (June-to-September) arrived at nearby Coronet Peak, morning hours no longer appealed. Luckily for me, I could play keyboards, and the Upstairs Downstairs bistro was looking for a honky-tonk piano player. With used but well-loved winter equipment, I hit the slopes by day, played music by night, and partied into the wee hours.

This was a place where I belonged. Up to then, and only once since, I had never felt so much a part of a community as I did in Queenstown. It was a travelers' hub, the far eastern extreme of the fabled "hippie trail" of the 1970s. People from nearly two dozen countries were a part of my life. Five decades later, I'm still in touch with many of them — people like Bret Lundberg, the California photographer with whom I later collaborated on travel books, and Gregory Jack Derwin, Australian bluesman and songwriter extraordinaire.

When the snow melted, I left Queenstown on a bicycle, pedaling through Wanaka, setting up camp beneath the Fox and Franz Josef glaciers, checking out the precious Maori jade ("greenstone") quarries near Hokitika. I was back on the North Island by November, kayaking the remote Rotorua lakes circuit with my Queenstown buddy Ted Hart. Alas, we didn't see a single nocturnal kiwi bird.

Just before Christmas, I flew to Brisbane and pointed my thumb in a northerly direction. I wanted to see the Great Barrier Reef. Hitchhiking somewhere near Proserpine, I was offered a job picking mangoes. I discovered that I was very allergic to mango sap. I had been on the road for a year.

Love and wine

I've always been drawn to the sea. It is, perhaps, a legacy of my Finnish grandfather, who served in the British Navy during South Africa's Boer War and later crewed on an America's Cup vessel in New York. Soon after my arrival in Cairns, I was wandering the planks of the small-boat harbor, a moorage for yachts of all sizes from all over the world. Thus was I recruited to join the crew of the *Mariah*. We cruised the Barrier Reef from Port Douglas to Townsville. Our exploits included a New Year's Eve masquerade on Dunk Island and a foray into waterfall-riddled jungles near Innisfail. ("Be wary of cassowaries," I was duly warned.) Had I not just arrived in Australia, I may have continued on the briny for a long time, living my best Jimmy Buffett as I sailed to Bali, the Maldives and Africa. I learned much later through the "coconut telegraph" that the *Mariah* had unfortunately put up on a reef in the Torres Strait between Queensland and Papua New Guinea.

I took the train south to Brisbane and tried my hand at door-to-door kitchenware sales. My Yankee accent should have given me an advantage, but a silver tongue would have helped me more. A failure at that pursuit, I took a bus to Sydney, where everything clicked. Twenty-five and broke when I arrived in Sydney, I found work first in a kitchen, then as a writer and editor for biweekly tabloids serving the restaurant industry and social clubs.

I made great friends and built new relationships. Those included my first serious girlfriend, Alison, an English woman whom I met in (where else?) a wine bar. A year later, we were still hanging out together in the U.K. and Holland. Then she met the man of her dreams. It wasn't me. Last I checked, she and Chris were happily married grandparents, together more than four decades.

Among my other new friends was Len Evans, the most influential wine lover in a nation of beer drinkers. Len owned the Rothbury Estate in the Hunter Valley, wrote the first major encyclopedia of Australian wine, and was a wine judge of international renown. Wikipedia calls him "the godfather of the Australian wine industry." Len encouraged me to "stop drinking the piss and learn to love the noble rot." I spent weekends at his estate, sometimes joined by Ali, learning how to make a decent shiraz. And I've been a wine guy ever since.

By July, winter was cloaking the Snowy Mountains and Ali got news from home that her father had fallen ill. She was off to England. I climbed the continent's highest mountain, Mount Kosciusko, on skis, then zipped down to Melbourne, where my Queenstown housemate, Bret, met me to celebrate America's 200th birthday with some other U.S. friends. We parted company in Adelaide. Then the adventure *really* began.

Beyond the wine-rich Barossa Valley, there was little but 3,000 kilometers of parched red dirt between Adelaide and the Top End, as the north end of the Australian continent is known. I was hitchhiking. The abridged version of this tale includes a pickup truck of Aboriginal sheep ranchers, an old Aussie pushing a wheelbarrow through the Back o' Beyond, and three young Brits who stuffed me into the boot of their overpacked Land Rover until the transmission blew, en route to the underground mining town of Coober Pedy. I threw up my hands in frustration, took a bus to Alice Springs and on to Darwin.

Asian kaleidoscope

In 20 months, I still hadn't encountered true culture shock. That came the moment my flight from Darwin touched down in Bali, the tourist mecca of Indonesia. (Keep in mind, this was 1976.) The sights, the sounds, the smells, the tastes, even the touches — I think back to my first traditional oil massage from a wizened old woman with arthritic hands — were nothing like I had ever experienced before. The *kecha-kechak* of dramatic dances and live animal sacrifices in ornate Hindu temples, the aromas of lemongrass and turmeric at public markets and tiny open-air restaurants, were a far cry from Australian meat pies and shrimp on the barbie.

The next four months were a blur. Motorbikes through the Balinese rice paddies. Batik art lessons in Java. Floating excrement on a freighter from Jakarta to Sumatra. A spiritual awakening, perhaps enhanced by elephant grass, at Lake Toba. ("Stop thinking. You're fine.") Fortune-telling by a renowned soothsayer on Penang Island. ("You will spend most of your life far from home.") A 26th birthday party on Bugis Street in Singapore, where just over seven years later my son would be born. Malay ghost stories in a primitive fishing village near Kota Bahru. The extravagance of the Grand Palace in Bangkok and the depravity of Patpong Road.

I ran out of steam in Burma, or Myanmar, as it is now known. I made it through the temples of Mandalay and the exquisite ancient ruins of Bagan, but dysentery hit me hard in Rangoon. I lost a lot of weight between Calcutta and Kathmandu. I thought I was on the road to recovery in Pokhara, gateway to Annapurna, but I wound up cloistered in a mud hut, unable to eat or drink for days. I might have died there. Anyone will tell you that if you don't like being sick at home, you will *hate* it when you're traveling. Either Ganesha heard my prayers or it was gut-check time. Probably both. I summoned strength to return to Kathmandu and check into a British hospital. A regimen of treacle, curd and saline solution got me back on my feet.

I scuttled any plans I had to travel overland through the Islamic world to Europe. Pausing only in Agra to adore the Taj Mahal, I hurried to New Delhi and flew Iraqi Airways, via Baghdad, to London, where Ali was waiting. We spent Christmas with her family in Sheffield, although it was a subdued celebration without her father, who had passed away, and with me in a weakened condition.

It was now *two years* that I had been on the road. What a two years it had been.

The fork in the road

I wasn't finished. As the calendar flipped over to 1977, I answered the summons of *mon ami* Claude, whom I had met in Yogyakarta as he was returning to France from his military service in New Caledonia. His family owned and operated a ski resort and hotel in the Vosges Mountains, on the border with Germany. Would I be interested ... Does a bear ...? Another winter of skiing was just what I needed to get my mojo back. In the spring, Ali met me again in The Netherlands, where I had found work tending bar in Amsterdam. Then my cousin Ulf made room for me in his small apartment in Gothenburg, Sweden, as I spent the summer rewriting a Yugoslavian publisher's political satire for an English-speaking market.

I turned down an opportunity to bartend at an American military post exchange in Berlin. I might never have made it home to Oregon. And I had been gone too long already.

I returned to London only to discover that Alison had succumbed to the charms of another during Queen Elizabeth's Silver Jubilee celebration. I flew to New York City, where I immediately felt out of place. Through the window of the Greyhound bus that took me west toward the Pacific coast, I was appalled as I viewed the conspicuous consumption of the America I had left behind. The cars were all gas guzzlers. The restaurants were fast-food cathedrals. The houses were far bigger than anyone needed.

As Nick also discovered, when you return home after an extended world journey, your old friends and family will no longer "get you." I had learned to be more than comfortable with a simpler lifestyle. I learned that money is a means to an end, but not an end in itself. I knew that life is all about learning, and my best place to learn is in my discomfort zone. And I learned that when you come to a fork in the road — always take it.

Reading departure signs in some big airport reminds me of the places I've been /
Visions of good times that brought so much pleasure make me want to go back again /
If it suddenly ended tomorrow, I could somehow adjust to the fall /
Good times and riches and son of a bitches, I've seen more than I can recall
— Jimmy Buffett, "Changes in Latitudes, Changes in Attitudes" (1977)

Chapter Thirteen

PARTING THOUGHTS:

The True Meaning of Travel

"Perhaps travel cannot prevent bigotry, but by demonstrating that all peoples cry, laugh, eat, worry, and die, it can introduce the idea that if we try and understand each other, we may even become friends." —Maya Angelou

What does it mean to travel as a quest for knowledge, not to simply check things off a bucket list? Is it better to "go local" when you travel, as opposed to vacationing in all-inclusive hotels, slugging down umbrella drinks, and steering clear of the from local culture?

When your time on this planet comes to an end, will you look back and think: "Man, I should have bought a bigger car! Or at least a 65-inch TV!" Or will you regret not having seen the Northern Lights?

We are advocates for movement. Along with changes in scenery, travel evokes a mindset that is altered with each new adventure. We have come to realize that the journey is more important than the destination itself. Adapting and blending into local society is where the trip begins. We are passionate about new cultures and keenly aware that sharing meals can change lives. Far from over-planning, we'll often just "wing it." More often than not, trips like a spur-of-the-moment overland detour from Nairobi to Cape Town have been life-changing endeavors.

Travel conjures up many images, from the freedom we feel when we hit the road to some stress and even fear when we think about making our way to unknown destinations. John can still recall severe headaches before his first solo trip to Europe at age 21. Once he hit the road, they magically disappeared.

The first time Nick went to Africa, he was uncertain about what might lie ahead. Perhaps he was a little frightened, traveling to a remote, distant continent. But when he encountered the Masai in Kenya, he found these noble warriors to be some of the kindest and most fascinating people he had ever met.

Travel changes our perceptions of how we see the world. To this day, we'll tell anyone who will listen that probably 99 out of 100 earthlings are good folk, not wishing you any harm.

We learned to become better world citizens by mingling and merging into new environments. The more we connect with people, the better we get to know them. Everywhere we've gone, our hosts have welcomed us into their towns and villages, their coffee shops and restaurants, indeed their homes and neighborhoods, walking and playing and shopping and being introduced to new friends. We trusted and learned from the locals, taking a leap of faith that human kindness is far more powerful than any malice you may experience along the way.

Embracing risk

Life, after all, is about risk. Take "Nothing ventured, nothing gained," and multiply it a hundredfold. Personal challenges are a part of the adventure in travel as in daily life. Never neglect common sense with regard to your safety, but don't be afraid to wander the road less traveled and immerse yourself in new experiences. Go to the off-the-beaten-track places that only the locals know. Follow them to fabulous cafes, markets, churches and obscure historical sites, canvassing unfamiliar places — the ones the guidebooks never mention — with companions you may have only just met.

Be willing to leap into new worlds. Your hosts want to learn everything they can from you, just as you wish to learn from them and their environs. Keep an open mind and you will return home with a new life perspective. The simple act of being removed from your day-to-day life opens limitless doors. Chance encounters happen when we stop adhering to an ingrained routine.

We should all be infected with wanderlust. With the advent of social media and the rise of peer-to-peer travel, it has never before been easier to live in a stranger's house or apartment, sleep on a couch, eat with locals in their home, share a ride, meet new friends, and find a tour guide who will take you to unique places that you would never find on your own. The thrill of any journey begins when you interact with local people.

The journey changes you. Each pilgrimage is different. No two trips are alike. Travel the world, learn from locals, and become the tolerant, globally educated, well-rounded person that you always imagined you could be.

Buy a couple of rounds of ale in a pub in Galway, climb Mount Kilimanjaro, work construction in a village in Peru, dine with an aspiring chef in Thessaloniki, travel overland through India on crowded trains and buses. Samba with the Cariocas at Carnivál in Rio, mend fences at an Australian sheep station, backpack through the Alps, eat raw blowfish in Japan, worship the shamanic Mother Goddess with the hill tribes of Vietnam, celebrate the Day of the Dead in Mexico. Whatever the journey throws at you, ride with it. It's a part of your new friends' lives: Make it a part of yours.

In every episode of our travels, we are reminded that through human interaction and by practicing sustainability, we can do our part to change the world. The billions of humans on this planet are far more alike than they are different.

By the decades

As we reflect on our lives in travel, we might consider each decade as an essential building block to who we have become.

We were blessed as young children to have parents who made every trip an adventure, whether it was a day's excursion to the mountains or an ocean beach, or a drive up the freeway to visit relatives. The mere thought of getting into a car excited us. Wanderlust was instilled into our character at an early age.

By our mid to late teens, we were already traveling independently. Nick left his San Francisco home to enjoy summer vacation with cousins in Greece. That stimulated his appetite, and not only for travel. As a schoolboy on the Peloponnese Peninsula, a three-mile walk with a pocketful of drachmas for fresh bread left him so famished that he finished the entire aromatic loaf before he made it back to the family home. The family soon realized they had to give Nick money for *two* loaves.

Later, his aunt taught him to bake his own bread. Soon he was playing soccer with other Greek youth and learning to scuba dive. By 16, he was hopping ferries across the Ionian Sea to Italy, where he boarded trains to explore other parts of Europe.

At 17, John took a summer job in Honolulu and learned to surf — after four full summers of backpacking the heights of his beloved Cascade Range, where he also spent winters ski racing. More significantly, Hawaii served as John's introduction to Asia's diverse cultures, igniting the spark that eventually led him to a life on the far side of the Pacific. The teen-aged Nick, meanwhile, when he wasn't in Europe, likewise was in the wilderness. Weeks spent amid the lofty wonders of Yosemite National Park provided many a John Muir moment, reminders that an affinity with nature can be essential to expanding your human interaction skills.

We learned how to travel in our 20s, the decade when we took the long-term, life-changing international journeys we described in the previous chapter. We were not afraid to venture to distant lands. Shorter business trips in our 30s had unique adventurous elements. Our previous experiences and encounters with local people had left us comfortable to mingle with anyone.

By the time we reached our 40s, some of our travel dreams were taking a back seat to our lives away from travel. John now had a family, and although he raised his son to be a traveler like himself, the opportunities were fewer. At a similar age, Nick had saved a bit of money from his travel business and was able to invest in some more costly adventures. On a luxury safari in Tanzania, he came to understand that the travel experience is subjective — that one need not have been a backpacking youth to appreciate the wonders of the world. He chatted with locals while sipping champagne at a Safari Lodge within an impressive African game reserve.

Now we're older, and we reflect with gratitude on our education in travel, which far outweighs anything we learned in a classroom. Now in our later years, we can look back on how different it was for us in the 1970s and '80s, without the internet, without cell phones, with postage stamps on envelopes as the primary means of communication with our families back home.

The differences can hardly be imagined by a new generation of "digital nomads" and "influencers," by YouTubers and Instagrammers. Then again, travel is never the same for any two people, even those who share instant gratification through video images in the 2020s. Ultimately, travel is a learning experience for explorers and wanderers of all ages. If, between pool parties and tropical island escapades, the young people of today can demonstrate the similarities between the people and cultures of the world, and minimize the differences, we will make each other better.

The essence of travel requires you to leave the comfort zone of your home confines to seek a deeper connection with people. To truly absorb a culture and the essence of a destination, you must be open to new experiences and people. Every person you meet has a story to tell.

"Two roads diverged in a wood and I — I took the one less traveled by, and that has made all the difference." —Robert Frost

About the authors

Nicholas C. Kontis:

Nicholas Kontis was born on Santorini Island in Greece and raised in America's cultural capital, San Francisco. After a 13-month whirlwind around-the-world-adventure, Nick returned to San Francisco and started the first travel agency in the United States specializing in discount around-the-world airfares. He is an award-winning travel writer, journalist, author, speaker, and *USA Today* photojournalist who has traveled to over 100 countries.

John Gottberg Anderson:

John Gottberg Anderson is a widely known writer, editor, photographer and educator. He launched his professional journalism career at the age of 16 in Eugene, Oregon, and since has taken it many times around the world, including Southeast Asia, his home since 2019. A former editor at The Los Angeles Times and the Paris-based Michelin Guides, he has been published in such magazines as *National Geographic Traveller*, *Travel+Leisure* and the *Southeast Asia Globe*, where he served as editor in 2023-24. This is his 24th book and the 10th he has co-authored.

Printed in Great Britain
by Amazon

57778110R00145